Assessment, Learning and Employability

SRHE and Open University Press Imprint
General Editor: Heather Eggins

Assessment, Learning and Employability

Peter T. Knight
Mantz Yorke

Society for Research into Higher Education
& Open University Press

Open University Press
McGraw-Hill Education
McGraw-Hill House
Shoppenhangers Road
Maidenhead
Berkshire
England
SL6 2QL

email: enquiries@openup.co.uk
world wide web: www.openup.co.uk

First published 2003

A catalogue record of this book is available from the British Library

ISBN 0 335 21228 X (pb)   0 335 21229 8 (hb)

Library of Congress Cataloging-in-Publication Data
CIP data has been applied for

Typeset by RefineCatch Limited, Bungay, Suffolk
Printed in Great Britain by Bell & Bain Ltd, Glasgow

Contents

Preface

A state of flux

Higher education is in a state of flux that arguably makes more demands on it than ever before. Governments typically base policy on the assumption that a highly educated workforce will assist economic competitiveness. Graduates, it is argued (amongst others, by Haug and Tauch, 2001, who take a pan-European perspective), should be attuned to the demands of the workplace. 'Key skills' and 'employability' are seen – and promoted – by governments as desirable components of first-cycle higher education curricula. The human capital approach gives higher education an instrumental twist which many academics find discomfiting.

We take as a premise that there is no necessary conflict between employability and traditional academic values. Good teaching and learning practices can serve both kinds of end, and assessment practices need to cohere with teaching and learning: Biggs (1999) would see this in terms of 'curriculum alignment'. The critical question, which we approach from the perspective of assessment, is, 'What is to be aligned?' This leads us to consider what an educational commitment to both learning and employability implies for the curriculum and, in particular, for assessment.

Assessment: a cause for concern

The Learning and Teaching Support Network (LTSN)[1] operated as a network of 24 subject centres charged with enhancing the quality of teaching, learning and assessment in UK higher education. In late 2001, 23 of the subject centres produced descriptions of the state of learning and teaching in their disciplinary areas. Their analyses, which were informed by reports of subject reviews conducted by the Quality Assurance Agency (QAA), provided a snapshot of practice in UK higher education.[2]

Of the six aspects of provision addressed in subject review, teaching, learning and assessment (TLA), together with quality management and enhancement, gave some cause for concern. The assessment component of TLA was particularly troublesome.

The QAA reports noted that, although some institutions' TLA arrangements were highly praised, there was concern that good practice was not as widely generalized as it might have been. Assessment issues were particularly problematical, especially when it came to creating practices that all members of a team or department would follow. Recurrent themes from the reports included the following:

- Teaching and learning sequences that were not matched to the pedagogical purposes claimed by module and programme teachers.
- The teaching of 'transferable', 'key' or 'core' skills.
- The underexploitation of information and communications technology in teaching and learning.
- The need for better integration into curricula of off-campus learning of various kinds.
- Many problems with assessment, including those of matching assessment methods to the range of intended learning outcomes, and the assessment of workplace performance, artefacts and productions.

One subject centre's report quoted the view that 'rapidly increasing student numbers are calling into question traditional teaching styles and relationships, demanding new skills of lecturers and requiring a broadening of the assessment base'. It went on to note that teaching was often not discussed within departments, that 'provision and take-up of staff development opportunities are poor', and said that 'there are few formal mechanisms in place for the dissemination of good practice'.

In another subject area, only one institution in three was awarded the top grade of 4 for TLA and questions had been raised about the effectiveness of assessment practices in more than half of the institutions visited, as well as about students' understanding of the arrangements for the development and assessment of key skills.

Yet another subject centre's report concluded that the following key areas required attention:

- Ensuring documentation and objectives were clear and detailed.
- Matching assessment and grading criteria to relevant objectives and intended outcomes.
- Ensuring the range of assessment criteria were appropriate for the level of study.
- Ensuring consistency and clarity in assessment criteria and in feedback to students.
- The development of appropriate methods of assessment for transferable skills.
- Encouraging and improving second marking, moderation and anonymous marking procedures.

The subject centres' analyses were almost completely silent about employability. Employability – understood in this book as a set of achievements, understandings and personal attributes that make individuals more likely to gain employment and be successful in their chosen occupations – has since emerged as a priority in the UK and is becoming an international concern, although other countries often label it differently.

The LTSN, like most other networks around the world of people interested in enhancing the quality of undergraduate learning, was concerned about the appropriateness, effectiveness and efficiency of assessment. Our argument is that such concerns, which have been manifest in the literature for the past 15 years, have been sharpened by increasing expectations of higher education, not least that it should contribute explicitly to the employability of new graduates and, by extension, to countries' economic well-being in times when 'knowledge economies' (Leadbeater 2000) are seen as prime sources of wealth. We now need to submit assessment to a sustained scrutiny and ask what happens when creaking assessment practices have to cope with new demands, such as promoting and describing the complex, fuzzy achievements that can be associated with graduate employability. We need to make clear at this point that this is not a book that details the variety of assessment methods that are available – there are already many good texts available to which those interested in such matters can turn (Brown and Knight 1994; Hounsell *et al.* 1996; Brown *et al.* 1997; Walvoord and Anderson 1998; Heywood 2000; Schwartz and Webb 2002 and the array of materials on the LTSN Generic Centre website[3]). Concentrating attention on assessment *methods* at the expense of concepts and theory is rather like trying to relieve symptoms of an illness without understanding what is wrong. Our claim is that good choices of assessment practices demand an appreciation of the range of assessment purposes; of assessment theory; of the nature of employability and the other complex outcomes that higher education is expected to foster; and of subsidiarity.

The concept of subsidiarity is used in the European Union to demarcate between central and national powers. Decisions taken by the EU are to be implemented at the lowest possible level in ways that are faithful to the directive or legislation and appropriate to local circumstances. The concept resembles 'loose-tight coupling' (Morgan 1997), which refers to organizations that set values and priorities centrally and insist that the whole organization adhere to them whilst leaving questions of implementation to the discretion of workers and workgroups. So too with assessment in higher education. We argue that complex outcomes of learning, such as those covered by 'employability', need to be seen as programme achievements and that assessment arrangements, whether primarily intended to support learning or to warrant achievement, also need to be seen as *programme* concerns. Although learning intentions need to be set at programme level and although programme teams need to make sure that the teaching, learning and assessment arrangements in the component parts come together sufficiently to make the learning intentions realistic, creativity and academic freedom need not be stifled in the process. Following the principle of subsidiarity, teachers would be free to engage learners with important subject matter in ways that were consistent with the programme goals and with the demands of the material itself. Plainly, there would be some degree of negotiation to make sure that the most popular modules in a programme form some kind of coherent set, but within this framework teachers would have considerable freedom. In one sense, then, this *is* a 'how to do it' book, not so much because we commend some assessment methods over others, but more because we claim that unless assessment issues are well understood, methodological enthusiasm will be fruitless, as many have found who have tried to measure undergraduate achievements that are in reality unmeasurable.

Our analysis is, then, more strategic than is usual in books on assessment. It offers ways of thinking about assessment that are intended to frame the methodological choices that need to be made. It is often supported with examples drawn from the UK, but as our set of references shows, we have drawn widely on work published elsewhere and believe that the case we make has significant implications for higher education practices across the world.

Navigating this book

Our book addresses the concerns of colleagues at a number of levels within the higher education system. Readers are most likely to be those who have an active engagement in curriculum design and implementation, since they are likely to need to follow through our argument in a fair degree of detail. Some of these readers will be programme or departmental leaders; some will be responsible for course components, such as modules; and others will be engaged in reflection on their practice as individual teachers, perhaps as part of their work towards a qualification as a teacher in higher education. Senior managers holding 'the institutional assessment brief' will, we hope, find food for productive thought in what we have to say, even though their interest is likely to be 'broad brush' in character. They may prefer to concentrate their attention on our diagnosis of what is wrong with assessment and on what we envisage being done to enhance it, whilst glossing over the finer points of detail.

Chapter 1 sets the contemporary scene in which higher education is expected to play a significant role in the development of economic success. The next two chapters show that assessment systems and practices are, globally, already hard-pressed to cope with the expectations being laid upon modern higher education. We argue that enhancing the employability of new graduates, in the interest of national economic well-being, puts severe pressure on ramshackle practices. We explain the difficulties of assessing in this context, and in Chapter 4 clarify some key, often unheeded, concepts in assessment and measurement theory.

In Chapters 5 to 8 we explore ways in which high-stakes or summative assessment might be put on a more secure footing, arguing that even though it might be a priority to get estimates of achievement that are tolerably reliable, some sorts of achievement resist reliable assessment and others totally elude it. The implication is that good summative assessment practices cannot be affordably applied to all of the complex, often 'fuzzy' achievements that constitute employability. They may be reached, though, by low-stakes assessments where the aim is to create feedback to improve learning.

Chapters 9 to 11 show in some detail how formative assessment can contribute to complex learning (hence to employability) and help students to lay claims to achievements which are to all intents and purposes beyond the reach of summative assessment practices, yet are of vital interest to employers. Low-stakes assessments engage students in worthwhile, often 'authentic' tasks and generate evidence that can be presented, perhaps through portfolios, in support of student claims to achievement. In this way a complete set of complex learning outcomes can brought within programme-level assessment systems (some – the simpler – summatively assessed, others formatively assessed), in the process helping students to make public claims to achievement.

The final three chapters address ways in which the strategic implications of our analysis can be realized at the level of the academic organizational unit (often the department) and at the level of the institution as a whole.

Notes

1. At the time of writing there were consultations in the UK about the future of quality enhancement arrangements. Although a new agency was to be established, it was not clear whether the LTSN would retain a distinct identity or not.
2. This section is based upon an unpublished synthesis done by the LTSN evaluation team.
3. www.ltsn.ac.uk/genericcentre > Projects > Assessment

1

Higher Education and Employability

Higher education and the economy

The connection between higher education and the economy is longstanding. In its review of higher education in the UK four decades ago, the Robbins Report listed four aims for higher education, opening:

> We begin with instruction in skills suitable to play a part in the general division of labour.
>
> (Robbins 1963: para. 25)

The Report placed this aim first in order to counter the risk that the importance of higher education for the economy might have been ignored or undervalued, and it went on to offer the view that few would enter higher education without an eye to subsequent employment.

In the UK, the nature of first-cycle higher education has in recent times been evolving, although the rate of change has been such that its magnitude has passed almost unnoticed (Yorke 1999a). The initial stimulus for the changes was probably the then Employment Department's Enterprise in Higher Education (EHE) initiative of the late 1980s which was designed to accentuate in higher education the notion of enterprise. Over time, this evolved into more of a concern with personal qualities and transferable skills, and lessened the emphasis on entrepreneurialism. It is probably fair to conclude that EHE has had a lasting effect on curriculum development.

The more recent Dearing Report on higher education (NCIHE 1997) drew particular attention to the vital role that higher education plays in a modern economy. Global competitiveness, it asserted, required that

> Education and training [should] enable people in an advanced society to compete with the best in the world.
>
> (NCIHE, 1997: para. 1.11).

Some commentators have questioned whether human capital is the key to economic well-being (Morley 2001) and whether 'employability' is anything but an empty concept. Even if the concept has value, it is debatable whether higher education can develop employability as governments suppose (Atkins 1999). Although these challenges have force, the notion of employability has far too much face validity for politicians to abandon it.

What do labour markets want of higher education?

When trying to appreciate the potential for higher education to contribute to economic well-being it is helpful to distinguish between the formation of subject-specific understandings and skills[1] and the promotion of other valued skills, qualities and dispositions. Whereas the world of employment has, by and large, been satisfied with the *disciplinary* understanding and skills developed by graduates, it has been less happy with their development of what have been termed 'generic skills', such as communication, teamworking and time-management. In the UK, the grumbles of employers about graduates' generic skills have been longstanding, although Hesketh (2000) provides evidence to suggest that there may be an element of myth contributing to general perceptions. If there is evidence from the employers' side, there is much less evidence concerning the satisfaction of graduates regarding their preparedness for the world of work. Initial findings from a survey of new graduates funded by the Higher Education Funding Council for England (HEFCE) suggest that graduates do experience difficulty with verbal[2] communication, time management and 'task juggling' (Leon 2002).

Harvey *et al.* (1997) showed that employers in the UK tended to value generic skills more highly than disciplinary-based understanding and skills. Whether the disciplinary aspect was being taken for granted by respondents to their survey is unclear. Brown *et al.* (2002: 19) quote one human resources manager as saying: 'Academic qualifications are the first tick in the box and then we move on. Today we simply take them for granted.'

For some employers (the computer industry and social work provide two contrasting examples), disciplinary knowledge and understanding are vital. Indeed, in the field of information technology, accreditation by major companies is competing with awards from higher education (Adelman 2001), corporate universities are growing in the USA, and there are hints of their potential growth in the UK as well. For other employers, a general 'graduateness', understood to include the possession of general dispositions, qualities and skills (HEQC 1997), seems to be regarded as sufficient, where the view seems to be something like 'give us a bright and engaged graduate, and we will build specific expertise for this organization on top of that'.

Robert Reich, Secretary of State for Labor in the first Clinton administration in the USA, has argued that advanced economies need two sorts of high-level expertise: one emphasizing discovery, and the other focusing on exploiting the discoveries of others through market-related intelligence and the application of interpersonal skills (Reich, 2002). The latter might be interpreted as entrepreneurship, whose inclusion in curricula at all levels was the focus of an investigation sponsored by the European Commission (EC 2002). In an earlier work, Reich (1991) suggested that these professionals, whom he termed 'symbolic analysts', had a range of achievements to their names. Symbolic analysts, he said, were imaginative and creative, had at their fingertips relevant disciplinary understanding and skills, and also the 'soft' or generic skills that enable the disciplinary base to be deployed to optimal effect. One important source of knowledge growth is the learning-by-doing that takes place in innovative workplaces. Another is the higher education system.

The key contribution of higher education to national prosperity, according to Reich (1991), lay in the development of graduates with the skills of the symbolic analyst at their disposal. The consequence was that undergraduate programmes should be concerned with four areas in particular:

- Abstraction (theorizing and/or relating empirical data to theory, and/or using formulae, equations, models and metaphors).
- System thinking (seeing the part in the context of the wider whole).
- Experimentation (intuitively or analytically).
- Collaboration (involving communication and teamworking skills).

Educational institutions are not always successful in preparing learners for the complexity inherent in the two main sorts of activity that Reich attributes to symbolic analyst's role: learners are often expected to learn what is put in front of them and to work individually and competitively, and subject matter may be compartmentalized. Plainly, the education of symbolic analysts – who are likely to be those at the leading edge of economic developments of one kind or another – requires that institutions make a particular effort to foster the achievements that Reich highlighted.

Higher education is, however, concerned with far more than the education of symbolic analysts. A massified system (Scott 1995) implies a highly variegated set of expectations regarding achievements: for example, mid-level qualifications have an important part to play in economic well-being (Robertson 2002). The US system, with its two-year and four-year institutions, and European systems (such as the German) with a differentiated higher education sector, seem to be more successful than the unified UK system in providing such qualifications. However, the introduction in the UK of the foundation degree (a two-year full-time equivalent programme involving work-based learning) is expected to fill a manifest national qualification 'gap' (DfES 2003).

As well as preparing graduates and diplomates initially for employment-related roles of various kinds, higher education has an acknowledged role in economic development through its contribution to lifelong learning – for example, in educating further the middle manager so that they can manage more effectively; in upskilling the teacher, teaching assistant, nurse or process worker; facilitating the development of active citizenship; and so on.

What is meant by 'employability'?

There are a number of interpretations of 'employability' in the literature, which can be reduced to three overarching constructs:

- Employability as demonstrated by the graduate actually obtaining a job.
- Employability as the student being developed by their experience of higher education (i.e. it is a curricular and perhaps extracurricular *process*).
- Employability in terms of personal *achievements* (and, implicitly, potential).

In the UK, a key performance indicator is the proportion of graduates obtaining jobs (HEFCE 2002) – currently, this indicator covers any job, rather than only those that would normatively be accepted as 'graduate jobs'. Even if this indicator could be refined sufficiently to include only 'graduate jobs', it would still be problematic since it would not take into account the fluctuations in the labour market, or the differential ease that graduates from different disciplines experience in getting a job (for example, when there is a shortage of teachers, graduates from teacher education have no difficulty in obtaining employment).[3] However, employability should not be confused with the *acquisition* of a job, whether a 'graduate job' or otherwise. It is also a mistake to assume that provision of experience, whether within higher education or without, is a sufficient condition for enhanced employability. The curricular process may *facilitate* the development of prerequisites appropriate to employment, but does not guarantee it. Hence it is inappropriate to assume that a student is highly employable merely on the grounds that they have experienced a particular curriculum.

The graduate exhibits employability in respect of a job if they can demonstrate a set of achievements that are relevant to that job. They are 'capable' in Stephenson's (1998) terms, which point beyond employability at the moment of graduation towards employability in the context of lifelong learning:

Capable people have confidence in their ability to

1. take effective and appropriate action,
2. explain what they are seeking to achieve,
3. live and work effectively with others, and
4. continue to learn from their experiences, both as individuals and in association with others,

in a diverse and changing society. . . .

Capability is a necessary part of specialist expertise, not separate from it. Capable people not only know about their specialisms, they also have the confidence to apply their knowledge and skills within varied and changing situations and to continue to develop their specialist knowledge and skills.

(Stephenson 1998: 2, minor presentational changes made)

Employability is context-dependent. A repertoire of attributes and achievements may have a general value, but may well prove insufficient for some specific situations. Employability is, then, a (multifaceted) characteristic of the *individual*. It is, after all, the *individual* whose appropriateness for a job is appraised by an employer.

Definitions of employability

In this book,[4] employability is taken as

> a set of achievements, understandings and personal attributes that make individuals more likely to gain employment and be successful in their chosen occupations.

There are a number of points to be made regarding this definition.

- It is probabilistic. There is no certainty that the possession of a range of desirable characteristics will convert employability into employment: there are too many extraneous socio-economic variables for that.
- The choice of occupation is, for many graduates, likely to be constrained. They may have to accept that their first choice of post is not realistic in the prevailing circumstances, and aim instead for an option that calls on the skills etc. that they have developed.
- The gaining of a 'graduate job' and success in it should not be conflated. Higher education awards describe the graduate's past performance but some achievements vital for workplace success might not be covered, not least because of the difficulty of placing a grade on characteristics such as drive, cooperative working and leadership. Large organizations may be able to fill in any gaps by recruiting through assessment centres which can call upon a greater range of (expensive) assessment techniques.

It is necessary not to lose sight of the fact that most of the discussion of employability implicitly refers to the full-time student who enters higher education at around the age of 18 and who graduates at the age of 21 or 22, and deals with matters beyond the boundaries of the subject discipline(s) concerned. For older students, employability may take on a different colouring, since those students may well have experienced employment and/or voluntary work prior to engaging in higher education: for them, the emphasis that they give to employability may be on the development of subject-specific understanding to complement what they have already learned about employability in general.[5] There is also a need to acknowledge the employment-relevant learning that ostensibly full-time students derive from part-time employment as they seek to fund their passage through higher education.

Alternative approaches to defining employability

Hillage and Pollard (1998) work towards a definition of employability that focuses on what is needed to secure and maintain a 'graduate job'. For them, employability is

> the capability to move self-sufficiently within the labour market to realise potential through sustainable employment.
>
> (Hillage and Pollard 1998: 2)

Unfortunately, the word 'capability' is ambiguous, suggesting both 'potential' or 'necessary characteristics' *and* the securing of employment (which then attests to possession of those characteristics). Brown *et al.* (2002) claim that Hillage and Pollard's view is ideologically loaded, because it does not acknowledge that the condition of local, national and international labour markets is a powerful determinant of graduates' success. The criticism could stem from the ambiguity inherent in the word 'capability'.

Brown *et al.* offer a different definition of employability:

> The *relative chances* of finding and maintaining different kinds of employment.
> (Brown *et al.* 2002: 9, emphasis added)

They see employability as a combination of the absolute and the relative: the absolute dimension relates to the individual's characteristics, the relative dimension relates to the state of the labour market. Following Hirsch (1977), they observe that, where many possess degrees, a degree confers no positional advantage in the labour market: 'at best, it enables the individual to stay in the race' (Brown *et al.* 2002: 9). The 'relative chances' proposed by Brown *et al.* are influenced by a number of factors:

- The programme choices made by individuals.
- The institution attended. (Some employers have a list of institutions from which they prefer to select graduates (Hesketh 2000). Further, criteria such as the match of a curriculum to the employer's business and the reputation of the institution can affect the graduate's chances.)
- An employer's preferences (perhaps implicit) in regard to the composition of the workforce (see Brown and Scase 1994: 130ff). Blasko *et al.* (2002) show, in the 'Access to What?' project, that these relative chances are not the same for all students with equivalent qualifications, since some groups face systemic labour market disadvantage.

'Skills' are more complex than is sometimes appreciated

Over the years, a variety of terms has been used to signal the kinds of achievement beyond the subject-specific that assist learners in higher education to demonstrate their potential value to the workplace. The literature includes 'core', 'common', 'personal transferable' (often without the 'personal'), 'key' and 'generic' skills, suggesting – as Bennett *et al.* (2000) do – that there is an underlying theoretical uncertainty regarding their status.

The Dearing Report (NCIHE 1997) recommended that higher education focus attention on so-called key skills (communication, numeracy, information technology and 'learning how to learn'). Key skills are now a curricular commonplace in UK higher education and are often to be found in specific modules where there is both some risk of 'ghettoization' and a perception by students that they are of little relevance to the main thrust of their studies. A more rounded view of qualities and skills relevant to employment and other situations, which is properly underpinned in theoretical terms, could lead to a more valuable – and valued – contribution to the profiles of successful graduates.

Wolf (2002: 117ff) tracks the policy commitment to 'core skills' and 'key skills' from their articulation in a speech on further education given in 1989 by the then Minister of Education, Kenneth Baker, and through a number of policy interventions, showing that their introduction can be laid at the door of the business community. She echoes Bennett *et al.* (2000) in remarking that they have nothing more than an ad hoc foundation.

There are two presumptions regarding skills, however linguistically qualified:

- They provide underpinning to a range of actions needed in employment.
- They are transferable from one realm of experience to another, relatively unproblematically.

Whereas the first is probably uncontentious, the second has been the subject of considerable debate.

In an early discussion of transferability, Bridges (1993) differentiated between skills that were in essence context-independent (the use of word-processing, say) and those that were context-dependent. Context-dependent skills can be demonstrated in behaviour that might be appropriate in one context (such as challenging received wisdom in higher education) but that might not be well received in another (challenging an employer's way of going about things). Far from transfer being a simple translation, its potential applicability required an appreciation of how the change in context might impact.[6] In the same vein, a recent analysis by Hinchliffe (2002) insists on the importance of developing situational understandings that are (at least potentially) able to cater for the unpredictability of happenings in the world.

Consideration of context-dependency led Bridges to a further category of skills which he termed 'transferring skills' – higher-order skills that enable the person 'to select, adapt, adjust and apply their other skills to different situations, across different social contexts and perhaps similarly across different cognitive domains' (Bridges 1993: 50). He points out that the exercise of 'transferring skills' involves very sophisticated personal/intellectual achievements that are much more attuned to professional behaviour than atomistic lists of competences. This is another way of describing metacognition.

Towards theory

In Chapter 10 we present a list of transferable or generic skills. Some would say, though, that it and others like it are little more than 'wish lists' constructed by interested parties. Two approaches which try to make connections between employability and theories of learning are:

- the model developed by Bennett *et al.* (2000) which links disciplinary content, disciplinary skills, workplace experience, workplace awareness, and generic skills; and
- Knight and Yorke's (2002) USEM model.

Bennett *et al.* (2000) offered the view that four personal management skills were relevant to a range of contexts:

- management of self;
- management of others;
- management of information;
- management of task.

Linked with this is their model of course provision, in which 'generic' skills interlock with disciplinary content, disciplinary skills, workplace awareness and workplace experience.[7] Their approach to skills development, whilst useful, is focused strongly upon the person's performance: the individual psychological conditions that *underpin* a person's performance are given little emphasis.

Employability is seen as being influenced by four broad and interrelated components:

U Understanding.
S 'Skills'.
E Efficacy beliefs, students' self-theories and personal qualities – of critical importance being the extent to which students feel that they might 'be able to make a difference' (not every time, but in a probabilistic way).
M Metacognition, encompassing self-awareness regarding the student's learning, and the capacity to reflect on, in and for action.[8]

The USEM account of employability is summarized in Figure 1.1, where it can be seen that the 'E' component suffuses the other contributions to employability.

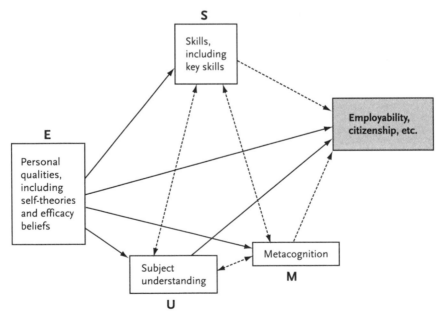

Figure 1.1   The USEM model

Understanding (as a term, preferred to 'knowledge' because of its implication of depth) is a key outcome of higher education and needs no further justification here. We follow convention by identifying 'skills' as a key element of employability, although we are critical of the term, believing that it lends itself to the view that skills are determinate achievements that can be readily measured and unproblematically transferred from setting to setting. These reservations are significant for assessment practices but it would intrude to elaborate them here and, for the sake of simplicity in this book we shall generally treat skills as a component of employability.[9] However, we make a sharp contrast with narrowly conceived notions of skills such as those appearing at the lower end of the NVQ framework,[10] or in some usages of so-called key skills.

Understanding and skills are not enough, though, if students tend to believe that their successes come from luck or from being innately smart and their failures come from malign forces or from a lack of ability. In the latter case students may succumb to the paralysis of 'learned helplessness' (Peterson *et al.* 1993) and, whatever their objective achievements, feel that effort will be wasted. As for students who believe that a high level of fixed intelligence accounts for their achievements, trouble comes when they encounter problems which defy quick solution. They are likely to lack persistence and to give up, which does not commend them to employers who want people able to chip away at problems that may be novel. It is better, argues the American social psychologist Carol Dweck (1999), to have malleable self-theories, to believe that strategic or reflective thinking, effort and persistence usually allow one to make some difference in most settings. Malleable self-theories go with a disposition to see tasks as opportunities for learning rather than as performance-oriented opportunities to demonstrate competence (or avoid showing incompetence). There are correlations between deep learning and a personal commitment to the pursuit of learning goals, and between surface learning and an orientation towards performance. Hence the self-theories that students – and their teachers – hold are likely to influence learning,[11] with those tending to malleable self-theories being likely to have more belief in their ability to be effective when faced with novel challenges. Entity theorists – those who rely on fixed traits in their explanations of actions, successes and failures – have less persistence and less commitment to learning. Dweck says that,

> holding a fixed theory of intelligence appears to turn students towards concern about performing and looking smart. Holding a malleable theory appears to turn students toward concerns about learning new things and getting smarter. We have also seen that entity theorists' concerns about looking smart can prevent them from seeking learning opportunities, even ones that could be critical to performing well in the future.
>
> (Dweck 1999: 23)

She argues – and we are inclined to agree – that graduates who incline to malleable self-theories can make better use of their achievements than those with fixed theories. She makes the further point that, 'it is students who are challenge-seeking and persistent and can tolerate periods of confusion who have the advantage' (p. 124).

'Metacognition' is a term not well known outside psychology, but we use it because it has an established literature which we find helpful when we think about how programmes can be designed to enhance student claims to employability. We mean three things by 'metacognition': knowing what you know, knowing how it can be used, and knowing how you get new knowings.[12] Underlying these three senses is the idea that the more we are aware of what we know and how we know, the more we are able to use our resources to good effect and go about acquiring new ones. Metacognition complements malleable self-theories (it provides the reflective or strategic thinking) and it contributes to the continued learning that professionals need to do if they are to grow and to keep pace with changes in the demands of their work. Those without this reflective capacity are likely to be professionally frozen and act on the basis of what has worked in the past rather than think analytically and reflectively about what it would be best to do. The virtues of metacognition are asserted by Mentkowski and Associates:

> Through a cycle of metacognitively monitoring performance, self-assessment of performance, reflective learning, and re-envisioning performance in some specific role, students and alumni gained a sense of self-confidence grounded in their capacities.
>
> (Mentkowski and Associates 2000: 196)

The employability-aware curriculum

Curricula in higher education are becoming more complex. Not so long ago the Modern History syllabus at the University of Oxford was a laconic statement which merely advertised that there would be, for example, an examination paper in British History 1066–1485. The tutors interpreted the statement as they chose, the students inferred from their engagements with their tutors what was expected, sat the examination, and succeeded to varying extents. It was tacitly assumed that success in the whole degree programme also signified employability.

Today, things are very different. Higher education institutions around the world are expected not only to continue to promote deep understandings of complex subject matter, but also:

- to work with cohorts of students from a diversity of backgrounds;
- to pay more attention to teaching, learning and assessment; and
- to support the development in students of a broad range of skills relevant to employment.

The words 'are expected' signal the concern of governments in many countries that their higher education systems should be accountable for the quality of the educational experiences that they offer and for the achievements of those who enter. The signal is given force in the various national systems of quality assurance that have been implemented. Further, governments have made clear their expectation that higher education should 'add value' to students so that they will become highly employable.

In a time when – as the cliché has it – the half-life of knowledge is steadily decreasing, and the virtues of lifelong learning are asserted, it makes little sense to think of the first degree as being more than the first step on the pathways that graduates subsequently take. 'Learning how to learn' is increasingly recognized as an important metacognitive achievement that is central to continuing personal and professional development. This is not to disparage understanding of a subject discipline; rather, it suggests that the first degree programme needs to consist of a new blend of content and process that will provide a launching-pad for lifelong personal and professional development. The curricular emphasis shifts towards *quality* of learning and away from *quantity* of learning, since quantity can accrete over time more easily than can quality.

Models for the employability-aware curriculum

There is no single model for the employability-aware curriculum, since contexts, student recruitment patterns, envisaged labour markets and institutional (and departmental) traditions are amongst variables that have to be taken into account when designing curricula. Further, major change designed to create an 'ideal' employability-oriented curriculum may engender prohibitive collateral costs.

The ways in which employability can be developed through curricula include the following, which are indicative of general structural options and are not clear-cut distinctions.[13]

- *Employability through the whole curriculum.* The best example here is of Alverno College in the USA, which requires its students to develop eight broad 'abilities' throughout the curriculum. UK examples of whole-curriculum innovation include the introduction of 'capability' at the former University of North London (Page 1998) and of transferable skills at the University of Luton (Atlay and Harris 2000).
- *Employability in the core curriculum.* The Skills *plus* project[14] argued the case for the USEM model informing 'core' modules in curricula, on the grounds that it would be more difficult to be systematic when modules, as optional components, were contributing in diverse ways to students' programmes of study.
- *Work-based or work-related learning incorporated as one or more components within the curriculum.* The most extensive incorporation of learning through work experience is in 'sandwich' or cooperative education programmes, in which a substantial placement[15] is built into the curriculum structure. A more modest approach is to award credit in respect of a module's worth of experience, such as reflectively documenting experience as a representative of the student body. Separate awards can be made available for work-related experience, and some examples are noted in Chapter 7.
- *Employability-related module(s) within the curriculum.* Work experience often does not fit conveniently into curricular compartments, even though successful experience can be accredited (see previous point). However, an important contribution to employability can be made by fostering skills of learning independently that

may not previously have been developed. Institutions, therefore, often include 'study skills' modules at the start of programmes, seeing these as an investment which will pay off in terms of students' autonomy as learners. Examples of skills-oriented modules at the beginning of study programmes can be found in Abramson and Jones (2001) and Booth (2001).

- *Work-based or work-related learning in parallel with the curriculum.* Many students undertake part-time work in order to support themselves financially through a full-time programme. Whilst this work may not be formally accredited, it nevertheless can be a valuable source of employability-related learning – provided that the student takes the opportunity to see it as such, and can take advantage of it when making an application for a job, or for some other purpose.

Employability and modular programmes

Many study programmes are modular in character. Modularity has both advantages and disadvantages in respect of the enhancement of employability.

The prime advantage of modular programmes is that they allow the student some (although not usually total) flexibility in choosing the modules to be studied. Where external constraints (such as the expectations of professional bodies) apply, the flexibility may be quite limited. Flexibility may also be limited where resources are constrained. A second advantage – for some students more theoretical than practical – is the opportunity that modularity offers a student to build up to a qualification by studying at more than one institution, or in one institution over an extended period of time. In the UK, credit transfer between institutions appears to have been little used, perhaps because of the lack of appropriate interinstitutional agreements and/or the fact that many students are restricted by residence to a limited range of institutions.

From the perspective of employability, a major problem faced by modular schemes is of accommodating 'slow learning' (Claxton 1998) – the kind of learning that may require more time than is available in a single module. The ability to deal with ticklish interpersonal situations, skill in tackling complex problems, and the development of powers of critical thinking are three examples where 'slow learning' is likely to take place. Slow learning is better assessed across a programme rather than at the end of a short modular slot. Hence a key challenge for modular schemes is to anticipate and forestall possible incoherence in the curriculum as it is experienced by the student.

Employability and assessment

The aim of enhancing employability brings into the open some longstanding problems with assessment. Awareness has recently grown that, for example:

- Some curriculum designs have inadvertently proved inimical to formative assessment, and consequentially to student learning. There is a need to review curricula in order to ensure that there is sufficient opportunity in them for effective formative assessment.

- There is a need to accommodate slow learning in the assessment regime, particularly at the level of the programme.
- Some achievements cannot be certified rigorously within the resources and time that are available to higher education. It is necessary to give thought to what can, and what cannot, be certified and, where certification is problematical, to consider alternative approaches.
- Students need to be knowledgeable about their achievements, to document them, and to be able to present them to putative employers in an appropriate manner. Supporting the development of 'knowing' students will require more than rhetoric if it is to be successful.

Contemporary higher education is expected to facilitate the development of a wider range of achievements than ever before. The implications for assessment are considerable. The need will be for some radical rethinking where the tweaking of existing approaches cannot do enough. The challenges posed by employability (and good educational practice in general) cannot be wished away. In the succeeding chapters we lay out the nature of those challenges, warn of some sterile or harmful responses, and suggest some potentially useful lines of development for heads of department, programme teams, educational development units and senior managers to pursue.

Notes

1. Later in this chapter we acknowledge difficulties with 'skills' (e.g. Holmes 2001; Hinchliffe 2002) and point to an alternative formulation, which we develop elsewhere.
2. The implication is that 'oral' is meant, since students claimed strengths in written communication.
3. Rushforth (2003) points out that the current set of employment benchmarks are adjusted to take account of the locality, and that future data will reflect job quality. Further, graduates will be surveyed three years after graduation.
4. This is also the description used on their website and in their print publications by the UK LTSN Generic Centre and the English Enhancing Student Employability Coordinating Team. (www.ltsn.ac.uk/ESECT)
5. The same general point applies to part-time students, many of whom will be studying in parallel with being in employment.
6. A similar distinction may be drawn between 'near transfer' and 'far transfer'.
7. See Bennett *et al.* (2000: 26ff) for a fuller account.
8. See Cowan (1998) for an extended discussion of reflection that can be directed towards students (in contrast to Cowan's intended readership of teachers in higher education).
9. Although we have a little more to say about 'skills' in Chapter 4, we develop our critique in Knight and Yorke (2003), where we explain our preference for 'skilful practices' and our dalliance with 'social practices'. Our point is that what are often called 'skills' are practices. The term directs our thinking to social theories of learning (Trowler, 2002) and away from psychometric ones. What holds for theories of learning holds for thinking about assessment as well.

10. Contrast the position taken by Hinchliffe (2002) who writes of 'skills in context' with the position taken by Jessup (1991) in respect of NVQs.
11. If the person holds a malleable self-theory, then in the USEM model there should logically be feedback loops back to the E from the U, S and M (not shown in Figure 1.1).
12. Pintrich (2002) subdivides metacognition into three: knowledge about strategy, about the cognitive task, and about oneself.
13. A fuller discussion can be found in Yorke and Knight (2003).
14. This project ran in four varied universities in the north-west of England between 2000 and 2002, and sought to bring fresh thinking to the incorporation of 'skills' in curricula in higher education.
15. UK placements tend to be of one year's duration. Elsewhere, shorter periods are more common.

2

Summative Assessment in Disarray

Assessment, judgement and measurement

Robert Linn, one of the USA's most eminent assessment experts, recently wrote:

> As someone who has spent his entire career doing research, writing and thinking about educational testing and assessment issues, I would like to conclude by summarizing a compelling case showing that the major uses of tests for student and school accountability over the past 50 years have improved education and student learning in dramatic ways. Unfortunately, that is not my conclusion.
>
> (Linn 2000: 14)

Paul Black and Dylan Wiliam argue that

> Students, parents, teachers, and others who use examination results to draw conclusions about individuals, or about the performance of schools, should understand that examination results are of limited reliability and validity,[1] and that they cannot be taken at face value.[2]

The point we are driving at is that the everyday trust we put in grades, marks and classes is not shared by experts in assessment. We add another quotation to drive this home.

> Assessing educational outcomes is not as straightforward as measuring height or weight. . . . One must therefore draw inferences about what students know and can do on the basis of what one sees them say, do, or make in a handful of particular situations. What a student knows and what one observes a student doing are not the same thing. . . . Assessment users always reason in the presence of uncertainty; as a result the information produced by an assessment is typically incomplete, inconclusive and amenable to more than one explanation.
>
> (Pellegrino *et al.* 2001: 42)

These three comments on summative assessment, or grading, come from experts on the assessment of schoolchildren. Public examinations have procedures that are far more rigorous than those commonly used in higher education. If there are concerns about assessment in the school sector, where public summative assessment is carefully done, then how much faith can we have in the marks and grades produced by higher education teachers whose understanding of assessment – especially of what assessment *cannot* do – is likely to be less developed?

This chapter is about assessment-as-grading and shows that commonsense higher education practices are not robust enough to allow us to make many generalizations about students' competence. Indeed, as far as some achievements are concerned, it is hard to see how grades could have anything except local, temporary and rather fuzzy meanings. If our argument holds good, much – perhaps most – of the time and money invested in trying to get accurate marks is wasted because we ignore decades of evidence about what can be measured, how accurately and at what cost. We shall build upon this analysis in subsequent chapters, mainly by using evidence from England to describe problems that cause concern in most higher education systems. These problems become more acute when teachers are asked to be explicit about the ways in which they promote and assess complex learning outcomes,[3] such as those that comprise employability. The familiar problems of grading essays reliably pale in comparison with expectations that colleges and universities will warrant students' all-round achievements as communicators, creators, motivators or leaders.

What is summative assessment?

As the name implies, summative assessment is designed to sum up achievement, to provide a summary. It is usually high-stakes assessment, by which we mean that the summary has an important purpose – it counts, typically towards the grade, class or mark that is shown on a certificate. High-stakes assessments with summative purposes include examinations, graded coursework and any performances that have to be satisfactory before one can proceed to the next stage of a programme of study. Because summative assessments tend to come at the end of a learning sequence, it can be difficult to use them to give feedback to help learners to do better next time. Indeed, there is often not a next time, in the sense that the material covered in a high-stakes assessment may never be addressed again. Although there might be useful general feedback that could be given to learners – about structuring examination answers, for example – exams are notorious for providing a mark and nothing else. By and large, assessment for summative purposes provides *feedout* in the form of a mark or letter. It has more to do with accountability and quality control than with providing feedback for learning.[4] The point is schematically developed in Figures 2.1 and 2.2, which use a conventional form to identify six elements of systems, in this case assessment systems with summative and formative purposes. The two look quite different. Summative assessment purposes give priority to getting secure estimates of achievement. The stakes are often high, as are the costs. In summative systems, power lies almost entirely with the assessor and 'final language' is common. When the purposes are formative the aim is to create feedback that

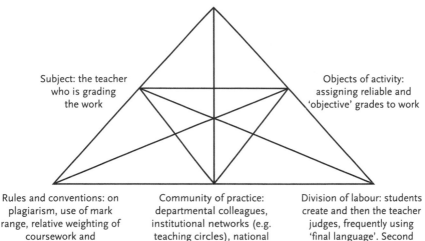

Mediating artefacts (assessment tools): low-inference tasks that can be reliably graded; secure grade criteria; possibly, norm-referenced mark distribution systems

Subject: the teacher who is grading the work

Objects of activity: assigning reliable and 'objective' grades to work

Rules and conventions: on plagiarism, use of mark range, relative weighting of coursework and examinations, standards and other local practices

Community of practice: departmental colleagues, institutional networks (e.g. teaching circles), national networks

Division of labour: students create and then the teacher judges, frequently using 'final language'. Second markers often involved

Figure 2.1 Summative assessment shown as an activity system from a teacher's perspective (after Engeström 2001)

helps student learning, i.e. it helps them to do better next time on a task of the same kind.[5] The emphasis is on valid judgements that tend to have local and provisional meanings. Power is more evenly distributed – the learner has more say. Dialogue and feedback are valued. Whereas one aims to generate assessment information with high exchange value, the other gives priority to use value.

It can be inferred that there would be undesirable effects of approaching tasks with a summative intent according to the rules of the formative assessment 'game'. Feedback is most useful when learners are prepared to show their weaknesses. That would, of course, be self-sabotage in summative assessments. So, any task should be clearly identified as formative or summative. Task *sequences* can have formative and then summative purposes, but any single task or activity should have one or the other. Teachers can also give general improvement-focused (formative) feedback on summative tasks.

Summative assessment and reliability

A central point about assessment-as-grading is that when the stakes are high, as with most summative assessments, reliability matters. A reliable assessment is one where the assessment process is believed to be objective and even-handed. By this we mean that:

• The assessment is fairly administered to all students who are working under the

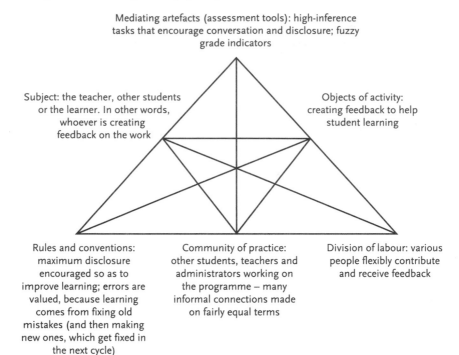

Mediating artefacts (assessment tools): high-inference tasks that encourage conversation and disclosure; fuzzy grade indicators

Subject: the teacher, other students or the learner. In other words, whoever is creating feedback on the work

Objects of activity: creating feedback to help student learning

Rules and conventions: maximum disclosure encouraged so as to improve learning; errors are valued, because learning comes from fixing old mistakes (and then making new ones, which get fixed in the next cycle)

Community of practice: other students, teachers and administrators working on the programme – many informal connections made on fairly equal terms

Division of labour: various people flexibly contribute and receive feedback

Figure 2.2 Formative assessment shown as an activity system from a teacher's perspective (after Engeström 2001)

same conditions[6] – for example, all students have the same amount of time; they all know whether they can or cannot use notes, books and electronic aids; and individual assessments are done in ways that prevent cheating.

- Room for administrative error is minimized. For example, there are routines to ensure that marks are correctly added up and that other clerical or transcription errors do not creep in.
- Markers work consistently to the same reference points. For example, there is an agreed mark scheme or set of grade indicators; markers are trained in using it; their consistency is monitored; each item is independently marked by more than one person, with the expectation that two markers would independently give the same mark.

It is not as easy to achieve reliability in human affairs as might be supposed. It might be supposed, for example, that it would be fairly straightforward to classify reliably causes of death. Box 2.1 shows the difficulties with devising, interpreting and consistently applying classifications of mortality.

Returning to the assessment of student achievements: reliability is greatest when assessments are simplest. There is a problem, then, if we aim to engender complex learning, because assessment processes that tend to simplify will undermine it. Suppose, for example, that creativity as an engineer gets tested by telling students to rate a number of solutions to engineering problems for their practicality and

Box 2.1 Reliability problems in the classification of diseases

The assessment of learning can be treated as a special case of the ways in which standards are set and used. If there are problems defining standards and applying them consistently, then there are reliability problems.

What are standards? Bowker and Star (1999: 13–14) say,

> The term as we use it . . . has several dimensions:
> 1. A 'standard' is any set of agreed-upon rules for the production of (textual or material) objects.
> 2. A standard spans more than one community of practice (or site of activity). It has temporal reach as well in that it persists over time.
> 3. Standards are deployed in making things work together over distance and heterogeneous metrics . . .
> 4. Legal bodies often enforce standards . . .
> 5. There is no natural law that says that the best standard shall win . . .
> 6. Standards have significant inertia and can be very difficult and expensive to change.

Against this list, we suggest that most of the standards and criteria we use in judging achievement in higher education are faulty. Faulty standards cannot support reliable judgements. Indeed, Bowker and Star document the problems attached to the international standards for the classification of diseases, arguing that 'while such [universal] standards may emerge in physical systems or under certain sorts of market conditions, for the class of phenomena described above, no universal standard is possible' (1999: 158). Moreover, agreements tend to be temporary:

> . . . we know from a long and gory history of attempts to standardize information systems that standards do not remain standard for very long and that one person's standard is another's confusion and mess. . . . We need a richer vocabulary than that of standardization or formalization with which to characterize the heterogeneity and the processual nature of information ecologies.
>
> (1999: 293)

Commenting on the history of attempts to set and apply criteria for the classification of disease, they said that

> the registrar general for England and Wales . . . noted [that] intranational (let alone international) comparison is difficult. Furthermore, doctors were too diverse a group to unite internationally around any given list. . . . The registrar's conclusion was that time spent on classification is wasted. . . . This solution . . . suggests that no list at all is valuable – local practices should be the focal point.
>
> (1999: 152)

Their case is that it is hard to classify the causes of death consistently, even when internationally agreed, long-established standards are to hand, along with the apparatus of pathology. This does not appear reassuring for hopes of achieving reliability in the assessment of complex outcomes of learning.

creativity. This is quite a high-inference assessment task in the sense that the answers are not obviously right or wrong but are matters of judgement. It would not cost too much to have the markers meet and agree on a marking scheme that they could all apply quite reliably. Even so, it is not a very valid assessment task because it implies that it is the ability to *recognize* creativity that is valued. It does nothing to help students to *be* creative engineers.

Chambers and Glassman identified seven desirable characteristics for assessments of competence (listed in Box 2.2) and argues that,

> Although all . . . characteristics are desirable they cannot be simultaneously maximized – trade-offs are unavoidable. For example, reliability can be increased in a straightforward manner by increasing the number of questions, raters, trials etc. . . . Generalizability and interprability [*sic*] are usually antagonistic. There are even situations where increases in reliability are known for theoretically sound reasons to decrease validity.
>
> (Chambers and Glassman 1997: 659–60)

Box 2.2   Seven desirable characteristics of assessments

1. Face validity – Does it look as if the assessments are really getting at the achievements in which we are interested? (For example, some mathematics tests will thwart people who can do numbers but who have trouble with reading.)
2. Efficient – Costs are low.
3. Interpretability – How easy is it to understand what results mean? How useful are they?
4. Non-reactivity – Assessments are best when they relate to authentic performances, rather than to exceptional shows for the benefit of the assessors.
5. Generalizability – 'Evaluation conclusions should be transportable from one context to similar ones; laboratory to clinic, lecture hall to clinic, school to practice, etc.'
6. Reliability – 'High reliability would be apparent if different raters agree, performance is similar from trial to trial, etc.'
7. Validity – 'Conclusions of evaluation should be accurate . . . high correlation between current and future, desired [assessments] . . . convergence of multiple, diverse lines of evidence.'

Source: after Chambers and Glassman 1997: 659

In a similar vein, Gibbs and Simpson argue that,

> The most reliable, rigorous and cheat-proof assessment systems are often accompanied by dull and lifeless learning that has short-lasting outcomes . . . we are arguing that we should design assessment, first, to support worthwhile learning, and worry about reliability later.
>
> (Gibbs and Simpson, 2002: 1)

There is a more fundamental reason why the concept of reliability is problematical. In their work on social measurement theory, Campbell and Russo argue that,

> Individuals can differ reliably in very specific settings, but the setting-person interactions are so strong that no trans-setting personality traits exist.
>
> (Campbell and Russo, 2001: 58)

This sits well with modern psychological research that emphasizes the degree to which our cognition and actions are contexted and specific to times and places, and with philosophies that place similar emphasis upon the particular and the contingent.[7] Applied to assessment, these theories remind us of the substantial difference between performance and competence, which is summarized in Table 2.1.[8] We tend to assume that the relationship between a performance and a person's competence is like that shown by points 1 and 4 in the table. Sometimes it is; often it is not. Fischer *et al.* (1990), for example, argue that people do not normally perform to capacity and although they can be stimulated (by tests, perhaps) to show their best, we also know that the high levels of stress that tests can evoke depress some people's performances. The implication of points 2 and 3 is that we need many samples of performance before generalizing to competence. Even then it would be wise to treat judgements as provisional.

If we add to this Campbell's pioneering work on threats to validity (Campbell and Stanley 1963), which identified over a dozen factors that make it hard, sometimes impossible, to be sure what any grades or marks *mean*, then it is not clear that summative assessment in the form of degree classifications is much use for

Table 2.1   Performance and competence

'Real' level of attainment	Is competent (can reliably do)	Is not competent (cannot reliably succeed)
Assessment assumption		
Competence can be inferred from a single performance	1. No problems	2. 'Success spikes' occur. They mislead, which is why high-stakes judgements should use multiple judgements that use multiple methods
Competence cannot be inferred from a single performance	3. We all make mistakes. When the stakes are high and judgements are based on too little evidence, mistakes are treated as evidence of incompetence, rather than as facts of life	4. Possible damage to self-theories but this does not cause *assessment* problems

Source: derived from Wood and Power 1987

differentiating between graduates – a concern expressed in the English higher education White Paper (DfES 2003).

Four limits of summative assessment

Making reliable judgements

We have said that the more complex the outcomes we hope to induce, the harder it is to assess them reliably *and* with validity *and* at a cost we can afford. Highly reliable assessments tend to tell us about simple achievements. Yet, even with complex achievements, such as classroom competence, counselling skill or project management, reliability can be increased to tolerable levels if enough costly effort is put into using more than one well-trained marker to judge a range of relevant performances against well-understood criteria. The quest for reliability threatens validity, and strategies that maximize both are expensive in proportion to the complexity of the achievements to be assessed. Where employability is concerned, they are complex achievements, expensive to assess with tolerable reliability.

Criteria-referencing (sometimes called criterion-referencing) is often held up as an answer to these problems. The theory is simple. Identify what counts as successful performance or good attainment, specify it precisely and judge evidence of achievement accordingly. The criteria provide agreed standards expressed in a shared language that become points of reference for markers to use when trying to put marks to students' work. Good criteria, carefully used by well-trained assessors reduce, but cannot eliminate, reliability problems, so criteria-referencing is not the solution that some believe it to be. Knight (2001b: 243–4) had five reservations:

- Difficulties with developing statements of learning outcomes, criteria for awards at different levels, and formulations of thresholds. These are not trivial disputes because they stem from ontological and epistemological uncertainties. Some consider that much that they try to describe cannot be captured by generic criteria because the phenomena are 'context-dependent, situational, uncertain and volatile' (Sadler 2002: 49). Others see value in such criteria but, as Coffield (2002) remarks of 'learning to learn', there is no shortage of lists 'all jostling to be included in any definition of "learning to learn" '. These lists 'are remarkably easy to construct' (Coffield 2002: 42).
- Attempts to produce precise criteria lead to a proliferation of sentences and clauses culminating in complex, hard-to-manage documents. Talking of the National Council for Vocational Qualifications' (NCVQ) attempt to produce criteria-related vocational qualifications, Wolf (2002: 74) said. 'As reality stubbornly failed to fall in with NCVQ's vision of perfect clarity, the level of detail required by the Council and the complexity of standards layout increased.' However, the obvious alternative – settling for fewer, looser statements – combines manageability with imprecision.
- It is important to remember that these are criteria-*referenced* judgements, not criteria-determined ones. The criteria are reference points in processes of judgement, aids not replacements.

- Even the most carefully drafted criteria statements have to be translated into concrete and situation-specific terms. What exactly is 'clear communication', or 'speaks with enthusiasm', or 'mastery of one common word-processing package'? What I call 'leadership' you call 'paternalism'; what you call 'good oral communication', I call 'bombast'. Wolf (1995b) has shown convincingly that it is not enough to provide statements of expectations – these need to be supported by exemplars and discussion of them if the fullest understanding is to be attained.[9] Note that the sharing of understanding encompasses both the assessors and the assessed.
- Ecclestone (2001) shows how entrenched teachers' individual judgements are. If greater consistency is possible, then it takes a lot of training before assessors feel comfortable with criteria-referenced marking and do it in broadly similar ways. In all high-inference summative assessments, reliability is expensive.

As higher education tries to do more than impart information it becomes harder to conceptualize the outcomes of learning and it takes longer to capture them in useful criteria statements. Once fixed on paper, these statements then have to become shared, understood and applied in common ways. In so far as this is possible, it is also time-consuming. Where criteria-referenced assessments involve high-inference judgements, they take longer to use than low-inference marking schemes and second and even third assessors are called for. The data they produce are often less wieldy than a simple but misleading numerical score.

The limits of number

We seldom realize just how commonly we attach numbers to judgements and then act as if those numbers can be fairly transformed by mathematical processes of addition, division, etc. There is no inherent problem with saying that people in the top 20% will be numbered 1s, those in the next quintile 2s, and so on. The problem comes if we then try to treat those numbers as anything other than shorthand for 'this person is in the top 20% of that group on that measure at that time'. We ought not, for example, to combine the 1 with a measure made at a different time – a 3, say – and conclude that this person is really a 2. The mistake is to treat numerals that were being used as tags or signs as if they were *numbers*. True numbers can be manipulated because they have the property that the interval between two numbers is known and constant. The gap between 1.5 and 2.5 is known and is known to be the same as the gap between 123.4 and 124.4, so we can perform all sorts of operations on true numbers. Assessments of learning are far more likely to produce tags or signs than they are to produce numbers.

There are other difficulties in combining data from different sources – from different sorts of task or different modules. Dalziel (1998) looked at the effect of varying the rules used to combine marks for different sorts of work in a first-year psychology module. One weighting favoured some students, another favoured others. This demonstration of the arbitrariness of grades based on manipulating numbers attached to different performances is confirmed by work done in England by the Student Assessment and Classification Working Group (SACWG). It shows, for example, that a first-class degree classification may not stay a first-class grade if different regulations and algorithms are used to weight and combine the numerical tags representing different achievements (Yorke *et al.* 2002b). Consumers of assessment data may sometimes value a headline summary – a 2:2 degree, *summa cum laude*, a GPA of 3.6 – but what does it really signify?

Meanings

Where achievements are reported in a simple form, for example as a grade point average or degree class, it is hard to know what is signified. Universities and colleges differ in the ways that they weight scores from the first, second, third and fourth years of study so that it is not clear whether a degree classification describes students' sustained performance across the programme or the level reached at the end of it (sometimes termed the student's 'exit velocity'). Again, we have been external examiners of programmes in which there are no examinations and have overseen ones in which there are (too) many. Since there is evidence that students who feel overworked may adopt 'surface' learning approaches (Chambers 1992), which should not lead to good marks, how are we to tell whether moderate marks represent overload or moderate effort/aptitude?

Although there are subject benchmarks that are to be used as points of reference in programme design in English universities and colleges, we find that there is a lot of variation in criteria used within a subject and between different groups of institutions serving different clients. So, although criteria-referenced grading may be good for student learning and equity *within* a community of practice, differences in the criteria used prevent, even impede, communication *between* communities. For example, difficulties are reported in getting agreement on criteria and their application within a subject (Greatorex 1999; Woolf and Cooper 1999) and even in one school (Price and Rust 1999; O'Donovan *et al.* 2000). Even if we accept that good criteria have been carefully used by trained markers, as outsiders we have little sense of what they *mean*.

Nor do scores and grades tell us how much scaffolding[10] students used, that is to say the degree to which achievements were their own. How are we to tell whether a number represents a performance achieved with the help of plenty of scaffolding or the same performance achieved with no help? In this sense, grades can mislead because the environment in which they were created is a significant, usually unreported, factor.

Achievements and communication

How are summative assessment judgements to be communicated, given this view that symbols – grade-point averages (GPAs) or degree classes – carry minimal, conventional meanings that have, in any case, been disrupted by the expansion of higher education and the proliferation of programmes and aims?

An attractive response is to tell consumers more. In England, progress files (QAA 2001d) are an attempt to do this. The files are to comprise transcripts, issued by the university or college and students' portfolio claims to achievement with accompanying evidence. The transcripts describe courses taken and marks but are essentially uninformative about learning. Personal development planning (PDP) and attendant portfolios,[11] may say too much. How are graduate schools or employers to process documents which, even expressed in summary form, will contain claims to achievements in respect of a programme's intended outcomes of learning – as many as 30 outcomes or more? How can this complexity be handled by employers who are already so harassed by the large number of graduates in the labour market that they use 'e-screening' to reject rapidly the majority of job applications?

Summative assessment: what can be done?

Universities and colleges are preoccupied with creating fair and reliable summative assessment data, yet summative assessment is in disarray (Knight 2002c), partly because of intractable problems with putting numbers on complex achievements, such as those subsumed by 'employability', but also because outside consumers do not always appreciate what it is that those numbers are supposed to signify. Local criteria, curricula and practices are rampant and national subject benchmarks seem to mutate into at least as many forms as there are departments using them. Yet universities and colleges are still expected to produce high-stakes assessments to warrant achievement in general terms.

Programme assessment plans

The most powerful suggestion we have for improving high-stakes assessment comes from our belief that assessment needs to be planned as a system that engages students from the time they enter a programme through to graduation. We appreciate that it is usual in some subject areas and in some universities and colleges to see a programme as something constructed by the student who chooses from a generous menu. In such systems it is hard to think in terms of programme teams making plans to enhance the coherence of the undergraduate years so that slow-growing and complex achievements have the best chance to develop and can be constructively assessed in some trustworthy ways. For some this is a cause for concern, as discussions of the undergraduate curriculum in the USA in Gaff and Ratcliff's (1996) *Handbook of the Undergraduate Curriculum* show. Our position is that programme-level thinking is necessary both to stimulate complex learning and to assess it. We argue that even in high-choice programmes it is possible to identify the most popular tracks that students beat through the modules available to them and to begin by trying to orchestrate those courses. In this chapter, though, our discussion assumes tolerably coherent programmes, programme specifications[12] and programme teams.

A starting point is for a programme team to review the programme specification and consider the outcomes of learning that could be assessed summatively. We have suggested that these will be the more simple and determinate achievements. Many teachers, for example, are keen to have regular assessments of fundamental information, formulae and heuristics.

The next step is, we suggest, to identify those outcomes of learning that are the least likely to be suitable for summative assessment. They will still get assessed and students will be *required* to treat seriously tasks that address them (see Chapter 9). These outcomes will not, however, be summatively assessed, except in the sense that non-performance or dilatory performance will be penalized.

Programme teams then consider the outcomes that are left. They will be those that, at a price, can be assessed with tolerable reliability and without severe damage to validity. Things to be considered in an appraisal of the opportunities and the costs attaching to tolerably-reliable high-stakes assessment arrangements are:

- How useful is it to have summative judgements of this outcome of learning? This implies considering who would want this information and how it could usefully be reported.
- What tasks could be set to allow reliable judgements to be made? Would they be sufficiently authentic?[13] This is a question about the trade-off between validity and reliability.
- Can the programme team afford the cost of getting tolerably reliable judgements of achievement when tasks such as these are likely to call for quite high levels of inference?
- Is it feasible to provide enough opportunities for repeated assessment across the programme? (Repeated assessment allows more reliable judgements.)
- Will these opportunities allow the outcome to be judged in a variety of contexts and through a variety of tasks?
- Can the team write grade indicators that will help judgement? That is to say, can indicators be written without relying on empty comparatives like 'more', 'better', 'poorer'?

Differentiated assessments

Most tasks tap several outcomes of learning. Take essays as an example. A typical essay will involve locating information, handling it, analysing, thinking critically, using English well, synthesizing, evaluating and following referencing conventions. Grade indicators are likely to run several of these achievements together: for example, a description of performance that would usually get a mark in the range 60–69% in an English research university says,

> An essay meriting an *upper second* mark displays an ability to handle the relevant literature and research in a critical and analytical matter. It is more than a good description of the various theories, studies and perspectives relevant to the question. It does not necessarily have a watertight argument, but it is clearly structured and its conclusion does not take the reader by surprise. An

upper-second essay develops a well-expressed theme or argument from a critical and appropriately referenced consideration of relevant literature. Competing claims, and the evidence advanced in defence of them, are examined and evaluated. An *upper second* essay avoids unsubstantiated assertions.

Notice that the indicator highlights some outcomes of learning – critical and analytical thinking, for example – and assumes a command of others, such as finding information, time management, problem working. Highlighted achievements may be directly appraised and inferences will be made about others. Notice that the extract does not mention giving accurate references and good English usage, although the department does assess them. Its approach is to make a background assumption that performance on these tasks will be satisfactory. A mispunctuated piece, or a paper accompanied by an incomplete set of references is summatively judged to have violated this assumption and students are told that a standard penalty (10%) will be applied *unless the failings are rectified within a week*. They usually are.

What we see, then, are three approaches to summative assessment at work in one task:

- Direct assessment of named outcomes of learning.
- Proxy assessment (in order to do X, Y has to be present but it is not directly assessed).
- Background assessment, where competence is an issue only if evidence of incompetence presents itself.

Box 2.3 shows how module handbooks can map the outcomes associated with the course on to the tasks. Students need to know this mapping, and so too do their teachers. Without shared understandings of the rules of the game, this differentiated approach to assessment collapses, and with it goes the hope that a programme can systematically stimulate complex outcomes of learning.

Assessment tickets

The way this department handles poor English usage is interesting on two counts. First, it shows things being required but being graded only as acceptable or not acceptable. This is a useful device, allowing teams to make some things compulsory and penalize poor performance without getting caught up in making fine-grained and expensive judgements. Only a minority of submissions, those on the acceptable/not acceptable borderline, need deliberation.

Secondly, it shows a nice blend of formative and summative purposes. If performance is summatively judged unacceptable, the student is told this but given an opportunity to rectify matters. If that is done there is no penalty. Although this looks like a violation of the principle that formative and summative should not be mixed in one task, they are, in fact, kept apart. The task is a summative one. Only in certain, well-defined cases, does it create feedback that has to be acted upon.

This practice can be generalized into the principle that staged tasks – tasks in which students have to do X, Y *and then* Z – can combine formative and summative

Box 2.3 The relationship between a module assessment plan and a programme plan

There are eight learning outcomes for this module, all derived from the programme specification. The links are not shown here but the table does show how outcomes and assessment tasks are related.

This table links these outcomes to the main pieces of work students do. The letters indicate the way the task will be treated: for example, A means that this outcome will be directly graded, D that there will be written feedback on this outcome from the tutor, and E that tutors will give oral feedback.

Learning outcomes, O1–O8, taken from the programme specification **Assessment tasks**	O1	O2	O3	O4	O5	O6	O7	O8
Coursework 1 – write a 2000-word literature review **(Summative)**	B	B	B		C	C, E	C	
Coursework 2 – designing a research inquiry **(S)**	A, B, E	B, E		A, B, E	C	C, E	C	A, E
Coursework 3 – write an evaluation of a published research paper **(S)**	B	B, E	A, E		C	C, E	C	
Submit bullet point lists related to each week's set readings **(Formative)**	D				C		C	
Examination – Q1 note-making **(S)**	A							
Examination – Q2 designing an inquiry **(S)**	B	B		A				

Source: based on Knight 2002a: 153

purposes as long as it is clear that a summative assessment of stage Z, for example, will not be influenced by feedback created in the formative stages X and Y. Let us illustrate this. Students are often told to keep learning journals, research logs or portfolios. These are complex products and it is expensive to try to get reliable assessments of them. One way of handling this is to make sure that students keep them (with penalties if they do not), check them to see that basic requirements are met (again, penalties for non-compliance), and provide plenty of opportunities for formative feedback (probably through peer feedback in a buddy system). A summative time-constrained assessment – say 30 minutes, done in a normal teaching period – is then set which requires students to use what they have learned through keeping the logs, journals or portfolios to resolve a novel problem. Their answers will need high-inference judgements but they will be short and a lot easier and cheaper to grade than the logs, portfolios or journals themselves. Indeed, it is likely to be a better test of learning, understood as the ability to transfer understandings, than any direct assessment of the portfolios, logs and journals.

A business studies module used an approach like this in requiring students to customize any software they liked so that it could run the accounts of a small hotel. They had plenty of formative feedback and were encouraged to work together, use the Worldwide Web and talk to the previous year's students. Time was provided for feedback about selected outcomes that were not going to be summatively assessed. The students then brought their disks to class and were given one hour to analyse a set of accounts. Those who had simply lifted other people's software solutions could not do the task *in the time available* because they did not understand the solutions well enough to transfer them to the new problem. As for the teachers, they had to invest in reliably assessing a short piece of work that showed achievement on half-a-dozen learning outcomes, but it did not take as long as previous attempts to assess this task. Their line was that the quality of the solutions should be assessed by students' use of them. This elegant combination of formative and summative assessment purposes plays to the strengths of both.

Summative assessment in higher education

This chapter aligns with Broadfoot's claim that

> any kind of data on student attainment, or indeed any other kind of assessment data, is the product of the interaction of people, time and place, with all that this implies in terms of a complex web of understandings, motivations, anxieties, expectations, traditions and choices.
>
> (Broadfoot 2002: 157)

She was commenting on data generated from the highly reliable tests used in the Third International Maths and Science Study. Higher education assessments are less robust. The implication is that a belief in the precision of assessment in higher education is likely to be misplaced. The more complex the achievements to be judged, the more misplaced the belief and the less trustworthy any generalizations based on scores, grades or other marks. A concern with student employability exacerbates the difficulties this causes for those who think that assessment should measure real achievements in ways that allow high-probability predictions to be made of future performance. As the 'assessment movement' in the USA and 'target-setting' managerialism in England have showed, there is no shortage of people who act upon beliefs that are at odds with social measurement theory

(Campbell and Russo 2001) and assessment scholarship, as represented by the quotations that opened this chapter.

Notes

1. When assessments are valid there is a good match between what they reach and what they are intended to reach. Validity questions include:

   - Does each component of the claim exhibit face validity (i.e. is it plausible, given what is known about the experiences of the portfolio compiler)?
   - Is each component of the claim backed up by credible evidence?
   - Is what has been put forward internally consistent?

2. See http://www.kcl.ac.uk/phpnews/wmprint.php?ArtID=238, accessed 10 February 2003.
3. We refer to 'learning outcomes' because it is a familiar phrase, although it is redolent of behaviourist approaches to learning. Preferred alternatives are 'outcomes of learning' or 'learning intentions'.
4. When students treat summative assessments seriously, good tasks can stimulate excellent learning in the revision period (Entwistle and Entwistle 1992; Entwistle and Marton 1994).
5. Pellegrino *et al.* (2001: 4) consider that '*One of the most important roles for assessment is the provision of timely and informative feedback to students during instruction and learning so that their practice of a skill and its subsequent acquisition will be effective and efficient*' (emphasis in original). They add that assessments' 'effectiveness and utility must ultimately be judged by the extent to which they promote student learning' (ibid.: 221).
6. With suitable modifications to put those with special educational needs on a comparable footing with others.
7. Reservations about the concept of 'skills' were established in Chapter 1. The discussion of criteria-referencing in this chapter amplifies this unease with claims that achievements are primarily stable and generalizable.
8. Medical colleagues seem to use the terms rather distinctively: to use 'competence' to refer to displays of achievement and 'performance' to describe more general, sustained achievement. As far as we know, no one else distinguishes the terms in this way.
9. Polanyi (1958: 54) earlier made the point that 'Connoisseurship . . . can be communicated only by example, not by precept.'
10. Scaffolding is a concept derived from Vygotsky's work. It indicates that learners have to be supported on their route to autonomy or expertise. This support may involve task design (tasks for novices spell out what needs to be done; those for more autonomous learners expect them to identify the problem and possible solutions); learning support (making helpful resources readily available for novices whilst expecting more experienced learners to identify for themselves the resources they need); and social support (by letting inexperienced students work together, often under close tutor supervision, whilst expecting more experienced students to work independently when necessary). These are three forms of scaffolding. We often find that students who can show evidence of similar achievements have experienced different levels of scaffolding. Good assessment systems help employers and graduate schools to appreciate how much scaffolding students have had. Apparent achievements should not, therefore, be taken at face value.
11. Chapter 11 says more about portfolios. We see difficulties with the assumption that staff and students will be enthusiastic about them. We are attracted by the alternative of

presenting PDP as an extended engagement with the necessary business of making, documenting, reviewing and updating CVs or résumés.
12. The idea is that all programmes should specify the outcomes of learning to be stimulated, identifying the concomitant assessment, learning and teaching practices.
13. 'Authenticity' pervades Chapter 7. For the moment we define it as the opposite of the simplified, artificial and decontexted assessment tasks that are commonplace.

3

Formative Assessment: Unrealized Potential

The concept of formative assessment

The basic idea is straightforward: formative assessment contributes to learning by informing students about their performances, creating the conditions for loops of reflection and action that, in theory at least, spiral ever more widely outwards (Figure 3.1). Although all feedback can evoke learning, it is helpful, from the outset, to declare an interest in feedback that draws attention to actions that, if taken, have

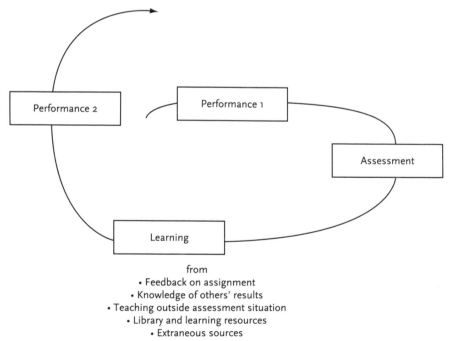

Figure 3.1 A schematic representation of formative assessment and the growth of learning

the power to make a difference to future work on different topics. Although many teachers give a lot of feedback on specifics, it is *general* feedback that has the greater power to stimulate learning. If general feedback relates to the learning intentions declared in course and programme specifications, then this is a clear benefit to the coherence of students' learning.

The literature tends to concentrate on feedback provided by teachers and its consequences, but to this 'supply-side' perspective should be added an acknowledgement that the student's 'tuning in' to messages (often informal) emanating from other sources is also part of the formative assessment process. Brown (1999: 6) suggests that formative assessment 'is primarily characterized by being continuous', but there is no necessity for this to be the case as far as formal assessment is concerned: formative assessment can be quite occasional, yet still embody the essential supportiveness towards student learning. If, on the other hand, Brown is taken as reflecting the student's perspective as a receiver of messages, then her point is more firmly founded.

Figure 3.1 implies that formative assessment spans 'a spectrum . . . ranging from the very informal, almost casual, to the highly formal, perhaps even ritualistic' (Rowntree 1987: 4–5). There is a fourfold distinction amongst

- informal formative feedback from peers and others outside the higher education institution;
- informal formative feedback from teachers within the higher education institution;
- formal formative feedback from peers; and
- formal formative feedback from teachers.[1]

In this chapter, by far the greatest emphasis is given to formal formative feedback, although the significance of informal feedback should not be overlooked.

Informal formative assessment can be provided by anyone, including people outside the immediate higher education context, such as parents or relatives, or from other students not involved in the same programme of study. It can also take place indirectly where the student sees assessments given to peers and is able to evaluate their performance with reference to these, or where they unearth new materials which throw light on the performance in question (reflective academics do this all the time when updating lectures or writing journal articles or books: from a quality assurance perspective, this would be seen as exemplifying 'continuous quality improvement').

Peers can be a fruitful source of informal feedback. Collaborative learning situations automatically create situations in which students learn from each other: this is clearly desirable, not only because it has the potential to augment the feedback provided by teachers, but also because it models situations that people routinely experience in employment, in voluntary work, and in life generally. There are two potential drawbacks.

The first is that informal feedback from peers may be misconceived and cause the recipient to veer off in an unprofitable (and, on occasion, dangerous) direction. Social psychologists remind us of the power of peer group pressure (the infamous Stanford jail experiment (Haney and Zimbardo 1977) being an extreme example).

Where students learn, within a programme, to assess well with reference to public criteria that derive from the programme learning intentions, the risk is reduced. The second borders on plagiarism: the student 'picks up' material from peers and presents it as their own. The risk of plagiarism can be reduced through a process of 'claims-making' and supporting the claim with evidence (Chapter 11).

Informal formative assessments by teachers take place as they use their professional expertise in the course of events, but are not specifically stipulated in the curriculum design. One example is the instantaneous feedback given when a graduate teaching assistant corrects the inappropriate use of equipment in a laboratory; another is when a tutor points a member of a seminar group towards an overlooked source of evidence. Formative assessment becomes less informal, and may need to be treated as formal, when a teacher comments on draft material produced by the student.

The value of formative assessment by students' peers should not be overlooked, though students need to be convinced that the task is educationally worthwhile for them (and not merely an example of the teacher abrogating responsibility for assessment), lest they refuse to take part.

Formal formative assessments can be defined as those that are stipulated by a specific curricular assessment framework. They require the student to do the work, and the teacher to assess the work and provide feedback from which the student can learn. Formal formative assessments are typically undertaken by academic staff or by supervisors of placement activity within a collaborating organization. The process may operate on a one-to-one basis, or may take the form of a group feedback session relating to an assignment that has been set (worked examples in engineering, for instance). Regarding the latter, when students have been surveyed about the value of organized formative assessment sessions, the relatively sparse evidence in the literature (Carroll 1995; Rolfe and McPherson 1995; Vaz *et al.* 1996) points to an overwhelmingly positive response.

This chapter argues that formative assessment in higher education involves (or should involve) considerations that are often given little attention in discussions about practice.

Formative and summative assessment: a fuzzy distinction

Bloom *et al.* (1971) made a sharper distinction between formative and summative assessment than many subsequent writers have done. Some assessments (for example, in-course assignments) are intended to be simultaneously formative and summative – formative because the student is expected to learn from whatever feedback is provided, and summative because the grade awarded contributes to the overall grade at the end of the study unit. Summative assessments in relation to a curricular component (the student passes or fails a module, for example) can act formatively if the student learns from them. Notice, though, our suggestion that it is best to keep formative and summative intentions apart because, as we showed in Chapter 2, different rules and expectations operate in each case.

There is also a problem because one of the less desirable effects of the unitization of curricula in UK higher education has been the reduction in the amount of formal formative assessment as the number of end-of-unit summative assessments has increased. The pressure on 'turnround time' for assessment is often too great. Any feedback is sometimes received too late for students' subsequent choice of study units and may also be insufficient, if only given as a mark or grade, for learning on subsequent modules.

Black and Wiliam (1998), in a substantial review of the literature in which higher education was much less well represented than school education, showed that formative assessment was effective in promoting student learning across a wide range of educational settings (disciplinary areas, types of outcomes, levels), and that the quality of the feedback received by the learner was an important factor. Formative assessment helps students to develop their capacity for self-regulation, by helping them to appreciate the standards that are expected from them and also to chart their development.

In their distillation of an accumulation of research experience at Alverno College in the United States, Mentkowski and Associates illustrate the significance for students' development that can arise from formative assessment:

> Students observed that feedback was given in such a way that they did not feel it was rejecting or discouraging or placing an unbalanced focus on negative aspects of performance. Instead, they experienced it as supportive criticism . . . [and] as an important support for learning and motivation.
>
> . . . Students observed that feedback procedures assisted them in forming accurate perceptions of their abilities and establishing internal standards with which to evaluate their own work. For some students, positive interactions with faculty or peers appeared to have been an important factor motivating achievement in the absence of grades. Students responded . . . to their teachers' expectations and personal recognition.
>
> (Mentkowski and Associates 2000: 82)

A problem with assessment generally is that expected standards, curriculum objectives or learning outcomes are often conveyed through the medium of a semi-technical language of assessment. These statements are generally insufficient to convey what is really expected of the students: this requires explanation, exemplification and discussion.

Purposes of formative assessment

Formative assessment has three purposes:

- To give credit for what has been done, with reference to the expected standard.
- To correct what is wrong, thereby helping the student to avoid repeating the error (hence merely saying that something is wrong is insufficient).
- To encourage emancipation by alerting the student to possibilities which they may not have hitherto discerned.

The psychologist Jerome Bruner made the point that

> Learning depends on knowledge of results, at a time when, and at a place where, the knowledge can be used for correction.
>
> (Bruner 1970: 120)

Although he alluded to other educational contexts, Bruner was writing about school education where 'getting things right' is given considerable weight. His use of the word 'correction' implies the existence of 'right answers', consistent with a homeostatic or single loop (Argyris and Schön 1974) perspective on education. 'Getting things right' is not to be disparaged, since it is easy to identify where 'not getting things right' had disastrous consequences – the examples of metal fatigue in the Comet airliner; the prescribing of thalidomide for pregnant women; the failure of the O-rings on the booster rockets of the space shuttle *Challenger*; and the collapse of the Tacoma Narrows suspension bridge come to mind.

Elsewhere, Bruner went further than homeostasis, a collection of his writings being entitled *Beyond the Information Given* (Bruner 1974). This implication of an intention to go beyond the current boundaries of knowledge (in personal and/or disciplinary terms) is more in tune with higher education, in which there is a significant dimension that can, following Barnett (1997), be labelled as emancipatory. From a higher education perspective, it would be more appropriate had the final word of the quotation from Bruner read 'development'.

Emancipation, in a strong interpretation of Barnett's educational intention, cannot be assumed to occur on its own. Few students at undergraduate level are likely to go beyond the boundaries of existing knowledge (although the creative arts might provide evidence to the contrary). In a weaker sense, emancipation can be seen as the movement of the student into richer intellectual territory. Students should be able to claim this as an outcome of their time in higher education, but the claims may be stronger where they have benefited from supportive formative assessment.

A model of formative assessment

Formative assessment is implicitly dialogic, since the student receives feedback on their performance from the teacher and may have the opportunity to engage them in face-to-face or online discussion about the assessment. Whilst the validity of the assessment has to be acceptable, its reliability is less important because of the developmental (as opposed to measurement-oriented) nature of formative assessment. In an ideal world, both teacher and student seek to interpret and understand what the other is saying, with the intention that the student will develop their learning. The mutuality of formal formative (and also informal) assessment is represented in Figure 3.2.

Figure 3.2 indicates that, at its richest, formative assessment is complex. In an idealized formal assessment, the task is constructed by the teacher, bearing in mind the structure and progression of the subject discipline(s) involved; an appreciation of the potential trajectory of students' general intellectual and moral development;

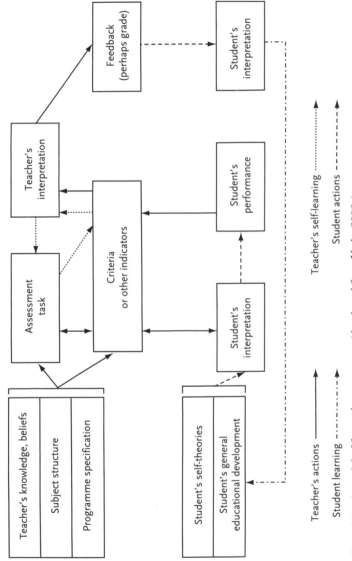

Figure 3.2 A model of formative assessment (developed from Yorke 2003a)

a knowledge of the current level of intellectual development of their students; and the students' self-theories. The specification of assessment criteria, supported by an elaboration of their implications, enhances the students' understanding of the task. The student interprets the assessment task and responds to it according to their knowledge of the subject and the level of their intellectual development, bearing the assessment criteria in mind. The teacher then judges the student's performance with reference to the specified criteria, and feedback is given through commentary and/or grades. At this point, particularly, there is potential for fruitful dialogue between student and assessor.

Reality tends to be rather different. The pressures on academics, and for many the lack of a grounding in student development, mean that their assumptions about 'where students are at', developmentally, can be fairly rough-edged. The assessment process (formative and summative) is not fine-tuned to the individual. However, it does offer the assessing academic the opportunity better to appreciate the students' understanding and capability, and hence – where the opportunity presents itself in the curriculum – the chance to tune assessment more finely in the future. The greatest opportunity for successive cycles of formative assessment and fine-tuning are probably to be found during the supervision of an undergraduate student's final-year project or dissertation, or during the completion of a thesis for a higher degree.

Formative assessment is threatened by two longstanding problems that apply with far greater force to summative assessment:

- Assessment design and instrumentation are often ad hoc and lack a theoretical base.
- Assessors typically do not have any substantial grounding in the theory (limited as it is) and practice of assessment.

Where the assessor is able to focus on supporting student learning, and offers a contribution towards a potential dialogue, these problems may well have little practical effect. The same cannot be said of summative grading.

Convergence and divergence

Torrance and Pryor (1998, 2001) make the distinction between convergence and divergence in assessment. Convergent assessments test whether students can fulfil pre-specified objectives, whereas divergent assessments test students' ability to succeed in more open-ended tasks. Boud (2000) argues – and we agree – that a key purpose of higher education is to facilitate the autonomy of learners in a world of lifelong learning, in which case formative assessments (and summative assessments, for that matter) must contain a significant proportion of divergence. Problems 'in the wild' are often open-ended, and solutions have to be reached relatively quickly, with incomplete information to hand. The reaching of solutions may involve the integration of understandings from a range of contexts, not all of them grounded in academic study.[2]

In their study of teachers in primary schools, Torrance and Pryor (2001: 621) found that 'in many cases their teaching seemed to close down opportunities for exploring student understanding rather than opening them up'; in other words, they 'missed tricks' as far as divergence was concerned. The use of expected learning outcomes in curriculum design could lead learning activities away from divergence, if the emphasis on assessment is focused too narrowly on the listed learning outcomes – something that could happen where higher education provision is under pressure. 'Teaching to the test' may make some appearance in pedagogical processes, for reasons that are honourable (teachers wanting not to disadvantage their students by going beyond what is stated in documentation, or not wanting to create a situation which might lead to an academic appeal), or less so (concern with retention figures, and with institutional or departmental income). This is where a broader perspective on student learning can usefully be brought into play, focusing on the third of the purposes of formative assessment that we noted earlier in this chapter: to encourage emancipation by alerting the student to possibilities which they may not hitherto have discerned.

Developing students' capability for moral action

Teachers in higher education are, in general, more *au fait* with the structure and progression of the subject discipline than they are with matters of student development. Whilst the constructivist Jean Piaget's work on developmental stages has been influential in school education, all students should – by the time they enter higher education – have reached the highest Piagetian level – that of formal operational thinking. Other theorists, amongst them Kohlberg (1964), Perry (1998/ 1970), and King and Kitchener (1994), offer accounts of student development.[3] The work of these developmentalists, though known to specialists in education for many years, has made few inroads into higher education curricula. Perry, for example, saw a continuum of developmental stages that were based on dualistic thinking at one end and on relativistic thinking at the other: in more vernacular terms, the cognitive substrate might be represented as extending from simple 'black or white', right or wrong, conceptualizing to an internalization of complexity, or 'shades of grey'. The person's actions reflected their position on the continuum. At the heart of Perry's work (and also that of both Kohlberg, and King and Kitchener) is a superordinate dimension which has acquiescence to authority ('I am told, therefore I do') at its lower end and, at the upper end, a personal autonomy that allows the individual to make complex judgements and to act accordingly (we return to this theme in Chapter 10).[4] With employability in mind, formative assessment should not overlook the significance of the 'acquiescence/autonomy' dimension. In curricula there occur many opportunities to encourage the student in the direction of autonomy. A curriculum that values divergence in assessment (see the preceding section), is one in which autonomy is likely to be strongly fostered.

The human capital approach to higher education that has been widely adopted by governments could be held to imply a need to support the capacity to act judiciously, with reference to a moral framework. This is one component of 'capability' (Stephenson 1998) which can be summarized as the ability to operate successfully in work, in voluntary service or more generally in the home and community.

In a political context in which higher education is expected to develop complex capabilities, the work of writers such as Kohlberg, Perry, and King and Kitchener has a place. In a liberal society there is a need to encourage students to develop the capacity to make moral judgements and then to act accordingly. For some, this is contentious territory. However, rarely will the graduate leaving higher education be able to prosper, protected from the wider world by the cocoon of their subject discipline. In medicine, there will inevitably be ethical challenges in respect of the terminally ill or the provision of expensive resources. In other people-related arenas, such as social work or education, the graduate will be faced with competing expectations. In industry, difficult problems can arise from the impact of the company's work on the environment. In all these types of circumstance, there is a tension (sometimes implicit, sometimes explicit) between acquiescing to what is taking place and taking a stand that could be organizationally unpopular and personally disadvantageous. One can imagine the consequences if an employee of one of the companies arraigned by Klein (2001) for subcontracting the production of 'designer goods' to third world 'sweatshops' commented adversely on the employer's economic behaviour.

A complex signalling system

At heart, formative assessment is a complex signalling system within which breakdown is possible at a number of points. Comment from subject overview reports from the Quality Assurance Agency (QAA) in the UK suggests that feedback to students could be improved. The first illustration is from business and management.

> In the best [institutions, feedback] enables students to focus on improving their levels of achievement; however, this was a weak feature of the provision [across the sector]. In more than 40 per cent of institutions, it was of variable quality, lacking in focus and being too brief. There was also evidence that formative feedback was provided too late for it to be of value.
>
> (QAA 2001a: para. 23)

Even in education – a subject area in which one might expect excellence in pedagogy – the performance regarding feedback was uneven:

> Good quality feedback characterised by detailed and constructive comment clearly matched to assessment criteria, features in 43 per cent of institutions. Particularly interesting is the way in which some providers allow dialogue with students as part of the feedback mechanism. This proved to be an especially useful approach where students are actively involved in teaching.[5] In 49 per cent of cases, marking systems could be improved particularly in respect of feedback to students. This sometimes lacked a critical edge, gave few helpful comments and failed to indicate to students ways in which improvement could be made.
>
> QAA (2001b, para 28)

We list the points at which the signalling system can break down, together with some amplifying comments, whilst noting the closeness of the connection between student learning and formative assessment.

Teacher[6] knowledge and beliefs, coupled with subject structure
It goes almost without saying that a primary requirement is that the teacher understands the epistemological structure of the subject discipline – what the main topics or themes are and how they are related. A newly appointed teacher may have a relatively sketchy appreciation of the subject discipline as a whole, perhaps because they have concentrated on a particular aspect whilst completing a doctorate, or possibly because, like many novices, they are preoccupied with covering the content properly (Gibson 1992). More experienced colleagues can help the novice lecturer to see how their specialism fits into the broader disciplinary picture. The teacher's beliefs about students, the students' state of development,[7] and students' capacity for learning will influence the ways in which teachers approach their task of facilitating learning – a matter that we discuss further in Chapter 9.

Programme specification
The programme specification provides a pedagogical 'overlay' to the academic structure of the discipline, which will reflect the way in which the department has chosen to teach the subject. A problem-based curriculum,[8] such as is increasingly being adopted in medicine and engineering, requires a very different approach to subject content from that implied in a more linear programme in which the subject is built up, accretively, from fundamental concepts. Where the demands made of higher education are changing (for example, as when participation is being widened), the way in which the 'espoused' programme is taught may have to be adjusted – and possibly quite radically – if the students are to maximize their chances of learning.

The assessment task and criteria
These are typically designed with reference to the curriculum as described in official documentation, such as the approved programme document, module templates and the student handbook. They will tend to reflect general assumptions about students' development. Some students may misperceive the demands being laid upon them.

The student's interpretation and performance
The student interprets the assessment task and criteria according to background characteristics that include their current state of educational development (taken here to subsume not only subject-specific understandings but also more general intellectual and social development) and their self-theories, and perform accordingly. A frequent interpretive error, which often has its origins in school curricula, leads the student to write descriptively when the expectation is that they take an analytical and critical approach. Consequently, they may not do themselves justice.

Self-theories (Dweck 1999) have received relatively little attention in the literature relating to pedagogy, although this is beginning to change. Dweck points out the importance of the student's self-theories (the set of beliefs that they have about intelligence, capacity to effect change, and so on). Some students in higher education tend towards believing that their intelligence (for example) is fixed; probably rather more, judging from a study conducted as part of the Skills *plus* project,[9] believe that it can be developed (i.e. it is 'malleable'). The psychological literature supports the proposition that there is more than one way of construing intelligence. For present purposes it is sufficient to point out the difference between 'academic intelligence' and 'practical intelligence', the former correlating broadly with the notion of an intelligence quotient (IQ) and the latter relating to the ability to solve practical problems (Sternberg and Grigorenko 2000). Practical intelligence can be developed, but this is assisted if the student differentiates between practical and academic intelligence, and believes in the 'developability' of the former.

The teacher's interpretation of the student's performance, and the provision of feedback
In some circumstances, such as in the performing arts, the teacher will assess the student 'live', and is able to tune into the cues about the student's intentions and abilities that are presented in the performance. There is particularly rich potential for formative feedback in situations of this kind. Where the performance is 'detached' from the student, the teacher has fewer cues, and hence it is more difficult to tailor feedback to the individual. Pressures on the teacher's time exacerbate the difficulties, and the provision of constructive formative commentary is likely to demand a high level of commitment on the part of the teacher. The minimalist, and least satisfactory, response in terms of formative assessment is simply to give a grade to the performance. Further, the teacher may interpret the performance as an indicator of the student's capacity and not allow for the possibility that the student may have misunderstood what was expected, and have underachieved as a consequence.

There is a general recognition that both formative and summative assessments are frequently multidimensional (Sadler 1989). Torrance and Pryor (2001: 625) observed, from their study of assessment in schools, that the teachers' feedback was more detailed regarding topics on which they felt secure, and more general when they were less confident of their ground. This has potential resonance for higher education. Expected outcomes of higher education stretch from students' competence in respect of their specialist subject to personal qualities and 'generic' skills. It is likely that teachers whose understandings of their subject discipline are stronger than those of pedagogy and employability will find difficulty in providing feedback in respect of achievements lying outside the specific subject discipline. Such teachers will probably need to add a professionally developed understanding of the issues (through experience, discussion with peers, and professional development) if they are to be in a position to give feedback to their students that is richly related to employability.

The student's interpretation of feedback
The tendency of the student to adopt 'performance goals' or 'learning goals (see Dweck 1999) is likely to have an influence on the way in which the student responds to feedback. Performance goals, in brief, are related to 'looking good' or 'not

looking bad' in relation to peers, whereas learning goals (self-evidently) make learning the focus. Pintrich (2000) has subdivided the notion of performance goals into 'approach' and 'avoidance' varieties – the former referring to doing well in relation to peers, the latter to not getting shown up as inferior to peers.

If the student is oriented towards performance goals, then the grade (or grade-type comment) is likely to overshadow the potential in the feedback for assisting learning. The minimalist teacher response, merely giving a grade, may indicate the general standard reached, but leaves it to the student to guess at the ways in which improvement could be secured in respect of future assignments. The student oriented towards learning goals is likely to benefit more from feedback, and may want to seek out the teacher in the interest of elaborating their understanding of how to reach a higher level of achievement. A grade can, of course, trigger such a dialogue: a teacher needs to be prepared for the student who, having received a mark of (say) 57%, asks what they have to do to obtain the remaining 43%.

Structural threats to formative assessment

Formative assessment is under constant threat from pressures on higher education whose origins are in large part external to the assessment of an individual piece of student work, and are largely structural in character. These pressures, which vary in intensity across the world, include the following.

- *Political.* An increasing governmental concern with attainment standards and accountability, which inevitably emphasizes the (summative) assessment of outcomes.
- *Cost-related.*
  - Increases in student/staff ratios, leading to a decrease in the attention being given to individuals.
  - The productivity demands placed on academic staff in addition to teaching, which include the need to be seen as 'research active', the generation of funding, contributing to public service, and intra-institutional administration.

- *Curricular.* Structures changing in the direction of greater unitization, resulting in the summative assessment of outcomes at short intervals and, as a consequence, less opportunity for formative feedback.
- *The legacy of history.* The legacy of the dominant paradigm of the twentieth century, which Shepard (2000) sees as reflecting behaviourist theories of learning, social efficiency and scientific measurement. Shepard's argument is that, whilst approaches to learning have taken a constructivist turn, approaches to assessment have placed undue weight on testing the attainment of outcomes (at the expense of assessment for learning purposes).

Unrealized potential

Our view is that the potential of formative assessment has yet to be fully realized across a broad swathe of higher education, even though there are some institutions that can claim to have been successful in this respect.

In the preceding section we listed some probable influences on the way in which institutions approach assessment. There is, at sectoral level, a loose analogy to be struck with the performance/learning goals dichotomy we noted earlier in respect of individual institutions. Higher education systems are expected to come up with 'measures' of their students' performances, such as grade-point averages and honours degree classifications. They are faced with external quality scrutiny of one form or another. Employers are often tempted, at the first pass of their recruitment effort, by the superficiality of the grading that a student takes from their experience in higher education. Institutions, therefore, may feel themselves implicitly being nudged in the direction of (institution-level) performance goals. The situation is exacerbated when the curriculum is subdivided into modules in which students see a primary need to perform well in order not to prejudice their overall grading according to the algorithm used to compute their final, overall, grading. The assessment stakes could hardly be higher.

Other contemporary pressures on institutions distract from the importance of learning goals. Teachers are pressed ever harder to fulfil a clutch of expectations beyond their immediate commitment to their students, in research, administration and community service. One does not have to be a teacher for very long in higher education before being faced with very real problems of allocating the time at one's disposal. Formative assessment is often a casualty – and, pedagogically speaking, this is tragic since feedback quality is (as Black and Wiliam (1998) have shown) very important for student learning. Further, we have pointed to the importance of students' self-theories for their approach to learning: the hard-pressed teacher may simply not have the time to gain even an inkling of 'where the student is at' in this respect.

Resolving the problems of providing adequate formative assessment is beyond the powers of most individual academics. It requires action at institutional level, and even political level. We address the former here, but hope that what we have to say will reach into the policy arena as well.

The main way in which the potential of formative assessment can be unlocked is through the creation, in the institution, of a culture in which student learning, and of course, formative assessment, are at the heart, and in which learning goals are given their rightful emphasis. The immediate reaction might be: 'But that's what higher education institutions have always done: they *are* institutions of learning.' And so they are – that is the 'espoused theory' of institutional functioning. The 'theory in use', though, is often rather different, despite the efforts of committed individuals.[10] Learning involves risk. If the stakes in the institutional assessment system are high, then risk-taking is implicitly discouraged, and some of the potential for learning is lost. Our view is that the curriculum needs to be developed so that it contains more low-stakes assessment, and more (and richer) formative feedback, if students' potential for learning is to be realized to the maximum extent possible. This implies a rethinking of the type and balance of formal curricular engagements. Tinkering at the edges is unlikely to be sufficient. The implication is that higher education has to 'work smarter'.

Notes

1. A similar distinction can be made regarding formative feedback in employment, in which case 'teachers' needs to be replaced by 'senior colleagues'.
2. Wagner (1993: 19) noted the importance of tacit knowledge deriving from work-experience: the 'practical know-how that usually is not openly expressed or stated, and that usually is not directly taught'.
3. Kohlberg focused on moral development, Perry on ethical and intellectual development, and King and Kitchener on the development of reflective judgement.
4. The work of other theorists overlaps with that cited. A summary can be found in Pascarella and Terenzini (1991), and Mentkowski and Associates (2000) give an indication of how such theorists might be related. Further, the latter indicate that there are a number of potential labels for superordinate constructs in this area. Ecclestone (2002: 34ff) discusses three types of autonomy – procedural, personal (practical) and critical. Our usage refers mainly to the last two.
5. Not all programmes in this area involve the training of teachers: some are academic studies of Education.
6. We take 'teacher' to subsume 'assessor' here, noting that formative assessment has a strong link to the former.
7. This linkage is not shown in Figure 3.2.
8. See Boud and Feletti (1997) and Savin-Baden (2000) for accounts of problem-based learning.
9. Seventy-two per cent of 2269 first- and final-year undergraduates from a range of programmes in five varied universities appeared to believe in malleability of intelligence, whereas 28 per cent appeared to favour a 'fixed' position (Yorke and Knight 2003).
10. In England, institutions are required by their funding council to produce institutional learning and teaching strategies. This could be used by leaders as a stimulus towards the further enhancement of student learning.

4

Key Themes in Thinking about Assessment

Introduction

This chapter highlights a number of the themes we have been using and, in so doing, clarifies ideas that will recur as we develop our analysis of assessment for learning and employability. The themes bear on most assessment situations, whether in the USA, Hong Kong, Belgium or Germany. And, as we have said before, although teachers may often have developed practices that insulate them from, for example, the concerns of social measurement theory (Campbell and Russo 2001), new demands upon higher education, notably that it should promote the achievements that make for good claims to employability, are disturbing old ways of doing assessment.

Sitting above the themes reviewed in this chapter is the idea that assessment arrangements should be:

- *Valid.* They should engage with the programme or module's learning intentions and not with pallid, easy-to-handle simplifications.
- *Useful.* Assessment is frequently symbolic (Airasian 1988), so data are widely collected and seldom used. We value useful assessments.
- *Reliable.* High-stakes assessments demand high reliability. Lower-stakes assessments with formative purposes should also be reliable, but primarily in the sense of being honest and careful.
- *Affordable.* Higher education has often ignored the political economy of assessment but, as slack disappears from the system, it cannot continue to assume that the costs of complex assessments can be treated as marginal costs to be absorbed by pliant teachers.

Pervading this chapter is the idea that the best way of achieving working balances amongst these competing priorities is to develop programme-level assessment systems. This was previewed in Chapter 2 and is further developed in Chapters 12 and 13.

Summative assessment and local judgements of achievement

High-stakes assessments with summative purposes are usually[1] module-level assessments – they have *local* meanings. However much meaning they have *in context* it does not get us very far if we are trying to make general statements about learners' attainments. We illustrate this by reviewing some mainstream advice on the assessment of learning outcomes (Otter 1992; Walvoord and Anderson 1998; Gosling and Moon 2001). Walvoord and Anderson suggest that teachers construct criteria by doing a primary trait analysis (PTA) for each assessed task they set. PTA, which has similarities with Gosling and Moon's (2001: 29–30) advice, involves:

- Returning to module learning outcomes to remind yourself of the module's declared intentions.
- Identifying the aspects of the task that you will mark to – the things you will value and those you will penalize.
- Writing a scale of between two and five points to describe different levels of performance. The descriptions should be precise and concise.
- Piloting it on a sample of student work: revising and then applying it to all of the assignments. (Walvoord and Anderson 1998: 69).

There can be little objection to these task-marking schemes or module grade indicators as local guides to what is being valued. But even where the criteria are derived from the programme specification, they are *local* judgements. For example, judgements about the weighting between elements are the tutor's judgements; Walvoord and Anderson's PTA for an original biology experiment seems to give equal weight to ten headings: title, introduction, scientific format, material and methods section, non-experimental information, experimental design, operational definitions, control of variables, collecting data and communicating results, and interpreting data (1998: 197–201). That is a defensible weighting but by no means an unchallengeable one. It is a local decision, nothing more.

A second reason for treating grade indicators as *local* is less obvious but more important. Suppose that a programme learning outcome was that students 'should understand experimental methods'. The score on this PTA would provide one, rather ambiguous, piece of evidence. A *reliable* verdict on the student's work, judged against this outcome, would need scores from different experimental tasks across the whole programme. One task by itself is not a reliable indicator. And if different tutors used different PTAs, then that would overlay any signal about experimental understanding with more noise. When the aim is to make judgements on programme learning outcomes, programme-wide criteria are necessary – a set of PTAs that all tutors have agreed and use in judging student performance on experimental design tasks. The subject-specific benchmarks promoted in the UK by the Quality Assurance Agency[2] may be helpful here as talking points but they are not grounded in a serious study of sufficient research evidence.

If an institution intends to certify that students show the attainments that it has defined as core elements of graduateness, then there needs to be some alignment between the programme specifications in different subject areas: there needs to be some core account of the nature of 'critical thinking', 'creativity' and other core elements of graduateness. Some have tried to transform local judgements into universal ones by benchmarking their standards to Bloom's (1956) taxonomy. His taxonomy was not designed to grade responses but to inform test-writing and the design of teaching units. It is arguable that the vision was to develop a tool that would help local actions (Bloom 1956: 1, 2), which is certainly the intention of the recent, and much better, elaboration (Anderson and Krathwohl 2001). As often applied, the 1956 taxonomy is open to severe, arguably fatal, philosophical and psychological challenge (Anderson and Sosniak 1994). In Marzano's (1998: 64) words, 'Bloom's framework only approaches a taxonomy'. The 2001 version is, we consider, a very useful heuristic with some claims to be a taxonomy in a loose sense.[3] Biggs' SOLO taxonomy is a popular and flexible alternative but it is not clear that his four levels of cognitive complexity are sufficient to support the transformation of a range of local outcomes into general warrants to achievement.[4]

Table 4.1 develops this distinction between local and general statements of achievement. Our claim is that if assessment is only a symbolic activity (Airasian 1988), then the rift between local assessments and general statements of attainment is insignificant. If assessment is believed to be the basis of warrants to achievement, the fault is serious.

Assessment as simplification

The claim that high-stakes assessment for summative purposes corrodes complex learning intentions has been presented in Chapter 2. It is developed here by asking how employability could be assessed in first-cycle higher education, examining each of the four elements of the USEM description in turn.

Understanding

There is uncertainty about what counts as understanding. Side-stepping some important philosophical issues, we suggest that a student who understands something is able to apply it appropriately to a fresh situation (demonstration by far transfer) or to evaluate it (demonstration by analysis). Understanding cannot be judged, then, by evaluating the learner's retention of data or information; rather, assessment tasks would need to have the student *apply* data or information appropriately. This might not be popular in departments that provide students with a lot of scaffolding because their summative assessment tasks only involve near transfer, not far transfer. Where far transfer and evaluation are the hallmarks of understanding, assessment tasks will not be low-inference, right or wrong tasks, but high-inference ones, judged by more than one person with a good working knowledge of agreed grade indicators.

We do not want to suggest that understanding cannot be assessed. Experts can together devise tests of understanding that are likely to be fair for a particular group

Table 4.1 Local and generalized assessments

Nature of learning outcomes	Generalized verdicts: assessment as warranting	Local meanings: assessment feedback and conversations
Well-defined learning outcomes	No great problems here, save only that few learning outcomes are really well-defined. Typical assessment methods include multiple choice tests, problem-solving exercises with correct solutions	Scores and test results give feedback, although exam scores tend to come too late (after the next set of modules has been chosen). Assessment conversations tend to be limited to correcting faulty algorithms
Learning outcomes are worked into a determinate shape. Treated 'as if' determinate but at some cost to their inherent complexities	There is no shortage of methods, for example essays, designs, problem-solving exercises with limited range of solutions	No trouble in using any methods that can be imagined as fit for the purpose for local assessments of these outcomes
	It tends to be expensive to get acceptable levels of reliability from them	There is plenty of room to talk about grade indicators and the way they're applied to particular cases
	The biggest difficulty is that the results are artificial because reliability has been bought by simplification. Sternberg (1997) shows how this makes academic tests poor predictors of career success	The main problem is a lurking belief that these local judgements are a fair basis for generalization – for making global claims about achievement
Complex learning outcomes	Generalized verdicts not possible without reducing complexity	Good assessment methods include conversations about portfolios and other descriptions of achievement. They are inherently formative, low-stakes and have local meanings. Others might try to generalize from them but any generalizations will be tentative and approximate
	However, others might be invited to make their own generalizations on the basis of evidence in portfolios and other descriptions of achievement	

and have acceptable levels of difficulty, and they can draw up grade indicators to help all markers to judge appropriateness in similar ways. Our points are that there is some uncertainty about judging understanding; there are costs involved in attempts to reduce uncertainty; and there are difficulties in claiming that judgements have a lot of meaning beyond the local community of practice in which they were created.

Skills

We see skills as context- and task-sensitive practices. Agreed, there is much about the practice of oral communication, for example, that is similar from situation to situation, but there are also significant differences, for example, between communicating well in high-stakes negotiations on the one hand and in brainstorming sessions on the other. We can say that if oral performance is observed on a number of occasions, in different contexts and for different purposes, then we could predict the probability of certain sorts of performance happening in the future, especially in situations similar to the ones in which the judgements of achievement were made. Notice, though, that many and varied observations are necessary if we are to make general estimates of the probability of any particular performance recurring. It is complicated, expensive and uncertain.

Efficacy beliefs and metacognition

Chapter 1 noted the significance of self-theories for personal action. Researchers have developed instruments to map differences in people's identities as expressed in their self-reported efficacy beliefs and metacognition. It is one thing to use psychometric tools to profile groups, but it is another to suppose that they could be used for high-stakes assessments of individuals' identities. Besides, students who remembered why a programme highlighted efficacy beliefs and metacognition would know enough to 'fake good' in psychometric tests, regardless of whether they really were metacognitively smart and given to positive efficacy beliefs.

Pellegrino *et al.* review modern cognitive research and say that

> One of the most important features of cognition is metacognition – the process of reflecting on and directing one's own thinking. Metacognition is crucial to effective thinking and problem solving and is one of the hallmarks of expertise in specific areas of knowledge and skill. . . . *Assessment should therefore attempt to determine whether an individual has good metacognitive skills.*
>
> (Pellegrino *et al.* 2001: 4, emphasis in original)

The assessment problems are similar to those for self-theories, with an extra complication if the concept of reflection is introduced. Described by Vygotsky as 'the internalization of argument' (cited in Valsiner and van der Veer 2000: 370), it is not easy to see how reflection could be summatively assessed.

Assessing complex achievements

Such problems would be even more pronounced if higher education were involved in the promotion of emotional intelligence[5] (Goleman 1996, 1998; Cooper and Sawaf 1997). Odd though this idea might sound, employers' lists of the attributes they look for in new graduate hires are replete with items that have strong emotional overtones (for example, networking, coping with uncertainty, self-confidence, and teamworking). There is evidence that life success may be associated more with non-cognitive factors than with cognitive ones, leading one researcher to suggest

> that more attention might be paid to the non-academic behaviour and development of children as a means of identifying future difficulties and labour market opportunities. It also suggests that schooling ought not be assessed solely on the basis of the production of reading and maths ability. There might be economic returns to thinking more imaginatively about the role of schooling and the way schools interact with families and children in generating well-educated, productive but also well-rounded and confident individuals.
>
> (Feinstein 2000: 20)

But how could we bring emotional intelligence and similar achievements under any high-stakes regime? If the programme learning intentions are stated rather loosely, as aims and statements of valuable learning engagements (in Eisner's (1985) terms, as 'expressive objectives'), which would allow students much greater latitude in responding to the expectations, reliability problems multiply and the burden on assessors tends to be higher than is typical for more traditional assessments. Since the resources available per curriculum unit are bounded, there are significant implications for the design of courses and programmes that emphasize the assessment of complex achievement. For example, the volume of assessment required to test the achievement of all the intended outcomes in a range of contexts can be enormous, as Wolf (1995a) demonstrates in the case of an NVQ in business studies. That has considerable cost implications.

Responses to authentic assessments of emotional intelligence and other complex creations will tend to be more open-ended than the right/wrong, more convergent sorts of answer elicited by tasks designed to be highly reliable. Convergent assessment tasks ask students to demonstrate their learning with reference to an externally determined expectation. Authentic assessments open up the possibility that (but do not require that) students may demonstrate the desired learning in a way that is unspecified by the assessor. The difficulties are compounded where assessors come with an 'excellence minus' cast of mind, which leads them to look for flaws to penalize, rather than with the 'threshold plus' approach of acknowledging achievements.

When it comes to portfolios (see Chapters 8 and 11), students usually are able to choose the evidence they cite to back their claims and often choose what weight to give to different claims. This introduces considerable variation in the product to be assessed, which then compromises attempts to achieve greater reliability. The example we give in Chapter 8 of portfolio assessment in one course shows how difficult it can be to produce reliable judgements of candidates' claims, even when the expectations are elaborated in some detail. When the purposes are summative, programme and, to a lesser extent, course portfolios present all imaginable challenges to reliability. When assessment relates to a performance that no other student is attempting (as in a research thesis), both internal and external assessors can only call upon their understandings of similar kinds of assessment (gained in a variety of ways) in coming to judgement. There is no crutch available to the assessor enabling a rank-ordering of performances, as is the case with examinations and other assignments given to a group of students. Reliability is therefore more problematical where highly individual achievements are being assessed. As a consequence, it is more difficult to state that a performance is of a particular standard, although a commentary on the performance may indicate where its strengths and weaknesses lie.

When assessment is concerned with authentic achievements, there is a sense in which variations in setting, task and student response mean that all performances and claims are individual, making it expensive to achieve the minimum tolerable levels of reliability when purposes are summative.

Hedlund and Sternberg (2000) offer a way out of this difficulty for those wanting to assess 'practical intelligence'.[6] They describe the development of a psychometric approach that involves measuring

> three domains of mental processing (analytical, creative, and practical) by means of multiple-choice and essay questions . . . [that] include questions such as what to do about a friend who seems to have a substance abuse problem, how to make chocolate chip cookies, using a map or diagram to plan a route effectively, and how to solve a practical problem in one's own life.
>
> (Hedlund and Sternberg 2000: 152)

Although their problems have an 'authentic' veneer, they have been simplified by being abstracted to provide assessment problems. The form of response – multiple-choice and essay – also encourages simplification. Reliability and simplification tend to be found in each other's company. Formative assessment can also simplify but, freed of the need to put reliability first, it can handle more ambiguity and cope with more uncertainty, *assuming that students and teachers know that those are the rules of the game.*

Differentiated assessment systems

A conservative conclusion is that, since the goals of higher education have grown and become more complex, so assessment must become differentiated. A summative approach to assessment may be fit for the purpose of establishing how much determinate information a student remembers, but not for making judgements related to a fuzzy social construct such as self-motivation or practical intelligence. It might be that the best judges of claims to be skilled at groupwork or to be 'self-motivating' would be other students, not the teacher, and that assessment would take the form of conversation amongst people of the same standing. There would not be the master–pupil relationship of traditional assessment and we would expect that the quality of the assessment conversations would differ as a result. There needs to be differentiation amongst assessment methods because those we have grown used to when assessing propositional understanding in humanities and social sciences, notably essay writing, are barely fit for the purpose of appraising practical competence. Related to this is a point made by Heywood (2000) that there is a need to use a range of assessment methods to tap a range of learning achievements: he calls this 'multiple-strategy assessment'. Again, the level of scaffolding attached to assessment tasks early in a student's learning career would be inappropriate towards the end.

Differentiation is primarily a programme or system-level concern. It is, of course, desirable to have differentiated assessment plans for modules, not least because different learning outcomes call for differentiated assessment approaches. However, there is not a lot of space in the typical module, which limits the amount of variation that can be accommodated. That, though, is not the main reason for thinking about assessment systems across three or four years. We want to highlight this point: complex learning takes time. Claxton (1998) writes about 'slow learning', saying that some learnings take weeks, months or years to construct. We would argue that complex learning is almost invariably slow learning, taking longer to grow than most modules last. Whilst information and inert knowledge can, in principle, be fixed in some form of memory in a fairly short time, and whilst the convergent use of formulae can also become quite quickly routinized (how long does it take to learn how to do statistical tests on a calculator?), complex social and academic practices can take years. The implication is that, whereas it has been usual to treat assessment questions as module-level questions, often paying the price of over-assessing students,[7] we would do better to design assessments at programme level. This systemic approach is also the only way that universities and colleges can generalize about competence because reliability demands multiple assessments of the same outcomes of learning.

Figure 4.1 shows how differentiated assessment practices could be organized in a degree programme, with some learning outcomes brought under cumulative summative assessment regimes, whereas others would be handled by formative assessment arrangements. If this sort of analysis is correct, then curriculum designers need to be concerned with the political economy of assessment. We use 'economy' to indicate that they have to decide how much it is worth investing in order to secure what levels of certainty in respect of which expected outcomes of learning. 'Political' is used as a reminder that these are value judgements and involve a choice, as does all politics, both amongst priorities and between priorities and practicalities. Programme-level assessment systems have radical implications for assessment practices, which is obvious, and for the design of student learning environments, which is not.

Generalizing about achievements

Can this differentiated view of assessment be reconciled with the expectation that higher education institutions will certify competence, warrant fitness to practise and attest to the 'graduateness' of their graduates? After all, many of the outcomes of complex learning resist measurement,[8] and without measurement how is there to be certainty about levels of competence and achievement, even assuming that in a programme there are enough assessments touching any one learning intention for generalization to be feasible?

Consider 'critical thinking' for example. There are North American tests of

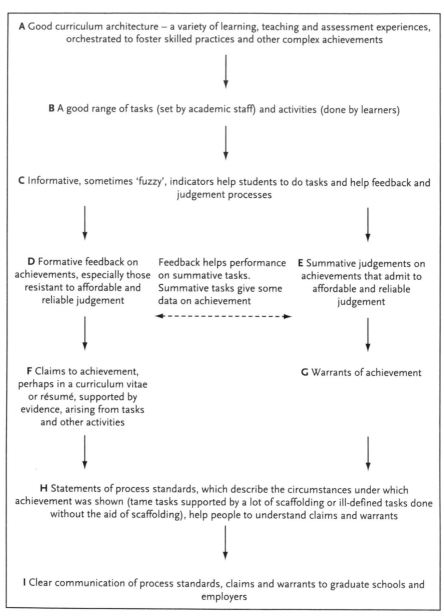

Figure 4.1   Differentiated programme-level assessment arrangements

critical thinking which can be objectively administered and reliably scored but they are more like IQ tests than estimates of the complex processes of informed criticism in fine art, history, sociology or philosophy. Even within those disciplines there is argument about what counts as criticism and there is disagreement between disciplines. If critical thinking is valued but escapes definition, how is it to be measured? What we find is that in *this* department, critical thinking is treated in *this* way and in *that* department it is understood like *that*. The same numbers, letters or degree classifications might be used to summarize these two different judgements, but nominal data such as these provide no basis for comparison or translation. But if local agreements on the meaning of complex learning outcomes are the best we can do, then we have locally reliable *descriptions* of achievement. Descriptions are not *measures* of achievement – 'precisely because they are individualized, neither the rationale nor the results of the typical classroom assessments are easy to communicate beyond the classroom' (Pellegrino *et al.* 2001: 41). Before we trust someone's judgement that a student from department Z is an original thinker, which is a judgement of a complex achievement, we want to know more about the process standards,[9] about what goes on there. What indicators are used? How are they interpreted? Does the department encourage original thinking or is there so much scaffolding that what it calls 'original thinking' we would probably call 'good synthesis'?

A partial answer to this question about the development of the shared understandings that are the basis for generalization is the view that explicit national standards are needed. They have the potential to reduce the range of uncertainty about any general statements of achievement, especially where the standards are widely used, supported by good training provision and monitored by a community of accreditors, external examiners or other consultants. The Quality Assurance Agency (QAA) has produced sets of subject benchmarks which can be treated as a first step to the production of national, subject-specific standards.

Whilst acknowledging effort being put into making generalizations more widely understandable, there are difficulties. As we have said in earlier chapters, researchers keep finding that criteria and standards, such as subject benchmarks, are locally interpreted in a variety of ways (for example, Wolf *et al.* 1997; Greatorex 1999; Price and Rust 1999). There are also questions to be asked about the quality of the benchmarks themselves. We wonder whether those who constructed them had the expertise in taxonomies and assessment that would be brought to bear in the USA by, say, the Educational Testing Service. The QAA did not invest as heavily in benchmark development. A good comparison here is the effort that has gone into the development and revision of the attainment targets for the subjects in the English national curriculum for schools. These targets are based on better evidence than the benchmark statements and have been refined over 15 years. Even so, Davies (2002) shows that the attainment level descriptions for geography do not fit well with the pattern of student learning nor, by extension, can they do much for teachers trying to develop students' geographical thinking. Similar faults can be found with national curriculum statements for other subjects. The investment in benchmark development, often comprising a few meetings by subject experts who sometimes had some appreciation of the educational research and conceptual issues, was slight in comparison. And what are we to make of the different profiles shown by the 24 sets of statements, differences which can only partly be explained by reference to disciplinary differences (Yorke 2002b)?

Teachers can, with care, learn to interpret and apply benchmark statements and other standards in similar ways, using external examiners and insisting on second, unseen, marking of anonymous scripts. However, this is expensive, works within subject communities of practice but may not cross subject boundaries so well, and is easiest when done with familiar evidence of achievement, such as that arising from traditional essay formats. Yet, it is not enough to have benchmarks or shared outcome statements. Generalizations that refer to these standards may come from excellent programmes and sound assessment systems but consumers of assessment data will not be in much of a position to know how to interpret them and how to relate them to similar statements coming from other programmes in other higher education institutions. Unless they know something of the conditions under which achievement was shown – unless they know about the programme's process standards, about the amount of scaffolding available to students – they cannot tell whether the assessments were far transfer tasks done by students who had experienced a wide range of methods and contexts, as Stark *et al.* (1998) recommend, or whether impressive outcomes are the result of coaching on near transfer tasks. Consequently, they have no basis from which to judge whether the achievement is liable to be robust enough for 'far transfer' and available to 'in the wild' problems, or whether its scope is near transfer to well-defined problems.

Generalization needs:

- sufficient samples of achievement to assure tolerable reliability;
- criteria, benchmarks or other accounts of shared standards of achievement;
- statements of programme process standards so that consumers can draw conclusions about the robustness of achievements.[10]

Differentiation again: limited warrants

Faced with problems of reliability, validity and generalization, we repeat our unease with unitary notions of assessment and conclude that:

- Some outcomes of learning, notably information retention and the use of algorithms, are fairly determinate and can be assessed cheaply and reliably.
- Others can be pushed into fairly determinate shape and assessed with tolerable reliability, but at a price. The earlier account of ways of assessing critical thinking illustrates the point.
- We cannot get – or we cannot afford to try to get – reliable measures of many of the outcomes of higher education. This means that universities and colleges are in no position to warrant them or to certify achievement in respect of them. Higher education institutions ought not to warrant achievements they cannot (afford to) measure.

The political economy of assessment involves differentiating between the outcomes of learning that can be assessed reliably, those that will be moulded so that some fairly reliable judgements can be made (albeit at some cost to validity), and those that will be assessed otherwise. This is counterintuitive for teachers who are at home in traditions that assume that anything of value can and ought to be measured as if it were a scientific phenomenon. We argue the contrary: that assessment is not all things to all outcomes, and the more complex the outcome (and the more it is central to the purposes of higher education), the less likely that it is to be measurable.

There are significant implications here for the ways in which awards, certificates and other warrants to attainment can be interpreted. They are in essence based on high-stakes, summative processes, which address only a selection of learning outcomes assessed in certain more or less artificial ways. Many outcomes cannot be warranted (even though awards may be attached to statements saying that a programme promoted all sorts of learning) because they are beyond the reach of affordable and reliable assessment. Users of these warrants need to know which outcomes are warranted because they have been assessed by sufficient and sufficiently reliable means.

Those attainments that colleges and universities cannot (afford to) warrant need to be assessed in other ways. We suggest in Figure 4.1 that low-stakes practices with essentially formative intentions are suitable for the purpose. Students would lay claims to achievement in respect of achievements that are not warranted by their awards. We begin to discuss the issue in the following section and extend our discussion in Chapters 9 and 11.

Ideally, consumers of warrants and claims would also know about the process standards behind the assessments, which means that reports on student achievements would be differentiated to include process standards, warrant and claims.

Assessment and claims-making

What of the achievements that colleges and universities choose not to warrant? Employers' accounts of what they look for in new graduate hires are full of achievements and qualities that resist reliable, let alone affordable, assessment. And, tempting though it is to look for proxy measures, the university or college's reputation is not a good predictor of student achievement,[11] nor can it be inferred that a period of work experience signifies employability.[12] Something of an answer to this problem is contained in the distinction between an authority, such as a university or researcher, making a generalization and saying that it ought to hold true across a certain range because good measurement methods have been used, and readers generalizing from evidence of varying pedigree. Those attracted by post-structuralist accounts of knowing will be familiar with the idea that the author does not determine the meanings that readers construct; rather, authority lies with readers as sense-makers, although the authorial voice is an influence on their sense-making. We see assessment contributing to sense-making by generating judgements which the institution is prepared to warrant confidently (judgements about information-processing, for example); generating other institutional judgements which are less robust (about groupwork or oral communication, perhaps); and, finally, generating student claims (about reflective practice and motivation, say) that are supported by evidence which will often, but not always, come from work they have done in their programme of study. This differentiated account of assessment in higher education places less emphasis on warrants because the range of achievement that universities and colleges can, and can afford to, warrant is less than the range which interests employers. It places more emphasis on generating claims to achievement in these areas and on supporting them with evidence which will largely come from tasks that have been formatively assessed with the help of fuzzy grade indicators. This opens up two new lines of thinking about assessment. The first is about providing consumers with evidence – with claims-making, which we consider in Chapter 11 – and the second is about communicating with consumers.

Communicating achievements

Portfolios are about learners judging, documenting and communicating their achievements, primarily for particular purposes (to get a job) for particular people (an employer or a graduate school). Having an audience and purpose makes it easier to communicate well, and the availability of rich evidence of achievement helps both the student and employer, if sufficiently interested, to work out exactly what a claim to skill in the use of information and communication technology really means. This is not the case with summative assessment judgements. Could educators do a better job of communicating them?

One common theory of communication sees it as the error-free transmission of information from one place to another (Fiske 1990). When information is intended for a diverse audience (and most educational information is), it has to be broadcast (as opposed to narrowcast), and contain a lot of redundancy – points should be spelt out clearly without assuming that the receiver has any particular prior knowledge or understanding. So, if we want others to understand the meanings of assessment judgements we need to say in good, clear language what the numbers and letters symbolize. Nor will it do to say that they mean someone has demonstrated skill at oral communication, or in numeracy. Broadcasting needs redundancy, which means spelling out what these terms mean. One way of doing that would be to elaborate on numbers, classifications and other symbols with prose descriptions of what they are likely to mean so that summative judgements would be broadcast along with transcripts that considerately say what they are supposed to mean. The difficulty of that task should not be underestimated, not least because we have already suggested that it is harder to get agreement on grade indicators and their meanings the more that attention moves from a single module to a programme team, national subject community or higher education institution. Even if such statements could be engineered, as they have been for the national curriculum and vocational qualifications in England, they are not enough, because people make better sense of the transcripts if they know something about the process standards – the learning, teaching and assessment processes associated with the achievement. For example, it matters whether a learner has regularly done independent reading, or whether an achievement comes from sustained classroom coaching. Broadcasting process standards – a summary of the learning teaching and assessment activities associated with the achievement – helps to communicate the message.

Furthermore, in times when educational qualifications and programmes are proliferating, conventions once used to interpret them have been disrupted. Some symbols – awards – are not recognized or not understood, whereas others may be recognized but the official reading may be distrusted (degrees from some higher education institutions can be seen as second-rate awards, even when claims for parity are based on external examiners' commentaries). In semiotic terms there is a need to broadcast clear and self-explanatory information *and* to try to establish conventional interpretations. But, to repeat the point, it is hard to see how conventional interpretations could be re-established. It is one thing to see that they are created where higher education and employers, for example, work closely together, as with good work placement schemes, but it is another to see how local agreements could be scaled up to cross institutions or disciplines. The irony is that institutions might restrict the range of learning to be assessed, simplify it and invest in multiple judgements of multiple performances, all in the name of reliability, only to realize that there is no guarantee that information will be understood in the way that assessors intended. 'Fixing' the reliability problem does not fix the communication problem. Strictly speaking, it is a problem that cannot be fixed because people will always construct individually hued meanings out of the same information, but we have suggested some ways in which communicators can try to limit the spectrum of constructed understandings. Communicating student achievements to outsiders is, we suggest, a strangely neglected and important issue, especially now, when the number of undergraduates continues to grow, corporate and online universities compete more directly with traditional institutions, and the range of courses and expectations continues to broaden.

Systems change

The principle nicknamed Romer's rule (Hockett and Asher 1964: 137) says that organisms generally evolve by changing just enough to maintain, as near as possible, their existing state. Complexity theories help us to see why change should be so hard to achieve. It has often been shown that dynamic systems tend to settle into cycles. The heart has its rhythms (Briggs and Peat 1999), as does human cognitive development (van Geert 1994). Changes may wobble a cycle, but normally the cycle is sufficiently strongly established to smooth out the change until it fades away. The point can also be made through activity system theory. Consider Figures 2.1 and 2.2 in Chapter 2, for example. The links between elements are multiple and strong, making change hard and there is a great deal of research evidence that changes in education often fail (Fullan 1991) or have marginal impact (Farrell 2000).

Suppose an assessment system was in essence about summative assessment (Figure 2.1) and innovators wanted to make it more formative in character (Figure 2.2). A comparison of those two figures shows how much would have to be done. It also suggests that changing one part of one element (introducing new assessment methods) would look puny against all the unchanged elements, and implies that continued, great force would be needed to break the hard bonds between the elements of Figure 2.1 so that they could be made more like the elements of Figure 2.2.

This, we suggest, evidences a problem with the view that we should try to make change at the point of greatest leverage (Hargreaves 2001): it is hard to look at an activity system diagram and see what would count as *one* point of leverage. It may be wise to continue to look for points of leverage *and* to act on as many points in the system as resources allow, trying to construct pervasive cultures and structures that support differentiated, cohesive assessments to stimulate complex learning. Plainly, this work of construction could take several years, with piecemeal innovations steadily coming together so that the assessment system at the end of the cycle would be quite different from that at its beginning.[13]

However, matters are complicated by mismatches between 'the system as planned' and as the system might be experienced by students taking one module. The difficulty is that interventions in the planned system might not affect the experienced system, which might be shaped by factors that the plans do not reach (Fullan 1991).

The right-hand column in Table 4.2 represents elements of a programme

Table 4.2   A student's experience of assessment shown against the elements that should be reached by a programme assessment system

	The assessment system as experienced by one student. Their priorities are getting good grades with acceptable effort, leading to a good job	*Typical elements of a programme assessment system that supports strong student claims to employability*
The subject of this system	A student, wanting teachers to tell them how to get good grades. They are willing to learn from peers but not if it takes too long: they have a living to earn and a life to live	Students with commitment and proven academic ability, who are committed to programme goals, have appropriate self-theories, and are willing to learn with others
The object of this system	Getting good grades and a graduate job. Also having enough money to eat, go out sometimes and enjoy themself	Good claims to complex achievements, supported by reliable warrants or other evidence
Tools	Cover/feedback sheets showing task specifications and task-specific grade indicators The library; the internet	Examples of good and less good task responses showing the sort of feedback that is given; programme specification and generic grade indicators; cover/feedback sheets showing task specifications and task-specific grade indicators The library; the internet; teaching accommodation; informal learning spaces, including mixing bays, coffee bars and seating in corridors/halls

Table 4.2 continued

	The assessment system as experienced by one student. Their priorities are getting good grades with acceptable effort, leading to a good job	Typical elements of a programme assessment system that supports strong student claims to employability
		Departmental academic support arrangements; scaffolding (which reduces as the programme progresses); central academic support provision; orchestration with learning and teaching arrangements
Rules	Module handbooks; organization of teaching time (pattern of contact hours, semester or trimester system) The tacit rules about setting 'far transfer' tasks and on how to get good grades	Programme and module handbooks; the institution's rules for aggregating grades and classifying degrees; organization of teaching time (pattern of contact hours, semester or trimester system); distinction between collaboration and plagiarism; rules; marking practices Expectations and standards Tacit rules on setting 'far transfer' tasks; about mark distribution patterns (e.g. almost all marks should fall between 45 and 68); and on how to get good grades
Community of practice	Teachers; the internet and virtual networks; other students following the programme; secretarial staff; friends and lovers	Teachers; library staff and other information specialists; the internet and virtual networks; teaching assistants; administrative and secretarial staff; advisers and counsellors Other students following the programme; friends and lovers
Division of labour	Teachers control the assessments but this student talks about tasks with friends, their partner and other students. They have only got so much time to spend on studying and they have to concentrate on what's going to count – they read what they need and write what they have to	Teachers control the high-stakes assessments and shape the low-stakes ones. The system is very much the product of teachers' individual decisions within a loose collective framework There is a change during the programme from teacher-managed, through peer-supported to self-directed learning, reflection and assessment. *However*, elements of all three are present throughout

assessment system. Notice that the system, even as sketched here, is quite extensive. Although presented here as a system, it will be less neat than depicted. Some teachers will resist enrolment in the system, continuing to do in *their* courses more or less what they have always done. Others will have different understandings of the 'rules of the game' and apply the same concepts ('student-centredness', for example) in different ways. There will also be slippages between the different elements, for example between tools, such as physical resources, and rules, such as the expectations of growing learner autonomy. In other words, the system will not work harmoniously: slippages and tensions will always be present.

There are also slippages and tensions between the system as intended and the system as experienced by learners. The central column in Table 4.2 imagines one learner's experience of the programme assessment system as it manifests in one module. Bear in mind that other learners are likely to experience the same system in other ways on this module and others. Divergent understandings are most likely to arise if a programme team has not paid a lot of attention to enrolling teachers and students into a shared network of practice and has not worked on creating 'knowing' students. Table 4.2 shows that assessment, as experienced by this student on this module, is not a good representation of the programme plan. Some gaps and mismatches are inevitable and there will always be some degree of disjunction between the modules that a student puts together to form a programme. As a result, someone, probably the student, has to do the work of integrating the different representations of the programme plan that get created in the modules. This is difficult work and in poorly orchestrated, inconsiderate programmes it has to be done by those least well equipped to do it – the learners. What we are seeing are multiple slippages amongst what is planned at programme level, what is enacted in a module and what is experienced by individual students. Together these slippages produce an unintentionally diverse range of objects and outcomes, many of which are unintended and perhaps undesirable as well. A major problem for those designing learning and assessment systems is limiting this diversity so as to encourage the production of the desired objects whilst knowing that they lack tools that will allow them to engineer a determinate system.

There are echoes in this account of slippages and uncertainty of work inspired by actor network theory (Latour 1999). Work based on this theory explores the ways in which shared meanings are created, maintained and mobilized – how integrated networks of people, meanings, objects and practices happen and work. Typical themes include uncertainty, slippages, the flows of power, and the divergence and contestedness of understandings. We infer from this literature that if a programme assessment system is to work out roughly as intended, then modules need to be orchestrated with the programme plan. A lot of work also needs to be put into enrolling students into the community of shared practice that the plan needs. Here we take the view that

> *For classroom or large-scale assessment to be effective, students must understand and share the goals for learning.* Students learn more when they understand (and even participate in developing) the criteria by which their work will be evaluated, and when they engage in peer and self-assessment. These practices develop

students' metacognitive abilities, which ... are necessary for effective learning.

(Pellegrino *et al.* 2001: 259, emphasis in original)

Table 4.3 represents this work of building shared understandings through a

Table 4.3   A representation of students adopting new assessment practices

Moment (or stage)	Explanation	Illustration
Problematization	Learners realize that a programme's assessment goals – its rules of the game – are different from those with which they are familiar, which means adopting the new goals if they are to play well	First-year students find that essays are not now judged on how much information they contain. Third-year students begin to see that high-scoring writing deals with all sides of an argument. Students notice that formative assessment, which they have treated as a skive, is highly valued in their degree programme. In each case, there is a dissonance between what they are used to and their emerging understandings of the programme's assessment goals
Interéssement	Learners begin to engage with the problem – mastering new assessment practices. They are beginning to break with old practices: to 'unfreeze'	They begin to think about what it would mean to put well-established practices to one side and follow the new assessment practices: writing essays that centre on arguments; writing pieces that look at all sides of an argument; creating and responding to feedback
Enrolment	Learners 'sign up' to mastering the problematical assessment practices and make use of the 'affordances' – the tools, rules and community of practice – that can help them	They try out new methods, making use of any tools available (course handbooks, advice on good essay-writing, skill-building sessions), referring to assessment rules (grade indicators), and drawing on the community of practice (tutors, other students)
		Ideally, they become skilled in the academic practices they need in order to play this assessment game well
Mobilization	New assessment practices are internalized by the learners on the course or programme	As individuals, learners buy into the new practices and become skilled in them
		As a group – as a learning community – they buy into the new way as *the* right way

representation, in the language of actor network thinking, of students learning new programme assessment practices. It should be said that some students will not follow this track but resist, avoid or stop before the fourth moment. The table represents the processes involved in adopting new views of assessment, not the counterprocesses that invariably engage some students.

Alverno College takes seriously the business of enrolling students into its distinctive 'assessment-as-learning' practices. Students often spend their first semester disoriented by Alverno's radical approach to assessment. Staff weather this student discontent and most students then go on to become advocates of Alverno's way (Mentkowski and Associates 2000). The College's approach to assessment has remarkably few slippages and mismatches. Elsewhere, students may find it hard to take up a programme approach to assessment because sometimes one simply does not exist and, even where there are planned approaches, slippages and mismatches characterize practice.

Creating assessment systems

If assessment systems are likely to be full of mismatches and slippages, then it is no surprise if students default to learning routines that served them well before they came to university; if they try to cajole teachers into simplifying complex tasks so that these strategies can work; and if teachers become complicit in this bargaining lest their course gets a bad mark profile and poor student evaluations (Doyle 1983). On this analysis, power in assessment systems lies not so much with the teachers as with students' learning histories. If new learning careers are to be built, that power needs to be opposed. A lesson from the literature on change is, as we have said, that sustained and systemic opposition will need to be supported by well-scaffolded procedures if students are to be habituated to new ways of doing things.

How, then, are assessment systems to be designed that reliably favour the development of desired outcomes when we know that slippages are endemic and that designers operate in realms of complexity, which are, of course, realms of uncertainty? The literature on school reform provides interesting indicators. Gray *et al.* (1999) and Leithwood *et al.* (1999) offer carefully researched suggestions about improvement processes. For example,

> If there was a common theme running across the schools that were improving more rapidly, it was that they had found ways of facilitating more discussion among colleagues about classroom issues than hitherto.
>
> (Gray *et al.* 1999: 144).

This is echoed by West (2000), who argued that improvement recipes cannot be transferred but the ingredients can. This line of thinking suggests that it is the alert process of engagement with improvement issues that matters, allied to a pervasive concern with students' learning. The evidence also suggests that improvement is slow and, if it lasts, due to incremental changes as much as to sweeping innovations. In the context of assessment, we suggest that the design of systems that have a good chance of supporting complex learning will involve the following:

- Programme leadership that maintains a focus on students' complex learning and what is designed to encourage it to take preferred forms. This involves paying attention to differentiation by task, purpose, level and audience; consistency with learning, teaching and curriculum arrangements; coherence; and progression.
- Leadership learning: leaders following a planned learning process so that they are not having to discover principles of effective change management, or principles of assessment and teaching practices that favour complex learning.
- An incremental and planned approach to system development, with the programme team starting with any issue that looks as if it could have high leverage and that *directly* concerns student learning and its valid assessment.
- Programme assessment and learning plans: a mapping of the assessment and learning provision as it affects students, taking the most common pathways through a programme in order to check that there will be a high level of consistency, coherence and progression in their experiences.
- Programme culture-building: the development of shared understandings amongst teachers about what assessment is for, what is possible and for whom assessment information is intended.
- Programme-structure-building: the development of rules and tools that bring modules within the boundaries of good practice, as the programme team sees it.
- Developing a student assessment-as-learning culture: making information about the assessment system easily available, linking individual assessment items to the overall plan, giving feedback that reinforces this vision of assessment, helping students to accommodate their practices to the programme's assessment rules and tools, etc.
- Communication: exploring ways of communicating judgements of achievement most aptly to internal and external consumers.
- Information management system: creating ways of using information from student assessment to improve assessment, learning and their concomitants.

It is not clear what part institutional leadership and support play in this process. Although there is a temptation to assume that good programmes are evoked by good institutional policies,[14] and although innovation is likely to be more widespread in 'learning organizations' than in 'stuck' ones,[15] Knight and Trowler (2001) have developed a case for treating mid-level units – departments, faculties and programme teams – as the most significant organizations in higher education. Chapter 12, on departmental assessment systems, is written from that perspective, whereas Chapter 13 complements it by taking an institutional perspective. Even allowing for limitations to Knight and Trowler's claim, their argument is sufficient to disturb assumptions that supportive institutional policies are necessary conditions for quality enhancement.

We are not claiming here that good, let alone perfect, assessment systems *must* come out of the nine actions listed above, but we are claiming that assessments intended to promote complex learning of the sort covered by the term 'employability' depend on manoeuvres such as those we have noted above. Without them there can be patches of interesting practice but they can do little to support slow learning. Worse, given a tendency to value summative assessment purposes, established assessment practices may bow to the power of past practices and, unwittingly, encourage students to concentrate on low-level tasks that are far removed from what they need in order to develop strong claims to employability.

In the following chapters these themes are developed as we examine specific assessment practices that favour the development and display of achievements that make for employability.

Notes

1. Capstone assignments and final year projects are likely exceptions.
2. See http://www.qaa.ac.uk/crntwork/benchmark/benchmarking.htm
3. Although Anderson and Krathwohl (2001) retain the idea of a taxonomy of levels of demand, arguing that 'create' is *generally* more demanding than 'analyse', they accept that there can be overlap between the six cognitive processes: 'analyse' is not always easier than 'evaluate'. There must also be doubts about the assumption that 'conceptual knowledge' always precedes 'procedural knowledge'. What we have is a loose generalization about the levels of demand that *tend* to be associated with different tasks and processes. This is of limited help to those trying to write precise standards or criteria to regulate high-stakes assessments.
4. They too may be too capacious and too dependent on the exact nature of the task, material and context. Sometimes SOLO level 2 is harder than SOLO level 3. Knight found kindergarten children giving replies to questions which, judged in context, were level 2. Many undergraduates also give level 2 replies, but their work is patently more sophisticated than Knight's 6-year-olds.
5. We dissect this concept in Box 6.3. We are using it here for illustrative purposes, to make the point that the less well defined and less well definable the achievements in question, the greater is the complexity of the assessment issues.
6. This is the 'intelligence' that bears on the way individuals deal with everyday problems. It calls upon but is more extensive than 'emotional intelligence'.
7. Where modules have been validated as if they were independent of each other, they have often taken on too many learning intentions and tried to assess all or most of them. In a systemic approach, any one module can concentrate on a limited number of goals in the knowledge that others are seriously addressed elsewhere.
8. Measurement entails judging something against a common scale with such reliability that we can generalize – by saying, for example, that a metre length is a metre is a metre . . . (assuming standard temperature and pressure at the times of measurement). We assume that true measurements have interval or ratio quality properties so that we can fairly compare and transform measurements because they are at least of interval quality. If we cannot measure using reliable instruments calibrated against a secure scale, then we are on shaky ground if we try to generalize. We can make the best local judgements possible but without a reference point, such as a common scale provides, we cannot say much about how they compare with other judgements.
9. The concept of process standards will be new to most readers. The idea is simple. Two essays presented for scrutiny might get the same mark but represent quite different achievements. The one might be the product of a well-supported task done with a lot of scaffolding and the other the outcome of a solo inquiry with virtually no scaffolding. In order to judge what a product, warrant or claim means, we need to know something about the conditions giving rise to it – about the process standards.

10. North Americans might consider that generalization merely needs good standardized tests. Maybe. We prefer feedout that says more about the breadth and depth of learning through a domain, noting that whilst 'Standardized assessments do communicate effectively across time and place', they constrain 'the content and timeliness of the message' (Pellegrino *et al.* 2001: 41).
11. Astin (1991) makes a strong case against what he saw as a common North American practice of basing many judgements of outcomes on institutional reputation and resources.
12. Blackwell *et al.* (2001) describe conditions under which work placements can enhance learning and employability.
13. It is usually required that students following a programme give their consent to significant changes in assessment patterns.
14. There may be some support for this view in the work of Wright and O'Neil (1995), who found that educational developers believed institutional policies to have an important effect on individuals' and teams' willingness to commit to the enhancement of learning, assessment and teaching quality.
15. The terms come from Rosenholtz's (1989) work on Tennessee elementary schools.

5

Diversifying Assessment Methods

Methods: varied perspectives

Knight (2002b) has suggested that, in the late 1980s and 1990s, a concern for the assessment of student learning tended to take the form of a concern to introduce new assessment methods designed to address achievements that were missed by the traditional methods. We have been suggesting that this international quest for better methods is misguided because it bypasses fundamental questions about what can be assessed, in what senses, by whom and how.

Methods

If we understand 'assessment' to be a synonym for 'measurement' then the range of assessment methods is much more limited than if assessment is seen as a form of judgement. Measurement demands reliable and valid instruments whereas judgement can be helped by whatever can be treated as evidence that is fit for the purpose. This distinction is close to that which writers on social science research methods make between the use of methods to test theory, which is often described as positivist research, and the use of methods to inform judgement, which is often described as hermeneutic or naturalistic inquiry. That literature contains extended discussions, relevant to those interested in the assessment of learning, of what can and cannot be measured, how and what conclusions can be drawn from data gathered in different ways, for different purposes (for example Schratz and Walker 1995; Bryman 2001; Knight 2002d). Since one of our themes is that the complex achievements of higher education resist valid measurement, as do complex social phenomena in general, we shall be liberal in our review of ways of creating evidence to support judgements of achievement.

We repeat that assessment issues are not solved by finding the 'right' methods. Of course it matters that methods are good methods, but their fitness is related to the purposes of judgement, to the people making the judgements and to the ways in which the methods and evidence are presented. Any method can be more or less suitable depending on purpose, people and presentation. It can also be more or less demanding according to how much help, or 'scaffolding', is given to the learner and whether it is used with well-defined or ill-defined tasks. The demands an assessment method makes if there is a lot of scaffolding, the purposes are formative and the task is well-defined are quite different from those made when there is little scaffolding, the task is ill-defined and the purposes are summative.

Purposes

We have already said that people tend to play the assessment game by different rules according to whether the stakes are high or low and the purposes summative or formative. A corollary is that a method which works well for a summative purpose might not create good enough feedback for formative purposes – a simple test score is not as helpful to a student wanting to improve as is an assessment method that is sensitive to the quality of problem-solving processes. Formative purposes tend to imply the use of more information-rich assessment methods. In the same way, if the purpose is to assess a complex achievement such as critical thinking, then there is not much point in using highly reliable tests because they tend to simplify the core concept and treat it – critical thinking in this case – as something that is content- and context-free. If, of course, critical thinking resembles that which IQ tests measure, then there is no problem. If, on the other hand, it is something more nuanced, then tests are less likely to be fit for the purpose.

The adequacy of any assessment method can only be assessed in relation to a purpose. Some methods are much better than others *for particular purposes*.

People

Teachers need to do the assessing in high-stakes assessment because they are most likely to have the expertise, authority and independence that are required. Since they are ultimately accountable for any high-stakes judgements, it is easy to see why there is such resistance to the idea of using peer assessment for summative, high-stakes purposes.

Yet we know that employers say they like graduates who can evaluate their own performances (self-assessment) and consider how to improve (reflection and personal development planning). This implies that there is a case for using self-assessment in higher education, if only as a way of beginning to stimulate practices which are valued outside it. We could imagine that students might use any assessment method to give themselves feedback on performance, for formative or low-stakes purposes. The same reasoning holds for peer assessment, although there is an academic industry devoted to finding reliable and affordable ways of using peer judgements for high stakes and summative purposes. Our point here is that any method takes on a different tone when it is a part of self-assessment as opposed to being used by teachers to pin down student achievements.

There is also the matter of who is being assessed. Usually it is the individual student, but as more and more use is made of groupwork, the focus becomes the group. If the group is being assessed for formative purposes, then it may be sufficient to stimulate conversations about how much each member put into the achievement. Consensus, expressed in the form of a mark, is not needed. When the aim is summative, things become complicated. Assume that the group's work can be graded in a tolerably reliable and valid way. Is everyone in the group to get the same mark, which should encourage students to take collective responsibility for group performance, or should stars and shirkers get different marks? The former course annoys those who work hard and carry an idler to success, whereas the latter route involves some complicated and rather arbitrary procedures for calculating differential marks.

Presentation

Assessment tasks can be presented in many ways – for example, in print, on the web, graphically, orally, on film, through video or in pictures. There is a view, represented by Gardner (1983) amongst others, that people differ in their preferred channels of communication. Some are happiest seeing information in graphical or pictorial form, others are accustomed to listening and some learn best by doing. An extension of this is that a task presented in one medium will favour some students, whereas an analogous task presented in another medium will favour others. There is also some evidence that there is an interplay between assessment methods and personality types, as established through the Myers–Briggs Type Indicator. Heywood (2000) reports that some Myers–Briggs types found it useful to keep a journal whereas one type did not.

Students can also be asked to present their work in any of these ways, as performance and through other creations, such as models, exhibitions, events, posters, designs, software and so on. Although we might hope that students could represent the same achievement through any of these media, psychologists know well that apparently small variations in task design can lead to significant variations in performance. We do not want to go into this topic here but we do need to insist on the non-equivalence of apparently equivalent tasks, assessments and awards.

Scaffolding

Why is it that higher education institutions say, in all good faith, that a student has consistently shown good levels of achievement in, say, critical thinking, and yet we fail to see it 'in the wild'? How is it that a good problem-solver in an engineering class can fail to demonstrate problem-solving in the workplace?

In Chapter 4 we suggested that an answer may lie in scaffolding, which is a term increasingly being used to refer to the amount of structure and help attaching to a task. The more scaffolding, the more prompts and cues given to the student and the more familiar the task, the easier it is to succeed. That leads to the conclusions that:

- Beginners should be supported with lots of scaffolding which is steadily taken away as they become more confident. One way of designing progression into a programme is to reduce scaffolding. (Others are to increase task complexity and fuzziness).
- If we say that someone is competent or can do something, we ought to be referring to what they can do with little or no scaffolding to help them.
- We need information about process standards – about the learning, teaching and assessment arrangements that lie behind claims to achievement – if we are to judge the meaning of those claims. This can be handled by issuing transcripts that are more than just lists of course titles, credit points and grades.

This note on scaffolding takes us back to the earlier point about the non-equivalence of ostensibly equivalent qualifications: two people may produce essays of similar quality but how is an observer to tell whether one essay is the outcome of a personal inquiry with minimal support from lectures, seminars or tutors and the other the product of hackwork on lecture and seminar notes? The more help learners get with tasks, the less those tasks tell us about the robustness of their achievement.

Ill-defined and well-defined tasks

The same assessment method can feel very different when the tasks are ill-defined as opposed to well-defined. Take a simple example. '10 + 5 = ?' is a well-defined task. Seven-year-olds will do well on that task but fewer will succeed if asked, 'How many sweets are there in a bag which has 10 red ones and 5 yellow ones in it?' They have to recognize that 'red ones' and 'yellow ones' fall into the class of 'sweets' and that the number of sweets is obtained by adding 10 and 5. In higher education we might hope that final-year students would be able to identify problems from raw data and decide upon an order of priority before attempting to work towards some provisional solutions. This could be introduced in year 1 as a structured exercise and lead, in the final year, to an in-basket exercise in which students have to identify the problems in the data that need attention, decide how to address them and offer provisional solution strategies. If we assume that ill-defined tasks have less scaffolding than well-defined ones, then this can be seen as a special case of scaffolding. The view is that graduates should be accustomed to complexity, which we associate with ill-defined problems and uncertainty in general. Ideally, *the* problem for graduates is finding the problem. It is only incidentally about working with little guidance on 'boil-in-the-bag' problems.

Table 5.1 summarizes these points and, in the process, paves the way for the extended treatment of progression in Chapter 10.

Assessment as judgement

If assessment is judgement, then anything that provides data for judgement is an assessment method. It is not possible to simplify by saying that only some methods

Table 5.1   Five factors affecting the demands made by assessment methods

Factor	Appropriateness for novice learners	Appropriateness for assessments of competence
Purpose: High stakes, low stakes; summative, formative	Low stakes tend not to be as intimidating. The intention is to help learning, which is especially appropriate to novices	A judgement that someone is competent is, by definition, high-stakes. We said earlier that we are not happy about the validity of many high-stakes assessments
People: Who assesses?	Peer assessments can be less threatening and there is some evidence that the quality of discussion with peers is better than it is with teachers (Moshman 1999). However, peer judgements need to be endorsed by teachers if they are to be taken seriously	Teachers have to assess competence, although they should benefit from using peer- and self-assessments as supplementary evidence
Presentation: In which medium is the task presented and represented?	As far as we know, one medium does not suit novices more than final-year students. Some students prefer some media, others prefer others. The more familiar students are with a medium, the easier they will find tasks presented or represented in it	
Scaffolding: How much help and how many cues does the task contain?	Lots of scaffolding, plenty of cues	Since judgements of competence are generalizations to a host of unknown situations that may be encountered in the future, exit tests should be robust and lifelike – little scaffolding, few cues, and ill-defined tasks
Task definition: Ill-defined or well-defined?	Well-defined	

can provide evidence for high-stakes assessments. Consider the descriptions in the appendix to this chapter, which summarizes 51 assessment techniques. It is not an exhaustive list of methods (and we have implied that it would be impossible to make one) and some of the 51 could be merged to shorten the list. The methods are loosely arranged so that those likely to make the lightest demands on the teacher and to be most susceptible to high-reliability judgements, come first. However, we cannot say that techniques 5, 32 and 48, for example, are formative assessment methods, good for low-stakes, low-reliability purposes, whereas 8, 33 and 44 are high-reliability, summative ones. It may be difficult to see how some methods could be used reliably, and in an institution like the UK Open University it is hard to see how markers could be sure that the work generated by some methods really was the unaided work of its distance learning students. That is not the same as saying that those methods are incompatible with summative assessment purposes.

Choosing assessment methods

In practice, assessment techniques are often chosen as the least bad way of resolving a number of competing contingencies – time, management demands, information and communications technology availability, need to verify student identity, staff expertise, 'the way we do things around here', and student expectations. Even though contingencies loom large, there are still general suggestions that can help with making decisions about assessment methods. We present some in Table 5.2 on the understanding that they point towards ideals, which are not always feasible in a particular setting.

The first point made in Table 5.2 is that there is a module–programme relationship that should influence the choice of assessment methods. Modules should, in Biggs' (1999) words, be constructively aligned with programmes, so that it can be

Table 5.2   Ten suggestions to guide the choice of assessment methods in a single module

Suggestion	Comment
1. Look for coherence between module assessment methods and programme specification	Programme assessment audits often show that some methods are overused, others are rarely used, and some that ought to be there are absent. Module assessment methods should be selected with an eye to their contribution to programme coherence
2. Assume that good assessments come from good task sequences	It is worth trying to devise good learning tasks first and then thinking about how they could provide evidence of achievement
3. Remember that one task can provide evidence of several achievements, although the evidence may not be direct	It is not necessary to get direct evidence in respect of all the achievements: a command of English and referencing conventions can be assumed and action taken only if there is evidence of poor English or anarchic references
4. Consider threshold or 'ticket' approaches – complex learning tasks leading to short, powerful assessment tasks	See Chapter 2 on 'assessment tickets'. Rather than directly assess complex products, such as reflective diaries, grade students on shorter tasks that draw on the learning done in the threshold task

Table 5.2   continued

Suggestion	Comment
5. Provide low-stakes practice tasks before high-stakes ones	Students might write three papers, the first two of which receive swift, pointed feedback (from the teacher or other students) before they do the third, which is graded
6. Reduce the scaffolding over the course of a module	This is difficult in short modules and more difficult if several different types of task are used, especially if each is used only once
7. Beware of assessment overload	Three forms of overload are: setting lots of peer-assessed tasks, so that students are overloaded whilst teachers have less grading to do; assessing everything, so that there are no 'spaces' left in the course, through which students all move in a lockstep; setting complicated, multipart tasks
8. Consider the economy of assessment	Set good tasks and look for efficient ways of getting assessment data from them (see also 3, above). Exams (or in-class tests) can be very efficient, especially if all non-exam work is formative
9. Try to see that low-stakes tasks and feedback do not get 'lost'	It helps to tell students how low-stakes tasks and formative feedback can contribute to achievement and to employability. This theme is developed in Chapters 6, 9 and 11
10. Make sure that you can explain to students what the assessment pattern is and why it is like that	If students know the intentions behind the assessment plan, they are more likely to work to specification and appreciate what they are doing. When students do not see the point, resistance and subversion follow

seen that module goals fit with programme goals and contribute to their advancement. By the same token, assessment methods need to be understood as a part of a palette of assessment methods. They have been chosen because they jointly promote programme goals. This need not be as constricting as it might appear if it is recognized that assessment methods are quite plastic. For example, it may be in the programme's interest for a course to have an assessment by short evaluations of target papers (method 17). As was said at the beginning of the chapter, there are many ways in which such tasks can be made more or less demanding.

But why should it be necessary to align course assessment methods with programme learning intentions? Consider the implications of saying that a programme aims to contribute to student employability. Suppose that employability were described as a combination of understanding some subject matter, being skilled in a number of practices and processes, believing that persistence and strategic thinking allow one generally to have an impact on most problems and situations, and having a commitment to reflection and the continuing learning that goes with it. It follows that there should be assessments, throughout the programme, that encourage reflection or stimulate the development of communication, inter-personal skill, creative thinking and the like. So, across the programme, assessment methods 4, 14, 25, 28, 29, . . ., could be regularly used to improve students' com-munication repertoires, whilst 18, 20, 42, 47, . . ., could be used to support reflec-tion, and so on. The underlying idea is that certain sorts of learning outcome are unlikely to occur unless certain sorts of learning, teaching and assessment activities are in place.

The Skills *plus* project asked participating departments to audit undergraduate modules to see how far the learning, teaching and assessment methods needed to stimulate programme learning outcomes were actually in place. Typical conclusions were that:

- Some outcomes were suitably supported by assessment methods.
- Some were patchily supported, perhaps addressed by a year 1/level 1 task and not again.
- Some were undersupported or not supported at all.
- Some (essay writing, for example) were overemphasized.

The project then encouraged departments to 'tune' the learning, teaching and assessment patterns they had discovered. This meant approaching module tutors and asking them to change aspects of their assessment practice in the interests of producing a more coherent programme assessment pattern. Examples included:

- Replacing overused assessment techniques with underused techniques, which often meant replacing essays with oral presentations.
- Replacing a summative purpose with a formative one, without otherwise changing the task.
- Reducing the amount of scaffolding in final-year tasks.
- Introducing group assignments.
- Replacing some time-consuming assessment methods with powerful but more efficient ones.

We are not saying that there is a close correspondence between assessment methods and learning outcomes, although we are making the important claim that certain learning outcomes are unlikely to materialize unless assessment methods of the right sort are in place: imagine promoting groupwork without having assess-ments of groups' achievements arranged across the programme in conjunction with instruction on progressively more advanced techniques for effectively working *in* groups and *as* groups; imagine saying that assessment promotes student learning and having a programme dominated by summative, high-stakes assessment tasks;

imagine trying to develop students' skill at interpreting numerical data in a programme which had no honours-level assignments requiring them to interpret statistical tables.

No simple solution

The design of assessment is an art in that there are many assessment methods available and those methods can each be designed to be more or less demanding. As with other arts, it is to some extent a matter of taste when it comes to choosing the methods from the palette and how to use them but, as with other arts, the methods need to be used in a context, for a purpose and an audience. Some suggestions to guide the choice of assessment method are presented in the appendix to this chapter, accompanied by the recommendation that module designers aim to align their methods with the needs of the programme. We illustrated that idea with a brief reference to the implications for assessment practice of saying that a programme should enhance student employability. That goal – enhanced employability – is a good and topical example of the complex outcomes of learning that should be associated with *higher* education. Because they are complex, these are also outcomes that cause serious assessment problems not only for those who see assessment as measurement, but also for the larger group whose concern is that achievements can be convincingly demonstrated. This chapter has been suggesting that these are not, at root, problems that will be solved by finding the right method or technique. To get a grip on the assessment of complex outcomes of learning we need to turn from assessment techniques, reconsider what assessment is for and remind ourselves what different approaches to assessment can and cannot tell us. Then we can return to technique. The next chapter develops this position by considering the relationship between assessment and that complex of achievements known as 'employability'.

Appendix: Fifty-one assessment techniques

Brief description of the technique	Strengths	Problems and limitations
1. Personal response assessments. Usually done in classes where each student has an electronic response pad. Teachers ask questions and they press a key to show their answer. Can be used for classroom assessment or test purposes	Similar to classroom assessment techniques (see 3), although some systems will provide data on individual student performance. Once the kit is in place, efficient	Not always easy for teachers to see how to use this in already-busy lectures and seminars. Danger of concentrating attention on factual questions. See also item 7

Brief description of the technique	Strengths	Problems and limitations
2. Assessment banks. Students have access to a question-and-answer bank. They have time to find out how to answer all of the questions and are then graded on their performance on a sample of them	If students have worked out the answers to all questions in a good bank, they have mastered the course. Efficient	Creating an item bank is difficult, costly and slow. Tendency to fill the bank with tests of information recall and of the use of standard formulae
3. Classroom assessment techniques (CATs). They are *brief* tasks that tell the teacher something about the *class's* grasp of the material. (See Angelo and Cross, 1993)	Good for establishing what *groups* of students have grasped	Hard to keep CATs to time and to find time for them in busy classes
4. Bullet point summaries. Students gain entry to classes only on production of summaries of set reading. Teachers may check a random sample each week or concentrate on finding summaries that are inadequate or plagiarized	Encourages preparation. Efficient	Copying from friends. Difficult with large classes
5. Computer-based self-assessment – students use a diagnostic programme to gauge their recall, application, understanding of material	Efficient for the teacher. Can help students to learn, especially where there are good feedback loops	The software costs can be excessive, especially when the application is developed in-house
6. Teachers use electronic monitoring of web searches, program use and communications to provide evidence for assessing the quality of online work	An unobtrusive, somewhat limited measure	Dependent on monitoring software being in place and students using the systems that it attaches to. Quite easy to subvert
7. Multiple choice questions (MCQs)	Cheap to mark large numbers. MCQs make students put course material into short-term	Hard to write MCQs that are not tests of information. Worries about the lucky guesser can be

Brief description of the technique	*Strengths*	*Problems and limitations*
	memory and some MCQs reach 'higher-order' thinking as well	accommodated by adjusting the scoring system
8. Making glossaries (under examination conditions)	Efficient way of establishing whether key terms are understood	Easy to plagiarize, unless done in exam conditions. Hard to mark reliably
9. Completing structured summaries of readings, debates, etc. The teacher prepares a framework, perhaps in the form of an incomplete flowchart, table, concept map, set of headings, etc., and the students complete it and elaborate upon it	Efficient	Danger of summarizing information only unless teachers frame the summaries so that students identify strengths, contradictions, new ideas, logical flaws, etc
10. New tests in which learners use old software, programmes and notes	Efficient tests of prior learning and its application	Takes some ingenuity to devise these assessment tasks
11. Objective Structured Clinical Examination (OSCE), which is where students move amongst 10–20 'stations', each of which engages them with a problem, task or activity representative of the clinical field being examined. Similar techniques can be used to test students' laboratory skills, etc.	Efficient way of sampling student skill in a number of professional practices – taking client histories, breaking bad news, interpreting test results, performing discrete routines. Could be used more widely than it is	Artificial and sometimes obscure tasks
12. Short answer questions (SAQs). For example, MCQs with the addition of 50–100 words explaining the thinking behind the choices	This deals with the concern that people can do well on MCQ tests by lucky guessing and helps teachers to appreciate the quality of students' thinking	As hard to write SAQs as MCQs. Take longer to mark
13. Fieldwork, lab work reports, etc.	Authentic, traditional and well-established	The volume can be overwhelming unless teachers decide to sample –

Brief description of the technique	Strengths	Problems and limitations
		for example, by marking some lab reports this week, others the next, or by concentrating on some sections of fieldwork reports in this course because other sections are carefully addressed in others
14. Posters	An efficient way of seeing how students understand complex content and relationships. Students can learn from seeing each other's posters	Best done by groups, it takes time. Danger of prettiness being students' main concern and of penalizing those with little artistic talent. No agreed rules for summatively assessing posters (but making posters is good for formative conversations)
15. Replication of published inquiries. Students take a report of a small-scale study and run the procedures themselves	Straightforward 'apprenticeship' tasks that allow students to gain confidence in inquiry procedures and interpretation of data	Hard to see what to reward when students are replicating someone else's inquiries
16. Seminar presentations (in or out of role; with or without use of video, overhead transparencies, PowerPoint, etc.)	Presentations encourage students to become better at oral communication, which is something employers value. They can be authentic and they invite peer assessment as a way of giving the tutor supplementary evidence for grading	Time-consuming, even with group presentations, which have their own difficulties. Reliability problems and a danger of valuing style over substance
17. Short evaluations of target papers, which will generally include appreciative and critical judgements	Efficient and encourage critical, analytical and evaluative thinking	Students are seldom familiar with this sort of task and need to learn how to write such evaluations. There is a tendency to be indiscriminately critical, which can be rather disheartening

Brief description of the technique	*Strengths*	*Problems and limitations*
18. Statements of relevance, which are short pieces of writing – 1000 words perhaps – making claims about the relevance of a workshop, article, field observation, etc., to another task or activity. See Bourner *et al.* (2000)	Good tasks for stimulating reflection and encouraging students to associate *this* learning with other learning	Can be difficult to identify grading criteria and to use them reliably. This sort of task will be unfamiliar to most students
19. Takeaway papers/ questions/tests	Help students to show their reasoning in the best light	Danger of collusion and plagiarism. Equal opportunities issues – not all students can use the 'takeaway' time to prepare their answers
20. Structured logs of project/ dissertation progress and reflections on it	Structured and staged reporting helps to pace students through complex assignments (i.e. a form of scaffolding) and helps teachers to mark them by breaking them into discrete sections (analytical marking)	Some say that complex products should be marked as a whole (holistic marking). Concerns that the structure can be a straitjacket and lead to dull uniformity
21. Terminal, unseen examinations and other individual time-constrained assignments	Traditional and valuable means of establishing what an individual can do on the basis of the learning that the course has stimulated	There is a legion of objections to exams – nerves; 'off days'; restricted writing times; the need to cram lots of information into short-term memory; rapid loss of information after exams; they favour fast writers
22. Writing memoranda, executive summaries or newspaper reports	Helps students to learn to write in a variety of styles for a variety of audiences. Short summaries, memoranda, etc., may be marked more efficiently than traditional essays	Students are not often familiar with this style of writing. Clear guidelines and criteria needed
23. Contributions to threaded electronic discussions	Students are assessed on their normal contributions	Online discourse tends to be brief and many people

Brief description of the technique	Strengths	Problems and limitations
	to online courses. Authentic	prefer to lurk rather than to contribute. Hard to grade contributions reliably
24. Devising exams/tests/ assessments to tutor specification	Like teaching, setting assessment tasks is a good test of one's own understanding of the topic. Potentially efficient, although the tests probably need an accompanying explanation, which reduces the benefits	Hard to see what would be a fair, robust and reliable way of grading these tests. Perhaps best treated as threshold or 'ticket' requirement
25. Concept maps. Students identify the main points in an argument, system or claim. They then group like points with like and arrange the points and groups on a sheet of paper in a way that shows the relationships between them	An efficient way of seeing how students understand complex content and relationships. Students can learn from seeing each other's maps. Concept mapping software is available	The technique is unfamiliar. Best done by groups, it takes time. No agreed rules for summatively assessing concept maps (but concept mapping is good for formative conversations)
26. Making annotated bibliographies for next year's students	Requires students to read quite widely and refine their web-search and data handling techniques. Can be quicker to mark ten-item bibliographies than essays	Hard to mark reliably. The technique is unfamiliar and students may need a disproportionate amount of help, especially where there is no other induction into electronic searches
27. Open-book, end-of-course exams	'The main cognitive benefit from open-book examinations would appear to be the raising of the level of the skills tested.' (Heywood 2000: 173). They penalize students who do not know the material (they spend their time looking for information)	Even good students can get snared by the books and give less thoughtful performances
28. Short-essay writing. Limit of 1000 words. Sometimes students are asked to write	Efficient. Cuts the blather, concentrates attention on the argument	Students find this hard. May give an unfair advantage to slick writers

Brief description of the technique	Strengths	Problems and limitations
this as if it were an article in a quality newspaper		
29. Bidding for funds or writing responses to invitations to tender. Students have to prepare bids or tenders	Bids often have to be short. This authentic task can be very efficient	Hard to write good briefing documents. Can take a lot of time in busy courses. The quality of the briefing affects the quality of student responses
30. Two-part assessments. Elements of a task are formatively assessed but the final product is summatively assessed	Supports learning and provides scaffolding for improved performance on the graded task	Time-consuming and possibly too big for some short courses
31. Essay writing – one 5000-word piece (make harder/easier by varying amount of scaffolding – tutorial guidance, range of reading expected, novelty of the topic/problem, time available, conceptual complexity, etc.)	Traditional. Arts and humanities students may not like essays but at least they have lots of experience of doing them	Expensive and often boring to mark reliably. Long essays can encourage narration at the expense of evaluation, analysis and critical thinking
32. Games and simulations	Can be good ways of seeing whether students understand the inner logic of events and situations. Authentic, often highly motivating. Efficient when the games/simulations produce results that can validly be used as indicators of understanding	Can be time-consuming and difficult to fit within a course. Availability of simulations and games is uneven
33. Peer assessment	Good for formative purposes, saves teacher time and paves the way for self-assessment	Complicated procedures needed if it is to be used for summative purposes
34. Self-assessment	Skill at self-evaluation is valued by many employers and it is also widely thought to contribute to learning	Enormous problems with using it summatively. When used formatively, a danger of self-affirming or superficial self-assessments.

Brief description of the technique	Strengths	Problems and limitations
		Critical self-assessments are not necessarily deep and insightful ones
35. *Viva voce* examinations	Useful for checking on points of uncertainty and confirming the authenticity of students' work	Expensive. Work against students who are nervous or do not speak well. Less ground gets covered than in writing
36. Exhibitions of work, posters, products. History students have curated museum exhibitions in lieu of doing a dissertation	Authentic and can inspire students	Time-consuming. Costly to grade reliably
37. Production of reviews of a book, website, paper, video or programme	Authentic and can inspire students	Students first need to learn how to write reviews – they often find it hard, especially as reviews usually demand tight length limits
38. Students have to make something – a common technique in fashion, fine art, design, engineering, etc.	Authentic and can inspire students	Time-consuming. Costly to grade reliably
39. Design and build models or, occasionally, the real thing	Authentic and can inspire students	Time-consuming. Costly to grade reliably
40. Role-playing, as when students take the part of judge, prosecutor, defendant, interviewer and then interviewee, a historical character, etc.	Can be very good ways of seeing whether students understand different perspectives. Authentic, often highly motivating	Can be time-consuming and difficult to fit within a course. Reliability problems and difficulty deciding what to reward in the grading process
41. Web page creation	An efficient way of seeing how students understand complex content and relationships. Students can learn from seeing each others' web pages	Best done by groups, it takes time. Danger of prettiness being students' main concern and of penalizing those with little ICT (information and communications technology) design experience. No agreed rules for summatively

Brief description of the technique	Strengths	Problems and limitations
		assessing web pages (but the task is good for formative conversations)
42. Submission of claims to achievement based on and closely linked to portfolios	The benefits of portfolios without the summative assessment difficulties. We suggest grading on the substantive quality of the claims alone *provided that* sufficient evidence supports them	Problems in judging to a common standard differing claims that refer to different evidence, but they are far less serious than the difficulties with trying to grade portfolios
43. Projects	Authentic and complex tasks, especially suited to final-year work when it is common to expect them to be 'capstones' – to show students using learning from several courses	Expensive to mark and supervise. Reliability problems
44. Dissertations and theses	Traditional academic tasks. Often ill-defined and with little scaffolding, which suits them to final-year work	Supervision costs can be high, as can marking costs
45. Small-scale research or inquiry	An empirical project, usually not a replication, and often presented in a dissertation. Often draws on learning from more than one course and usually quite complicated	Expensive to mark and supervise. Tendency to concentrate on the mechanics of inquiry and to sideline the academic side – making sense of findings and relating them to the wider literatures. Reliability problems
46. Assessment of logs and journals	Authentic and can encourage highly prized reflection, especially when used formatively to support assessment conversations	If used summatively, there are considerable reliability problems and difficulties deciding what sorts of comment to reward. Sampling recommended as a way of coping with the volume of reading this method generates

Brief description of the technique	Strengths	Problems and limitations
47. Portfolios	Allow students to establish their own claims to achievement, using what they see as the best evidence to hand. Encourages reflection, planning and learning conversations. From 2005, all students in England should have opportunities to construct them as a part of their progress files	No great formative problems, beyond encouraging students and staff to take them seriously and make time for them. Formidable summative problems (reliability, analytic *vs* holistic marking, what to reward), which can be eased at a price (Baume and Yorke, 2002)
48. Performances. Students put on a play, show how they take patient histories, teach a class, operate a programme, etc.	Authentic and can inspire students. Simulations sometimes an acceptable alternative – often necessary in anatomy and other procedures that would put human or animal life at risk	Observation of performance is expensive and there are massive problems assessing complex performances fairly and reliably. May be less problematical when simulations are used, especially if the software produces performance data
49. 'General' assessments, drawing together learning in several modules	Good way of exploring understanding and the degree to which learning is transferred and applied	No scaffolding, ill-defined tasks, considerable cognitive (and emotional) demands – many students hate them
50. 'Real' problem working, which involves defining 'fuzzy' situations, bringing some order to ill-defined issues, analysing the problem and suggesting solutions	Authentic and complex tasks, especially suited to final-year work when it is common to expect students to address tasks by drawing on what they have learned from the range of courses they have followed. Success on these tasks can be treated as a robust indication of secure learning	Can be expensive to mark. Students often feel very disoriented by ill-defined tasks which are replete with uncertainty. Performance and course evaluations can be low in comparison with other courses
51. Assessment of work-based learning, which involves using evidence from the workplace (paid or	Authentic, can inspire students and bridge the academic/work divide that puts some potential	Low reliability, unless it is done in a variety of ways, many times, by a variety of people

Brief description of the technique	Strengths	Problems and limitations
voluntary work) to judge whether students have achieved learning specified in the course specification or in a learning contract	students off higher education	

Source: after Knight 2002a: 146–7

6

Assessing for Employability

Employability and higher education

Although this chapter centres on assessment and employability, its analysis illumin-ates a question that is causing a lot of difficulty in many countries: how are complex achievements to be assessed? One answer, developed in this chapter, is to recognize that they are complex and to assess accordingly.[1]

We have argued that assessment methods are versatile, that one method may be variously moulded to serve different functions. The corollary is that thinking about assessment calls for thinking about what higher education is *for*. Decisions about how to assess learning may involve nothing more than recalling a technique that 'works'. More formally, decisions may stem from learning theory, as when peer assessment is given a prominent place in programme assessment. Many of these decisions are shaped by what the course and its host programme are intended to promote. For example, a programme that is designed to enhance professional competence needs assessments of performance; one intended to encourage 'far transfer' needs assessment tasks that pose novel problems calling upon learning from the programme as a whole; and a programme concerned that students should command a lot of scientific information is likely to be test-rich (although lots of testing may not be the best way to encourage learning for information mastery).

The idea that the quality of learning and teaching in UK higher education should be enhanced (Cooke 2003; DfES 2003) calls for similar analysis of the goals of higher education. To some, enhancement means relating curriculum design and pedagogical practices to research evidence about effective student learning, although this is not as straightforward as is sometimes imagined because prescrip-tions for practice cannot just be read off from unproblematical research findings (Evans and Benefield 2001; Pawson 2001; Davies and Nutley 2002.) Yet there remains the question, 'better learning for what?' The practices that help students to analyse, evaluate and argue are not the same as those that help recall and 'near transfer' (Peterson 1979).

In order to choose which research to use we need to have a sense of what the curriculum is for. By way of illustration, consider the implications of two views. One line of thought[2] concentrates upon the contribution of higher education to knowledge economies – to economies that are based less on agriculture, mining and heavy industry and more on software, bioscience and media – and sees higher education producing graduates who are steeped in new, research-driven ideas and techniques. Here higher education produces knowledge that commerce uses to its, and by extension to national, advantage. Another view sees higher education producing graduates who have general achievements of the sort that make for flexibility, openness to learning, creativity and drive. Knowledge decays fast, so, from the latter perspective, universities and colleges can best contribute by helping graduates to become people who can thrive in turbulent times, enhancing the employability of *all* students through its general approach to teaching and learning. The two are not incompatible, although there may be a tendency to focus on one – usually the first one – rather than the other. Our point is that different views of the ways in which higher education might enhance employability can steer thinking about curriculum and pedagogy in different directions.

The first view has obvious merits but we will concentrate upon the second for three reasons. First, it is inclusive, in the sense that it can be applied to history, nursing and biochemistry graduates in the making. Secondly, it has more profound implications for the goals of higher education. The first view can easily lead to the position that higher education will contribute best to national well-being by running more computing, nanotechnology and project management programmes. The second view implies that higher education contributes to national wealth by concerning itself with the qualities of *all* graduates. Thirdly, employers, when asked what they look for in new graduates, frequently talk in general terms. Many are indifferent to students' first degree subject (Purcell and Pitcher 1996), and those who require a degree in a certain area seem to discriminate amongst applicants on the basis of their general achievements, such as creativity, drive and interpersonal fluency.[3] Even where specific knowledge is required, having it is an entry ticket to a game which is usually decided on the basis of generic achievements. And, of course, employability is not a one-off achievement but an identity that demands continued work and renewal.

Although the terms used differ, there are striking similarities in the lists researchers produce. Box 6.1 provides a sample of the characteristics believed to be important for employment.

There are objections to these lists:

- Some argue that they typically come from middle and senior managers who are detached from the operational realities of the organizations in which they work.
- There is a view that they are 'wish lists' and over-idealized. There may be some support for this position in Coleman and Keep's (2001) contention that many enterprises do not need and cannot use to best advantage graduates who are prepared for high value-added enterprises. What employers say they want and what their businesses are able to use may be two quite different things.
- Some talk about employability in terms of skills whereas others refer to qualities, dispositions and self-presentation.

Box 6.1   The characteristics of highly employable graduates

- Harvey *et al.* (1997) found that employers want graduates with knowledge, intellect, willingness to learn, self-management skills, communication skills, teamworking, interpersonal skills.
- Hawkins and Winter (1995) identify the following 'career management skills and effective learning skills': self-awareness, self-promotion, exploring and creating opportunities, action planning, networking, matching and decision-making, negotiation, political awareness, coping with uncertainty, development focus, transfer skills, self-confidence.
- Yorke (1999c) found that small enterprises especially valued skill at oral communication, handling one's own workload, teamworking, managing others, getting to the heart of problems, critical analysis, summarizing, and group problem-solving. Valued attributes (part of the 'plus' in the Skills *plus* model) included being able to work under pressure, commitment, working varied hours, dependability, imagination/creativity, getting on with people, and willingness to learn.
- Brennan *et al.* (2001) identified the following 12 competences as those that UK graduates believed they possessed on graduation: learning abilities; working independently; written communication skills; working in a team; working under pressure; accuracy, attention to detail; power of concentration; oral communication skills; problem-solving ability; initiative; tolerance. The 10 required in current employment were: working under pressure; oral communication skills; accuracy, attention to detail; working in a team; time management; adaptability; initiative; working independently; taking responsibility and decisions; planning, coordinating and organizing. Graduates from elsewhere in Europe and from Japan provided different lists.

- There are some national variations (for example, see Brennan *et al.* 2001). This is awkward for those promoting international labour market mobility.
- Should higher education have any truck with shaping the self? There is no shortage of critiques arguing that modern 'fast' capitalism (Gee and Lankshear 1997) is colonizing workers' identities, in the process demanding emotional labour (Hochschild 1993) and corroding character (Sennett 1998).
- Whilst it is often assumed that skills can be taught, people are unsure whether qualities and dispositions can be. Can education make a difference in these areas?

We do not advocate any particular list, although we observe that many of the things that employers say they value are things that university teachers value in their own right (such as autonomy and critical analysis), or value because they make for good learning (for example, management of self and action planning). To us there seems to be no necessary tension between employability, understood as the promotion of achievements such as those listed in Box 6.1, and the sorts of learning valued in higher education.

To recap: the argument is that higher education is expected to encourage the development of complex outcomes of learning. Knowing, as we do, that assessment influences what students learn and how, we face a problem in seeing how we can reconcile assessment, which in its summative form tends to be simplifying because of the need for reliability, with complex learning goals. Our position is that this implies having differentiated assessment plans. One face of differentiation is drawing generously from the range of assessment methods described in Chapter 5. Other implications of differentiation are now considered.

Assessment for employability

In Chapter 1 we described employability as a constellation of understandings, 'skills' (by which we mean 'skilfulness'), efficacy beliefs and metacognition. There are other ways of representing the clutch of achievements subsumed by USEM. We might align it with what Wagner (1993) has called 'practical intelligence' and Sternberg (1997) calls 'successful intelligence', and we see points of contact with Goleman's (1996) account of 'emotional intelligence'. Rather than haggle about ways of representing such employability, we prefer to cut to the main point which is that, given that we are concerned with complex achievements such as the promotion of 'emotional intelligence', we face a serious assessment problem. In Box 6.2 we illustrate the difficulty of offering any resolution, let alone one that will satisfy those who see assessment in terms of measurement.

Our approach takes a cue from pioneering work done at Alverno College, Milwaukee. There,

> Faculty define assessment as a multidimensional process that is integral to learning, which involves observing performances of an individual learner in action and judging them on the basis of public criteria that are developmental, with resulting feedback to that learner. . . . Faculty define the ability to judge one's own work – self assessment – as integral to the student assessment process.
>
> (Mentkowski and Associates 2000: 58)

This broadens the notion of assessment in three ways.

- First, we suggest that assessment should serve learning and not hinder it.
- Secondly, the idea of multidimensional assessment suggests that a range of methods should be used. Heywood endorses the related concept of multiple-strategy assessment, quoting the view of the National Governors Association of the United States that

> Because the nature of undergraduate education requires many skills and cognitive abilities be acquired and developed, colleges and universities should use a number of assessment approaches and techniques. An

Box 6.2 Assessing 'emotional intelligence'

Employers' wish lists imply that they want graduates with emotional intelligence (EI). The high sales of *Emotional Intelligence* (Goleman 1996) shows the concept's appeal. It therefore seems reasonable to say that education should promote EI. By extension, it should then be assessed. Six problematical assessment issues are:

1. Does EI really exist? Alternatives include social competence (which includes, but is not the same as, social skills), social intelligence, practical intelligence and personal intelligence.
2. If it exists, what does it comprise? Mayer *et al.* (2000a: 101–2) argue that Goleman's initial account of EI comprised a set of 'broad . . . definitions [that] . . . is finally extended to cover almost all of personality. Included are traits based on motivation . . . as well as on emotion . . . and also characterizations of broad areas of behaviour . . . that encompass the entire model of how one operates in the world.'
3. Are displays of EI in essence responses to mood and context? If so, then it will be unwise to generalize from one display to other occasions, and substantial samples of EI will be necessary before any generalizations (warrants are generalizations) should be ventured.
4. Assume there is to be an attempt to measure EI. Three main approaches present themselves (Mayer *et al.* 2000b):

   (a) Tests of ability might be devised but procedures for the development of rating scales are demanding. We could not get a technically adequate self-efficacy scale despite piloting with some 200, then 400+ and then 2200+ subjects.
   (b) Observations need trained observers who are able to watch enough samples of behaviour for generalizations to be defensible.
   (c) Self-reports: 'People are notoriously inaccurate reporters of functioning, including the self-assessment of ability: self-reported intelligence correlates only modestly with actual measured intelligence' (Mayer *et al.* 2000b: 324).

5. Assume EI can be measured. Can EI be improved by educational interventions? If not, then why are we assessing individuals' EI? There are views that it is possible to intervene effectively in some of the areas covered by EI (Cherniss 2000; Topping *et al.* 2000).
6. Finally, there is no certainty about which methods work best, let alone about why (Topping *et al.* 2000).

In sum: without agreement that there is such a thing as EI (1 above) and on its definition (2), no assessment is possible. If it is a plastic phenomenon (3), then judgements can be made but generalization is hazardous. Attempts at

---

Box 6.2   continued

measurement rest on methods that are unreliable (4c), expensive to use (4b) or expensive and difficult to develop (4a). It is hard to see many universities or colleges having the expertise to develop assessment methods, the funds to do this properly, or wanting to warrant achievement on the basis of such assessments. If EI can be enhanced (5), there is disagreement about the best approach and the sorts of long-term impact that might be anticipated (6).

---

assessment programme that uses multiple measures of student learning will more accurately and fairly depict a student's knowledge and abilities.

(Heywood 2000: 59)

Notice the well-chosen word 'depict'.

- Thirdly, we observe that teachers are not the only people who assess and it implies that they may not be the best.

We add a fourth point, which is the reminder that assessment may be summative but there is also great value in formative assessment (Chapters 3 and 9).

Here is the basis for a sketch of the ways in which higher education might foster employability without being sabotaged by assessment practices that tend to compromise complexity. Differentiated approaches, which use a range of methods and have formative and summative ends in mind, may preserve complexity and, in that way, support rather than undermine good learning. This should be understood as a programme approach with implications for modules. Three reasons are as follows.

- As we have said, complex achievements are slow-growing achievements and are not normally the result of single lessons or even of modules: months and years may be needed. The implication is that modules *contribute* to the promotion of achievements that are *programme* achievements. Both learning and assessment need, then, to be conceived in programme terms.
- We need to design progression into the sequence of engagements. By this we mean that learning should be expansive, in two senses. First, that the problems on which students work should be progressively less well-defined and progressively more complicated; secondly, that they should be asked to transfer their understandings and skilled practices to problems that are progressively further removed from the contexts in which the learning originally took place.

    By definition, this progression has to be planned at programme level so that tasks, particularly assessment tasks, towards the end of the programme make different demands from those at the beginning.
- This is a complicated approach. It is one thing to use a good range of tasks to support a set of broad achievements, sometimes having teachers judge achievement, sometimes having other students judge, and sometimes requiring self-evaluation, but it is another thing to avoid tokenism, where something is touched a couple of times and no more.

If the aim is to build confidence and skill, then students need to do enough peer assessment, starting in year 1, to become confident enough to do the far transfer of applying what they do in peer assessment to self-assessment. So, too, with the assessment of group projects, with portfolio assessment, assessment of oral presentations and so on. If students and teachers are to become fluent in the practices of differentiated assessment, then programme-level planning is necessary to make sure that there is adequate, paced and progressive engagement. This means that no one module will try to cover all programme learning aims or use all the assessment techniques we can imagine. Rather, modules will make strategic contributions to the programme plan of campaign.

Programme assessment plans

A programme assessment plan is a device for keeping track of the several forms of differentiation that are needed in order to sustain complex learning. Figure 4.2 in Chapter 4 sketched the territory that a programme assessment plan might describe.

As we said in Chapter 4, the point is that some outcomes of learning are subject to formative, conversation-creating assessment and others are subject to summative, grade-creating assessment. Programme teams normally have little problem identifying achievements that are well-suited to summative assessment – information retention, use of common problem-solving routines in standard circumstances – and those that are obviously so unsuited to summative approaches that they call out for formative, low-stakes assessment. They do have problems with the rest, achievements that might be assessed with tolerable reliability *if* the team invested enough time, effort and money in devising, mastering and using assessment indicators (or criteria) and in making sure that they were used on more than one performance of the achievement in question by more than one trained assessor. These are not easy decisions to make and, although there is a tendency to see them as assessment decisions, they are largely economic decisions – you can make tolerably reliable judgements of all sorts of achievement if you are prepared to spend enough on doing so. These economic decisions are also plainly management decisions because they mean freeing resources to assess more systematically and somewhat reducing teachers' freedom. This reduction can be seen in terms of subsidiarity, in that teachers have considerable scope to plan and teach as they wish, *as long as they work within the framework provided by the programme assessment plan.*

When trying to make these economic decisions it is useful to have a view of which outcomes of learning are going to get *particular, direct and sustained* attention in which of the programme's components. Colleagues teaching the modules shown in Figure 6.1 said that most programme learning intentions were touched in most modules but, when pressed, they agreed that two or three outcomes were a particular priority in each. Box 2.3 in Chapter 2 showed the relationship between the programme plan and the pattern of assessment in one module, and together Box 2.3 and Figure 6.1 show how a commitment to diverse assessment methods is orchestrated across a programme and related to individual courses in the interests of coherence, progression and slow learning.

Skill outcomes (Programme Specification, section 10.2)	101	102*	103	200	201	202	203	204	301	302	303	304	305	306	300*
Critical capabilities													■	■	■
Argumentation	■				■			■				■			
Open-mindedness				■			■								
Tolerance of ambiguity										■				■	
Information-handling		■									■			■	
Research skills								■	■		■				
ICT	Students go to ICT workshops if they need to uprate their knowledge. WWW used in most courses												See left		See left
Number	Students read and make sense of numerical data in all courses														
Conventional	The expectations laid down in the first term are reinforced by normal course practices														
Presentational	■						■		X			■			
Reflectiveness			■	■											
Independence			■		■										
Problem-working						X			■						
Work organization	The expectations laid down in the first term are reinforced by normal course practices												■	■	■
Interpersonal				X	X	X									
Groupwork															X

The shaded cells identify skills that will get particular attention in a module. Students wishing to improve a skill are advised to use this information when choosing modules. 'X' shows skills that are not identified as learning priorities in a module.

* Learning opportunities in these two cases vary according to students' option choice.

Figure 6.1 The contribution made by key courses to programme learning outcomes

It might be said that this degree of coherence is only possible in simple programmes and not when students can construct a pathway to an award from a menu of a hundred modules or more. In those cases, though, analysis of students' patterns of choice often shows that there are a few pathways that students regularly create. Some coherence can then be achieved by orchestrating the demands of the modules that make up the pathways students have beaten through the thickets of choice. This means concentrating on the coherence of a core of modules, which is a necessary compromise in many cases, especially in high-choice modularized programmes. Non-core modules should still contribute to the programme goals, even if planners cannot assume that most students will take any particular one of them. The trick is to 'watermark' the elective modules so that they are recognizably part of the family of modules contributing, in their various ways, to the achievement of programme learning goals. Where students know what a module is going to concentrate upon, though, they are free to choose it to enhance their claims to be skilled in any particular outcome.[4]

Although it may seem to be common sense, the claim that assessment for employability is intimately related to programme planning, especially to the coherence of a programme's core or spine, is important. The 'capability envelope', described in Chapter 7, describes a complementary approach that could be applied to high-choice modular programmes.

A note on assessment centres

In concentrating on what higher education can do to assess employability, this chapter has been following the line that it is hard to afford tolerably reliable assessments of complex achievements. However, employers do need to make what they take to be reliable judgements of employability when they hire new graduates. In England we continue to hear stories of the invalid and discriminatory practice of rejecting applicants whose A-level scores are not high enough. It is also common to use some standardized tests, although it is open to argument whether these tests are fit for the purposes to which they are put. Survivors are often invited to a residential event at an assessment centre where they can expect to be appraised by several trained observers whilst they do group and individual tasks which are mainly intended to be fairly authentic representations of workplace activities.

The aim is to get high validity through authentic tasks, and high reliability through extended performances on multiple tasks observed by trained assessors. Although they seem to satisfy the employers who pay a great deal for them, researchers suggest there are modest correlations between career success and assessment centre results. Heywood (2000) reports that 42 per cent of those predicted to reach middle management after being appraised at an assessment centre had done so 25 years later. Sternberg (1997) is more sceptical of the relationship.

We wanted to make three points in this aside on assessment centres.

- First, employers' selection practices may be neither wise nor effective.
- Secondly, it is expensive to assess complex achievements with validity and reliability.

- Thirdly, assessment centre results may not be good predictors of achievement in the workplace.

This mismatch can be seen as a special case of the performance–competence gap mentioned in Chapter 2.

Differentiated, programme-level assessment

We have presented the assessment of employability as:

- an example of the assessment of complex learning;
- a problem that cannot be solved by applying brute force to summative assessment practices so that they become fit for the purpose of assessing employability;
- a demonstration of the usefulness of differentiated approaches to assessment;
- a planning problem and a programme problem, rather than a module problem to be tackled by ad hoc actions.

In the Chapters 7 and 8 we consider some ways of enhancing the quality of summative assessment, where summative assessment is called for. In Chapter 9 we do the same for formative assessment. The answer we are therefore offering to the question, 'How do we assess employability?' is, 'By taking a systemic, differentiated and programmatic approach: nothing else will do.'

Notes

1. A Danish colleague of the authors was unhappy that the English concept of 'skills' was being taken up in her university. She said that they were having trouble with the assessment of these skills because the language implied that skills were real, measurable things that one had or did not have. A change of terminology – substituting 'practices' for 'skills' – suggested that measurement would seldom be possible and helped educational developers to get out of the trap of trying to measure skills.
2. It will be recalled that we take an interest in enhancing student employability to be consistent with an interest in learning that is compatible with academic values and which may also contribute to postgraduate life as a citizen and person generally.
3. See Chapter 1.
4. It also helps them to avoid working on a particular programme outcome. A good support programme for personal development planning will help students to make informed decisions about 'dropping' programme learning intentions.

7

Authenticity in Assessment

Towards authenticity in assessment

The previous chapter advocated a systematically differentiated approach to assessment, particularly when the purpose is that assessment should support a programme aim to enhance student employability. The suggestion that some achievements resist affordable and reliable assessment opens questions about how achievements are to be assessed, with a view both to enhancing learning and to describing achievement.

Some responses, which mainly capitalize on recent reappraisals of formative assessment purposes, were previewed. In this chapter they are developed through an examination of programme portfolios as an assessment method, paying particular attention, for the moment, on the ways in which portfolios and other assessments of authentic achievement may be used for summative purposes. Formative uses will be considered in later chapters (especially Chapter 11), where there will be a greater concern for the ways in which students can make claims to achievement. The process of making and revising portfolios is seen as a useful spur to systematic reflection and, to an emergent feature of higher education in the UK, personal development planning (PDP).

Course portfolios have become increasingly common in the past 15 years (Wright and Knight 2000; Cambridge 2001) but our interest in the development of complex achievements leads us to concentrate upon programme portfolios. When used for summative purposes, issues of reliability, validity, usefulness and affordability present themselves particularly sharply.

'Authentic' assessment

'Authentic' assessment has been a preoccupation in the UK schools sector for a considerable time, as the desire to identify 'what pupils really know and can do' pointed towards assessments that were more practical, realistic and challenging than 'traditional paper-and-pencil tests' (Torrance 1995: 1) – in other words, assessment tasks with greater ecological validity. We noted in Chapter 4 that 'assessments of authentic achievement', as Cuming and Maxwell (1999) say they should be known, are different from traditional tasks which, according to Hedlund and Sternberg (2000: 137), tend to be:

- formulated by others;
- well-defined;
- complete in the information they provide;
- characterized by having only one correct answer;
- characterized by having only one method of obtaining the correct answer;
- disembedded from ordinary experience;
- of little or no intrinsic interest.

'Authentic' assessment may often be distinguished by its greater emphasis on documenting achievement, in contrast with forms of assessment in which 'what the pupil can't do' has comparatively more significance.[1]

The 'authenticity' movement has had some influence on accountability oriented testing in US schools, where there has been a lot of interest in trying to augment standard multiple-choice and short-answer test items with writing tasks, on the grounds that writing enables the pupil to demonstrate and apply knowledge and show linguistic fluency (Resnick and Resnick 1992). This has been developed in some state-wide assessment systems (see, for example, Koretz *et al.* 1993; LeMahieu *et al.* 1995; Koretz 1998), although the costs of reliability are notable (Breland 1999); the tasks are still seen by some to be artificial; and there are reports of students learning model answers which they use in the tests. In North American universities there has also been interest in assessing authentic achievements or achievements in natural settings, particularly in the wake of Barr and Tagg's (1995) call for higher education to give priority to student learning rather than to teaching. Course portfolios have been a common response in professional courses and in the mainstream of the arts and humanities (Hult 2001; Jenkins 2001).

Whilst authentic assessment is an attractive concept, there are problems. Cuming and Maxwell (1999) elaborate the criticism that many 'authentic' tasks are nothing of the sort, being artificial tasks of the type described by Hedlund and Sternberg that have been gilded to look more authentic. In reality, they are no more authentic than the questions that used to be set in arithmetic classes which asked students to calculate how long it would take ten people to dig a hole, empty a bath with buckets or run a relay race. Furthermore, some performances displayed in naturalistic settings may be narrow, dis-integrated actions produced in response to checklists of tightly defined learning outcomes, such as the 'competences' developed under the umbrella of the UK's National Vocational Qualifications (Jessup 1991). There are also concerns that assessments claimed to be authentic may not properly probe depth of understanding, which may be assumed to be sufficient if students merely demonstrate that they can succeed at the specified task. Finally, the reliability problems alluded to in Chapters 2 and 4 are compounded by 'in the wild' assessments of achievements that are complex and which elude precise specification. Complete coverage has considerable cost implications if authentic assessments are to be used for summative purposes.

If the learning outcomes are stated rather loosely, as aims and statements of valuable learning engagements (in Eisner's (1985) terms, as 'expressive objectives'), thereby allowing the student much greater latitude in responding to the expectations, reliability problems will multiply (Chapter 4, above) and the burden on assessors will probably be higher than is typical for more traditional assessments. Since the resources available per curriculum unit are bounded, there are significant implications for the design of courses and programmes that emphasize the assessment of authentic achievement – assessment costs are likely to be higher and savings will have to be made elsewhere, which may lead to radical changes in pedagogy, as in the case of the introduction of problem-based learning programmes which are designed to maximize authenticity.

Performances offered as authentic assessments have a strong individual component which may well not fit normative expectations of an assessment system. The standardized (using the term in a non-statistical sense) assessment task asks the student to locate their learning with reference to an externally determined expectation, whereas the authentic assessment opens up the possibility that (but does not require that) the student may demonstrate the desired learning in a way that is unspecified by the assessor. This is compounded where assessors come with an 'excellence minus' cast of mind, which leads them to look for flaws to penalize, rather than with the 'threshold plus' approach to acknowledging achievement.

Authenticity in higher education

In higher education there have been similar tensions, in that governmental concerns for standards and accountability can hamper assessment approaches that are more practical, realistic and (perhaps) challenging than most written tests have been. However, in this sector, academic freedom allows academic staff more scope for divergence and students generally have a greater opportunity than their counterparts in schools or further education to interpret assignment tasks in ways that suit their predilections for learning. In other words, they have greater scope for performing 'authentically'. Later in this chapter, when the use of portfolios in assessment is discussed, it needs to be borne in mind that a portfolio can encompass a range of performances (only some of which may be 'authentic' even under this relaxed interpretation).

Work-based learning, in 'sandwich' (or cooperative education) programmes, has plenty of potential for the student to demonstrate 'authentic' performance, even though its summative assessment is not without problems. The placement experience is widely held to benefit the student (anecdotal evidence attests to greater self-confidence and awareness of the challenges faced in the world of work, the acquisition of tacit knowledge, and so on), but the full accreditation of the learning from the placement period(s) has proved problematic in the UK where modular structures based typically on a three-year (full-time) model of enrolment have found it difficult to accommodate the additional placement period(s). A few institutions have offered students, as an adjunct to sandwich degree awards, the opportunity to gain a Licentiateship of the City and Guilds of London Institute in respect of work-based achievements that would otherwise not formally attract credit (Jackson *et al.* 1998), although this is accompanied by the disincentive of additional cost.

Students are required to write a report on the sandwich placement in UK programmes. This is intended to be an authentic record of the experience. Ideally, it should include reflection on what has been gained thereby, but the low weighting often given to the report in the final assessment militates against the extraction of the maximum educational value from the experience.

Many UK institutions formally accredit work-based learning as an integral part of their (non-sandwich) curricula – offering a module's worth of credit, for example[2] – and extend the opportunity to work-*related* learning (such as for the mentoring of more junior students, or engagement in student representative activity). Awards are now available outside degree structures, of which two examples are the York Award[3] and the Work Experience Award developed as part of the JEWELS project.[4] Outside higher education institutions, the CRAC Insight Plus programme assists students to represent to best effect the enhanced employability that should derive from paid, often part-time, employment.

Some students, particularly those whose subject disciplines are less obviously employment-oriented, might welcome a joint honours programme involving a particular subject discipline and what might be termed 'employment-related studies'.[5] The assessment of the latter component might most appropriately be through the compilation of a portfolio in which students reflect on what they have learned from their academic and work experiences, and on how the developed academic and practical understandings inform each other.

Validity and reliability in authentic assessment

This section concentrates upon two questions. How can the validity of the assessment be judged? (We introduced the concept of validity in Chapter 2 and develop it further in Chapter 11.) And can the assessment be reliable? In discussing these, questions of cost and usability are implicitly drawn into consideration.

The assumption is made that portfolio assessment entails the examination of a claim made by the candidate which is backed up by relevant evidence. In other forms of authentic assessment – the assessment of work-based practice, for example – teachers observe and weigh other evidence against course or programme criteria.

If the assessment relates to work carried out in an organization (for example, a work placement, period of voluntary service, or internship), then it is usual for the judgement of the workplace supervisor to be brought into play. The supervisor may, for example, comment on the person's effectiveness as a colleague, thereby offering a cross-validation of what the candidate has claimed. This would provide some external validation which would augment an assessment based on internal consistency.

However, the assessment of workplace performance may bring a clash between the academic's and the employer's frames of reference, since different parties will bring different concatenations of criteria to bear, as Brennan and Little (1996: 120) note. Academic staff are likely to be mindful of the need to make judgements that are generalizable to other contexts, whereas employers are better placed to comment on local achievements. There is also a risk, as Winter and Maisch (1996) note, of academics making a 'category mistake' of judging practice with reference to criteria derived from theoretical study; the reverse, of employers judging theory with reference to practically-grounded criteria, seems relatively unlikely. Risks such as these can be mitigated when the opportunity is taken by both parties to share their expectations and agree the assessment criteria – something that can occur comparatively easily where there is a close-knit relationship between the educational programme and an employer, but would be difficult to implement where students' work experience was spread across a number of employers.

Winter and Maisch (1996: 100ff) discuss the need for assessors to be convinced that what the student puts forward is genuine, and provide a list of types of evidence considered appropriate for portfolios compiled for the ASSET (Accreditation for Social Services Experience and Training) programme (Box 7.1). This programme, with its emphasis on professional practice, required that the practice be documented since evidence could be needed in the case of a subsequent complaint or legal proceedings.[6] Winter and Maisch themselves provide, appropriately, examples of students documenting their practice – and how circumstances can make this less than a straightforward process.

In dealing with the question of validity, that of reliability, which has been explored in general terms in Chapters 2 and 4, has been opened up. The more complex the claim proffered for assessment, the more open is the actual assessment

---

Box 7.1 Types of evidence appropriate for portfolios compiled under the ASSET programme

- Report from an observer of the learner's practice.
- Practice-generated documents (e.g. practice notes; case history; letters and memos), plus an explanation of their relevance.
- Audio-recording of practice supported by transcribed excerpts and an explanation of their relevance and/or a commentary by the learner on their actual practice.
- Audio-recording of discussion(s) with other professionals with a commentary on relevance and/or matters of significance.
- Video-recording of practice plus an explanation of its relevance and/or a commentary by the learner on their actual practice.
- Analytical and evaluative (i.e. reflective) commentary on practice, training or training materials.
- Analysis of issues relevant to the planning of practice.
- Records of clients' responses plus learner's commentary.
- An authenticating statement from colleagues or managers.

Source: based on Winter and Maisch 1996: 89

to assessor variability. Moreover, the more complex an achievement then, by definition, the less it can be specified in the unambiguous terms that make for reliable
assessments. When it comes to portfolios, a further reliability problem is that students usually are able to choose the evidence they cite to back their claims and often
choose what weight to give to different claims. This introduces considerable variation in the product to be assessed, which then compromises attempts to achieve
greater reliability. The outcomes of assessments of portfolios discussed in Chapter
8 show how difficult it can be to produce reliable judgements of candidates' claims,
even when the expectations are elaborated in some detail. When the purposes
are summative, programme portfolios and, to a lesser extent, their course-level
counterparts give rise to a slew of difficulties as regards reliability. By extension, the
same applies to the assessment of authentic achievements and performances in
general.

The key to maximizing reliability resides in having:

- clear statements of what is intended,
- associated assessment criteria and, in particular,
- information on how the criteria are to be applied in practice (and, where
  possible, exemplars of the application of the criteria).

Wolf (1995b) has shown convincingly how important the last of the three points
is. It is not enough to provide statements of expectations – these need to be supported by exemplars and discussion of them if the fullest understanding is to be
attained. Note that the sharing of understanding encompasses both the assessors
and the assessed, although, when the issue of reliability is being considered, it is
primarily the assessors' context to which the point applies.

In assessing for an educational qualification, standards are normative expectations that are sometimes codified in formal terms, and are sometimes more
implicit.[7] The QAA subject benchmarks for higher education (even though not
claimed to be standards as such) fall somewhere between the two, being reference-
points to be acknowledged by curriculum designers in setting out the standards that
pertain to their first degrees. When these statements are examined, it quickly
becomes apparent that there is considerable scope for interpretation, and that the
actual standards reside within the relevant disciplinary community (including,
where appropriate, professional and statutory bodies). Although there is continuing
unease regarding its effectiveness (DfES 2003), the UK external examiner system is
intended to exercise a normative role relating to students' performances at perhaps
two points: in the setting of tasks (especially examination papers) and in the judgement of students' actual performances. Neither task is easy, as most external examiners would acknowledge. However, when the assessment relates to a performance
that no other student is attempting (as in a research thesis), the internal and external
assessors can only call upon their understandings of similar kinds of assessments
(gained in a variety of ways) in coming to judgement. There is no crutch available
to the assessor to enable the rank-ordering of performances, as is the case with
examinations and other assignments given to a group of students. Reliability is
therefore more problematic where highly individual achievements are being
assessed. As a consequence, it is more difficult to state that a performance is of a

particular standard, although a commentary on the performance may indicate where its strengths and weaknesses lie.

When assessment is concerned with authentic achievements, there is a sense in which variations in setting, task and student response mean that all performances and claims are individual, making it expensive to achieve the minimum tolerable levels of reliability when the assessment purpose is summative.

Portfolios

A major attraction of portfolios as vehicles for assessment is their potential to represent claims to achievement on authentic tasks in authentic settings (Klenowski 2002). They are becoming increasingly important, particularly in professional development: for example, Seldin (1997) indicates their significance in the discipline of education, Pietroni and Millard (1997) do the same for general practice in medicine, and Campbell and Russo (2001) provides case studies of electronic portfolio assessment in nursing, the humanities, English and management. Portfolios, which make claims to achievement based on the student's own experiences (often, but not exclusively, in employment-related settings), are seen to have advantages over exercises and examinations that are related less closely to the demands and realities of professional life: portfolios have an ecological validity. They are also authentic in that the student is able to shape them in a way that is not possible in response to more traditional assessment methods.

A portfolio typically includes evidence drawn from practice, although writers hold differing views regarding what should be included in a portfolio (Stecher 1998; Simon and Forgette-Giroux 2000). It is possible to include in a portfolio items of evidence that spread across a spectrum of contexts, some items being 'authentic' on the most stringent definition, whereas other items might – on their own – be deemed not to meet the criteria of authenticity.

A portfolio in higher education usually contains a section of reflective commentary, in which the course participant shows how they have interrogated their experience and related their practice and understandings to cognate evidence from the literature and elsewhere. It is typically expected that the portfolio will be scholarly and draw upon relevant theoretical constructs. The assumption here is that theory is an important component of bridges being built between practice in different contexts (Taylor *et al.* 1999).

The portfolio is used as the basis of a *claim*[8] that the participant has fulfilled the aims of the programme on which they have enrolled. Participants will fulfil the programme aims in differing ways, just as it can be argued that graduate status can be justified in a number of ways, depending on the emphases that have been given to the various aspects of 'graduateness' (the 38 attributes listed in the HEQC's (1997) Graduate Attributes Profile implicitly suggest that students can satisfy the broad criterion of graduateness in a multiplicity of ways).

The use of portfolios is consistent with constructivist perspectives on learning in which the influence of theorists such as Piaget, Dewey, Vygotsky and Bruner can often be discerned. Portfolios involve students in making (ordered) sense of their learning experiences, many of which will have had a social dimension, and in reflecting upon those experiences. Students construct their own interpretations of their experiences and of how what they have learned can help them to cope with the challenges that the world throws in their direction. Hence employability may well be assisted if students are encouraged to stand back from their experiences and to reflect upon them. However, some students – and their assessors – do not find reflection easy: a project team from Sheffield Hallam University discovered that

> most of the reports accompanying students' portfolios . . . were more like engineering project reports on learning. . . . It appears that self review and evaluation of knowledge, skills and competence does not come naturally to engineering undergraduates or their assessors.
>
> (Sheffield Hallam University (1996: 10) quoted in
> Brennan and Little (1996: 126)

Many learners, especially those engaged in professional updating, have developed a considerable capacity for managing their own learning. They have identified what they want to achieve, and go for it. Lester (1999: 105) suggests that to assess such self-managing learners is a contradiction in terms. Lester's argument is that self-critical evaluation and the value of the learning process are undermined if an assessor decides for the learner how good their performance is. Lester seems to be referring to summative assessment and 'final language' (Boud 1995) here, and not to assessment as part of a (formative) dialogue. Regarding summative assessment, Lester's argument has some force, though he is sufficient of a realist to acknowledge that, for a variety of reasons, some form of summative certification is usually a necessity. Certification is not straightforward, though. Some of the issues are raised here and there is a fuller treatment in Chapter 8.

Although the ecological validity of portfolios is attractive, practical considerations will affect their uptake. At the first level, and assuming that they appear on the curriculum specification, there is the potential for students to 'tell a good story' via the portfolio, whose reality may be less compelling. There needs to be some form of validation of the portfolio in the assessment process, which would seem to require conversation between the compiler and the assessor. The issue of the availability of time immediately rears its head.

Where the programme is homogeneous and involves relatively small groups of students (as is the case with many professional updating courses), the portfolio may be the main – perhaps the only – medium for assessment. In such circumstances, the time required for the assessment process can quite easily be built into the programme, *as long as other summative assessment demands are few.*

However, the span of studies comprising, say, a first degree programme poses a more difficult problem, especially where a student is following a multidisciplinary programme, such as a joint or combined degree. Whilst the use of the portfolio in assessment is not vitiated in these contexts, it would require a very different conception of the way that assessment operates across a programme from the approaches that are typically used. The 'capability envelope' (Stephenson and Yorke 1998; Stephenson 2001) is one approach relating to the whole curriculum (or, perhaps more likely, part of a curriculum) that could be used in some disciplinary areas (in others, the requirements of professional and statutory bodies could make its use problematic).

The 'capability envelope'

The 'capability envelope', sketched in Figure 7.1, was proposed as one curricular structure through which engagement in matters such as portfolio construction could take place throughout the duration of a programme: the general approach is adaptable to part-programmes and modular programmes (Yorke and Knight 2003). The capability envelope has four components:

1. An exploration stage, in which the student is supported in planning, and gaining approval for, their programme of study.
2. A series of learning engagements appropriate to the approved programme.
3. A progress review stage running alongside (2), whose purposes include tutorial support of reflective/metacognitive activity, the adjustment of plans in the light of experience, the creation of 'learning logs' or other records of attainment.
4. A demonstration stage, in which the student is expected to integrate what has been learned via the prior stages, and to demonstrate what they can do as a result.

It should be noted that the exploration phase aligns well with the development, in UK higher education, of personal development planning, and that the 'progress review' stage does likewise with expectations that students will prepare progress files. In the latter, there is considerable potential for formative assessment. The

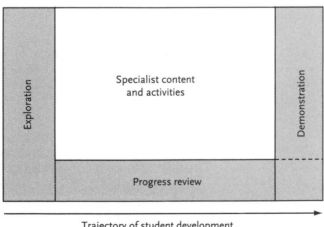

Trajectory of student development

Student control of overall strategy of the programme

Figure 7.1   The capability envelope (after Stephenson and Yorke 1998; published with the kind permission of John Stephenson and Kogan Page Ltd)

demonstration phase can subsume a variety of kinds of performance, such as the outcomes of computer-marked tests, project reports or dissertations, and evidence from work placements (coupled with reflective comment).

Practical realism suggests the inclusion, at intervals during the programme, of formal assessment points (which might be points at which the emphasis is formative, but where 'ticketing' of progress is also undertaken), or else there will be a significant risk that students will not take the requirement seriously.

Further, relatively few staff will have engaged with students in the development of portfolios and in judging whether portfolios have reached an acceptable standard, and so there would probably be a considerable need for staff development to help them develop these capacities. It would probably be wise to try out the 'capability envelope' approach on a relatively small scale – for example, during a year-long module – before any large-scale adoption is considered.

Formative advice on portfolios produced for summative purposes

One approach to raising intersubjectivity between the main parties to the course has been the commenting, by assessors, on first drafts of sections of the portfolio. This has disadvantages and advantages. A disadvantage, noted in respect of formative assessment generally, is that the feedback could be used by the student to construct a portfolio that would satisfy official assessment expectations, without the student having progressed in their learning (except in respect of fulfilling the course requirements). The advantage is that the student, instead, might make the desired leap in learning to produce a soundly grounded portfolio. On the evidence of the portfolio alone, the assessor cannot be entirely sure.

There is a risk that formative feedback could exacerbate the potential for the compiler of the portfolio to exhibit skills in presenting a text, rather than developing an improved response to the criteria set for the programme. Regarding this presentational issue, Winter and Maisch comment, in relation to portfolios compiled to fulfil the requirements of the ASSET programme:

> . . . there is a danger that the grades awarded may reflect candidates' ability to manage the selection and presentation of evidence and to articulate its relationship with the competence statements and the Core Assessment Criteria, rather than variations in their practice (and their understanding of practice).
>
> (Winter and Maisch 1996: 99)

Academics who have been faced with responding to the expectations of external quality scrutiny in its various forms will appreciate how attention to 'the text' can lead to the veiling of actual performance.

In offering feedback on draft sections of a portfolio, a balance has to be struck regarding risk. Where the broad thrust of the course is developmental, with an implicit expectation of the person's success (for example, to help participants to gain accreditation by the Institute of Learning and Teaching in Higher Education as a teacher in higher education), the formative aspects of feedback are important. If the student subsequently demonstrates through the portfolio that appropriate learning has ensued, then the risk that this is a misrepresentation may be low. Where the stakes are higher, with the pass/fail decision having a major impact on the person's future, then the risk is heightened. The stakes are quite high where portfolios are used to assess the attainment of externally set standards across an educational system (as has been the case with a few school systems in the USA), but there seems not to be evidence available as to the extent of the 'backwash' effect of the results on teaching and assessment practices.

Beyond summative assessment

Portfolios have a practical value for their compilers, aside from any considerations of assessment. If accompanied by reflection, they constitute a personal repository of understanding about experience that can help compilers to present themselves to employers and others. Few, if any, receivers of applications would want to be faced with extensive documentation, but they do appreciate well-constructed arguments as to why a person should be considered. Indeed, with the strong competition for jobs in the graduate-level job market, the presentation of self becomes an important ability. The portfolio, as a consequence, has a value beyond that derived from an institution's summative assessment requirements.

Notes

1. There is a need to note the other meaning of authenticity – that the performance is genuinely that of the student, and represents an appropriate response to the expectations laid upon them. The latter point reflects the risk of a good text-production dominating other, perhaps more valued, aspects of the performance.
2. Some examples are given in Watton and Collings (2002: 33).
3. This is a certificated programme of transferable skills training and experiential learning, offered by the University of York in partnership with a number of public, private and voluntary sector organizations. See www2.york.ac.uk/admin/ya/ for details.
4. JEWELS is the acronym for Joint Systems to Enhance Work Experience Levels of Service and Satisfaction, a project run jointly by the Universities of Exeter and Plymouth. See Watton *et al.* (2002); www.jewels.org.uk/finalreport.htm and associated papers.
5. A lifelong learning perspective would encourage such students to extend their studies of subject X beyond the boundary of the first degree (Yorke 2003).
6. Winter and Maisch (1996: 101) note that tutors found some difficulty in convincing students of the value of collecting evidence of practice, although when students acknowledged the importance of collecting this evidence they became empowered through realizing the value of their day-to-day professional activity.
7. Recall, also, the discussion in Chapter 2 of the limits to which any criteria or other standards can be fully explicit in the sense of being unambiguously specified.
8. Chapter 11 has more to say about claims-making, Chapter 8 about reliability and portfolio assessment.

8

Optimizing the Reliability of Assessment

The best reliability that can be achieved

The more complex the learning to be judged, the harder it is to reconcile validity (as with the need for assessments of authentic performances), affordability (especially time and opportunity costs), and reliability (or, as it is sometimes called, objectivity), whilst engaging students and teachers in processes of worth to themselves and other stakeholders. These issues are most pressing in high-stakes assessments with summative purposes, although they are also raised in low-stakes judgements when the purposes are formative. The preceding chapter explored validity issues through authentic assessment; this chapter concentrates on what might be done about the reliability problems raised in Chapters 2, 4 and 6.

'Optimizing' conveys the idea of striving for the best result in the circumstances, bearing in mind that circumstances include the levels of available expertise, time and money. These qualifications of 'best' imply that perfect reliability is not possible.

Improving reliability

We distinguish between tasks where low-inference scoring procedures apply (where there is little or no dispute about the best answers) and those more typical of higher education which call for high levels of inference in assessment. A computer can score low-inference responses to tasks because the rules are unambiguous ('In question 4, answer iii is right. All others are wrong'). Reliability levels should be very high and, once the costs of the hardware and software have been written off, cheap. However, high reliability does not sit well with complex learning intentions that tend to elude valid appraisal by questions that are expected to produce low-inference answers. Complex tasks, of which the construction of a portfolio is one example, are generally more appropriate to higher education but produce responses requiring high levels of inference on the part of the assessor. Where reliability is a concern, a lot of effort goes into trying to develop tasks that restrain the scope for legitimate divergent responses; developing assessment criteria to limit unusual variations in judgement; training markers; and checking that no human errors creep in at the data entry and processing stages.

Reliable markers

Panels of mathematics examiners were asked to rate features of school mathematics examinations (Jones 2002). They did not agree, which is to say their assessments had low reliability. Figure 8.1 shows the range of responses when asked to judge how clear the distribution of marks available in each question was. It is hard to see this as a high-inference task, yet interobserver reliabilities are low. Figure 8.2 shows the range of responses when asked to judge whether the non-mathematical

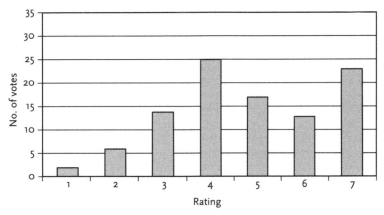

Figure 8.1 Mathematics examiners' ratings of the clarity of the distribution of marks in questions in a mathematics examination

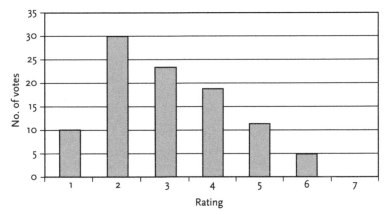

Figure 8.2 Mathematics examiners' ratings of the demands made by the non-mathematical language in a mathematics examination

language used in the question papers made high or low demands on the candidates' language skills.

Higher education programmes, which have ambitious learning intentions, use tasks that make higher inferential demands on assessors than these two did. That augurs badly for reliability.

Commenting on attempts to enhance marker reliability in public examinations, Izard said:

> Comparability between examiners is difficult to achieve without taking special precautions. Use of expert examiners can help in the assessment of open-ended items from traditional examinations. All examiners will not reach perfect unanimity, but equity arrangements do imply that there should be some reasonable measure of agreement between examiners. . . . How can we check that examiners agree to a reasonable extent? Devising marking schemes for examiners to use is *not* a sufficient requirement to ensure that scoring will be consistent. . . . If the examiners do not use the schedule correctly or at all, then the assessments will almost certainly be flawed. Analysis needs to show the extent to which the assessments make sense and indicate where there is room for examiners to work on attaining shared meanings for the assessment labels they use.
>
> (Izard 2002: 263, emphasis in original)

It is worth emphasizing that Izard refers to teams of examiners who grade a single paper taken by thousands of students. At this scale it is possible to see ways of enhancing reliability that are neither feasible nor cost-effective on a smaller scale. This analysis of the flaws in assessment systems that are technically superior to much higher education practice has interesting implications for the certificates and awards made by universities and colleges around the world.

We now review some standard ways of getting more reliable judgements of performance on complex tasks and then explain why they have limited power in many higher education settings.

Setting clear standards

Students and markers need to know what is going to be valued. That knowledge helps students to do what markers want and helps markers to judge it fairly and consistently. There is a strong move to set up rating scales, which are also known as a set of criteria, grade indicators or primary traits. Describing how this is done for the assessment of projects, Izard says that it

> involves a number of steps. Experts are invited to describe what they look for when assessing student work. The resulting list of descriptors is circulated amongst the group of experts for discussion and modification. An edited version of the list is used to assess some real projects. (These projects should include both high quality and low quality projects.) Each expert is required to assess more than one project. . . . Item Response Modelling is used to look at the ways in which students/projects vary, examiners/judges vary and descriptors vary. [This] allows checks on which descriptors work or do not work,

which overlap or are redundant, and which are controversial. . . . The list of descriptors is discussed in the light of the analysis; examiners are advised of their performance relative to their professional colleagues. . . . The list of descriptors is revised and submitted to further trials.

(Izard 2002: 271)

Professional examining bodies take very seriously the development of robust descriptors because the quality of the descriptions of what is to be rewarded is fundamental to the quest for reliability. When it comes to thinking about descriptors for use in undergraduate programmes, matters are compounded by the problem of specificity.

What we see is a tendency to proliferate achievement statements or grade indicators, which was remarked upon in Chapter 2. We have *programme learning outcomes*, which should tint all *module learning outcomes*, although many modules will add their own specific outcomes to the set. Then there are *task learning outcomes*, which should be a selection from the module learning outcomes and which are rephrased to illuminate each particular task. To this programme–module–task outcomes series we should add two forms of differentiation: first, task outcomes are usually elaborated as *grading outcomes* and should be written to identify the sorts of performances that will attract the various bands of marks available ('a mark of 80 per cent is achieved by . . .'); secondly, *level outcomes* need to be written to show how an 80 per cent mark awarded at level 1 differs from 80 per cent at levels 2, 3 and 4.[1] The pursuit of this degree of clarity demands considerable ingenuity in writing indicators that draw fine distinctions. Some wonder whether this is either sensible or possible, noting that many of these indicators depend on heavy use of comparators (better, weaker, stronger) and 'empty' terms (excellent, poor, good). In this view, clarity becomes a semantic operation which does no one any good because complex achievements cannot be described in terms of content-free hierarchies.

There is another difficulty with the quest for precision, namely that the chance of disagreement between markers grows as the number of decision points increases. Let us revisit the case, summarized in Figures 8.1 and 8.2, of the mathematics examiners who were asked to judge how clearly each individual mark in the paper was specified to the candidate. On a seven-point scale there are six ways for any other observer to disagree with any particular judgement and, as these figures showed, people tend to exploit those degrees of freedom. Suppose, though, that the task was simply to rate the clarity as high or low – and for many purposes a yes/no, competent/not competent judgement suffices. Markers have just two decision points and one way of disagreeing with each other. We would expect a much higher level of intermarker agreement as a result. And more judgement points mean more disagreements and higher assessment costs. Either each pair of markers has to resolve differences, which takes time, or third – even fourth – markers are brought in to adjudicate. No wonder that universities that have the data – the Open University, for instance – find that assessment costs are rising.

Nevertheless, we are faced with a situation in which we have to write and use detailed indicators of achievement. Detailed advice on primary trait analysis is given by Walvoord and Anderson (1998), who write for a North American audience. Gosling and Moon (2001) advise UK teachers how to write the state-ments of learning outcomes from which assessment criteria and indicators can be derived. Anderson and Krathwohl (2001) provide a sophisticated approach in their revision of Bloom's *Taxonomy*, although English audiences may find problems aris-ing from its distance from the subject benchmarks that have been enjoined upon them. Recall, too, the view in Chapter 2 that the use of criteria will lessen reliability problems but cannot erase them.

Marker training

Laws, rules, criteria and similar prescriptions have to be interpreted. Left to their own devices, people will interpret them differently. They also have to be applied to different contexts. People again differ on how to do so – how realistic it is to expect people to agree whether a piece of work is original, fresh or evidence of divergent thinking? This is why marker training is necessary – partly to get agreement on what is generally likely to count as evidence of performance judged against the indicators, and partly to agree on the 'work-arounds' or local customs for dealing with tricky practice. (An example would be the convention that if a marker was convinced that an answer which appeared to be essentially narrative contained an *implicit argument*, then a mark in the range 59–61 would be appropriate.)

Training can reduce the range of disagreement but it does not (and cannot) eliminate it. This will shortly be illustrated in an account of one programme's use of portfolio assessment for high-stakes purposes. Yet the idea that training will ease problems is attractive because it clearly specifies *something to be done*, which is what policy-makers need. This is not the place to review the rather disappointing evidence about the impact of workshops and training sessions generally on professional practices, nor to go beyond remarking that, because higher education training is voluntary, it misses the majority of teachers who need it. Our point is that it is one thing to put faith in training and quite another to see it happen in ways that make a sustained difference, a theme developed by Knight and Trowler (2001).

Marker monitoring

It is not easy to interpret and apply indicators. We know that markers' performance deteriorates over time, is affected by irrelevant cues, such as a candidate putting a little circle where the dot should be in the letter *i*, and by the quality of the answers marked immediately before the one being marked now. Markers have preferences which incline them to give credit for some ideas and to be cool towards others. They may apply criteria inconsistently both within a paper and between papers.

The system of second marking is intended to redress these problems, but there must be doubts about it. Where marker 2 knows marker 1's scores, there is a tendency to mark in the same area, possibly to drop the mark a little to demonstrate one's own intellectual rigour. Where no scores are known to marker 2, marking can take longer especially when the second marker is less expert in the field. It will then take longer to reconcile differences between the two markers because there will be more differences. Given the costs of this approach to monitoring, many teams sample the scripts to see whether, in general, the first marker's grades are confirmed by the second. Concern arises if this monitoring identifies problems and does not then lead to a complete re-marking of the scripts. Public examination boards have available to them statistical techniques to help them detect where there might be problems, but statistically based methods are seldom appropriate for higher education programmes because the number of students taking modules is usually too small for the analyses to produce useful results.

In public examinations there are plenty of other markers with whose scores any individual marker's scores can be compared and, if marking standards do not come into line, the delinquent is dismissed. In higher education we are often talking about pairs of markers, one of whom is expert in the field. When there are disagreements, it is hard to say who is right and, partly as a result, hard to change the behaviour of the one who is out of line. Nor does the system of external examiners used in UK higher education resolve matters. Partly this is because the idea that an outsider can carry and apply 'pure' standards is naïve and partly it is because externals are increasingly asked to audit the assessment system and told not to change marks. There is no system of external examiners in the USA, and accreditation agencies – which could have some standardizing impact – review programmes every ten years and tend to concentrate on inputs, rather than on evidence of learning.

Task design

No one task can provide a reliable measure of achievement. We need to have a bigger sample of evidence before concluding that there is a good chance that someone will show similar levels of achievement in the future. It is also important that the tasks from which we make inferences and generalize really address the learning we want assess. This is not easy to ensure because task design is not rule-governed and there is no formula that guarantees that all the tasks we design as valid probes of achievement will be equally valid and at the same level of difficulty. Two tasks that seem logically to be the same can turn out to be psychologically different, evoking quite different levels of performance. This validity problem creates a reliability problem if we suspect that variations in scores are due to differences in the assessment instrument – the tasks – and not to differences in levels of achievement.

Four steps used by test developers to deal with this are:

1. Writing large numbers of tasks which are intended to access key curriculum outcomes or other target achievements.
2. Reviewing the bank of tasks and checking, by means of expert judgement, that they appear fit for the purpose.
3. Piloting surviving tasks with large numbers of people who are similar to those who will be involved in the finalized version of the assessment.
4. Using statistical routines on the pilot data to identify the tasks that come closest to the specifications.

Few teams in higher education could do anything as sophisticated as this, but the principles – write many tasks, review, pilot, analyse and identify the best – are worth using. With the possible exception of external examiners and others who work cross-institutionally on learning, teaching and assessment issues, teachers in higher education are poorly placed to appreciate that the results they see are products of *particular* assessment tasks. Care is needed before assuming that these performances are indicators of general competence (see Table 2.1 in Chapter 2) and it is prudent to treat performances on any one task as nothing more than provisional and local indicators of achievement.

That said, thoughtful task design, which is orchestrated at a programme level, can allow greater confidence that a sequence of tasks is indicative of target attainments rather than if the tasks were devised idiosyncratically (Knight 2002a).

Representations of achievement

We indicated in Chapter 2 that there are problems with handling the grades and marks produced by high-stakes, typically summative, assessments. Although it is not strictly a reliability problem, because any decent data-processing system gives accurate arrays of marks, weights them, calculates means, and reliably produces final scores according to the prescribed algorithm, it is treated as one because the same array of marks can lead to different qualities of award when different translation practices are applied. The problem is really whether the formulae involved produce useful representations of achievement or whether the signs that emerge (*summa cum laude*, 2:2, β^{++}, 3.8) are just artefacts of processing rules that warp the intentions expressed in the programme specification. We comment here on the processing of marks in order to make decisions about awards, but the same points apply to the ways in which module grades or scores are calculated: different calculation principles can lead to the same set of marks being translated into different signs of achievement.

Classification algorithms

Universities and colleges differ substantially in their procedures for combining marks from different sources to get aggregate scores for conversion into classes and grades. For example, there are three common measures of the central tendency in an array of numbers: the mean ('average'), mode (most common) and median (mid point). Some English universities rely on the mean in their rules for getting degree classes from strings of numbers; others use the median. Some use a combination of the three measures. A number of studies conducted by the Student Assessment and Classification Working Group (Woolf and Turner 1997; Yorke *et al.* 2002a, b) and a survey conducted by the Northern Universities Consortium for Credit Accumulation and Transfer (Armstrong *et al.* 1998) have pointed to the variation of these algorithms between institutions and the potential effect that this has on students' awards. It appears that institutional algorithms have evolved 'naturally' over time, with little consideration given to the underlying assumptions and the technicalities. The problems with combining grades awarded for a variety of kinds of performance at (in many institutions) two qualifying levels (levels 2 and 3) seem insurmountable. In addition, the degree classification is a poor filter for employers, for whom the employability of a graduate involves not only the academic intelligence which the assessment system tends to index (albeit not unproblematic-ally), but also the personal qualities and 'practical intelligence' (Wagner 1993) that contribute to a person's being effective in dealing with the kinds of challenge that employment tends to throw up.

Universities and colleges also have different rules on how many marks contribute to the final array; whether any poor marks can be routinely discarded; how differ-ent sorts of marks, such as coursework and examination marks, are weighted and combined; how work done in different years is treated; the treatment of work not done because of certified illness or for other 'good' reasons. Even if the raw marks were reliable, it would be hard to see how such a variety of rules and practices could be squared with the belief that a 2:1 degree from one university, with its degree classification methodology, is comparable in standard to a 2:1 from another university with a different methodology (Yorke *et al.* 2002b).

Finally, we note that the weighting at module level of coursework against examinations is significant, with there being fairly consistent evidence (Elton 1998; Bridges *et al.* 2002), that coursework marks tend to be rather higher than examination marks.

Norm-referencing

City University, Hong Kong, provides a guideline for the distribution of awards to its examination boards. Less than 10 per cent of awards should be at first class, less than 35 per cent at upper second class or above, and so on. Consequently, roughly the same proportion of top grades should be awarded if a class of keen, able students is taught well as in a class routinely going about a workaday course. This is norm-referencing, whose logic is that achievement is routinely distributed through the population in stable proportions and that grades should be awarded in those proportions. Suppose that students are assessed, algorithms applied to the array of marks and their overall scores are converted to grades by the formula that 10 per cent will get 'A', 30 per cent 'B', 30 per cent 'C', 20 per cent 'D' and 10 per cent 'E'. Table 8.1 shows the way this works out on two cohorts of ten students. It also shows the effect of criteria-referenced grading, where the rules are that a score of over 84 per cent = 'A', . . ., 35–39 per cent = 'E'. Notice that the marks needed to get a particular grade differ considerably between the two cohorts. Notice, too, that for cohort 1 there is only one difference in the grades produced by norm- and criteria-referenced methods but for cohort 2 there are seven.

Norm-referencing is sometimes useful. For example, Alfred Binet, who invented the intelligence test which led to modern IQ testing, was interested in measurement in order to identify those with severe intellectual limitations so that they could be given special, compensatory education. His test was to be used to identify 'outliers', the Parisian children with severe limitations who could benefit from special educa-tion. Numbers were there to warn, not to rank, people; to call for care, not to distribute life chances. Used like this, norm-referencing can be helpful, assuming that we know that the characteristics being reliably and validly measured are stable ones. However, the whole point of higher education is to improve learning, so the more successful higher education is, the *less* stable the distribution of achievement should be and the less appropriate it is to use norm-referencing.

Table 8.1   The effects of norm-referencing (NR) and criteria-referencing (CR) on two arrays of marks

Cohort 1 student	Mark	NR grade	CR grade	Cohort 2 student	Mark	NR grade	CR grade
Angie	56	C	C	Berry	54	C	D
Aretha	59	C	C	Betty	61	B	C
Beverley	44	D	D	Carla	75	A	B
Curtis	72	B	B	Carlos	69	B	C
Lamont	63	B	B	Dobie	22	E	F
Martha	87	A	A	Frank	52	D	D
Marvin	40	D	D	Nina	64	B	C
Otis	25	E	E	Rufus	36	D	E
Patti	55	C	C	Timmy	60	C	C
Tina	67	B	C	Wilson	58	C	C

When criteria have been carefully devised, are used to shape curriculum, learning and teaching, and are summarized on degree transcripts, then the criteria-referenced approach is much better for two reasons:

- It is informative. We have no way of knowing anything about the group with whom any student is compared in norm-referenced systems, so we know little about what their grade means. Criteria are far from perfect but, when well-devised, they are considerably more informative;
- Norm-referencing gives good grades to indifferent marks in years when achievements are depressed. Criteria-referencing should lead to more stable standards.

From the point of view of the consumer, the referencing procedures used to transform marks into awards are a source of unreliability. An employer, for example, would be hard-pressed to know whether marks have been transformed to awards by norm-referenced principles (and if so, what is the ratio of top to good to acceptable to poor awards?), or by criteria-referenced ones (and if so, what are the criteria describing top . . . poor awards?).

Malpractice

Malpractice covers cheating in examinations, whether by impersonation, employment of a 'jockey',[2] using unauthorized notes, equipment or software, and plagiarism. We concentrate upon plagiarism because some of the answers to the problem are also answers to the broader cheating issue and because concern is growing as the internet makes it easier to plagiarize.[3]

Self-report evidence implies that most English students have plagiarized (Franklyn-Stokes and Newstead 1995; Ashworth *et al.* 1997), by which we mean that they have passed off another's work as their own. Plagiarism is roundly condemned. Carroll's (2002) advice includes:

- Give students specific instructions ('creating assessment criteria that positively reward individuality and arriving at a unique solution sends a strong message to students' (p. 13).
- Ask for drafts.
- Use peer review for formative feedback.
- Reconsider essay titles.

These practices can be supported by considering the following:

- Markers need to be more diligent.
- Few of us are original thinkers, so when we are faced with a task that does not involve generating new data, what are we to do but read others' work and produce a digest? Is the difference between this and plagiarism nothing more than a matter of giving enough references?
- The problem is not in the students but in the tasks. If you set questions that can be answered by malpractice, you can expect some malpractice.

The first point implies more demands on academic staff who, across the world, feel that they are already juggling multiple demands on their time, and who are seldom well-disposed to 'backstage' work like this (Knight and Trowler 2000). However, plagiarism-detection software may produce an affordable solution within a few years.

The second point implies that we could limit plagiarism by helping students to understand what it means (they are often ignorant of academic convention regarding the use of sources) and how to make sure that legitimate use of others' material is not passed off as their own work. More fundamentally, it might mean that academic staff should be open about their own research and writing practices so that students understand the difference between writing with, say, Heywood's *Assessment in Higher Education* to hand and plagiarizing his work. This is sound academic practice, regardless of any concern about plagiarism.

The third point provides a basis for effectively discouraging plagiarism. If high-stakes questions can be answered by plagiarism, they are poor questions.[4] It is hard to see why the same question should be set year in, year out, and why tasks cannot be topical or fresh[5] – the appendix to Chapter 5 contains a number of ideas for development. In the sciences the problem is different and there are many ways in which takeaway problems can be solved by others, not by the student. The answer here is surely to set such tasks as formative, low-stakes work, checking that it appears to have been done. Then set, in class or in an examination, high-stakes work that cannot be plagiarized and where success depends on having mastered the routines covered in the low-stakes work. Good designers ensure that high-stakes tasks do not lend themselves to routine plagiarism and that tasks are done in conditions where the opportunity for plagiarism is minimal. An example of this approach in a business studies class was described in Chapter 2.

Optimizing reliability: two cases

Employability and the assessment of work-based learning

If employability is intrinsically a fuzzy concept, then precision in assessment cannot be achieved. For some aspects of employability the best that can be done is to produce broad statements of performance, acknowledging that there is an inevitable trade-off between the reliability of the assessment(s) and the validity of the assessment task(s).[6] Across a programme, the trade-offs made in one task that addresses particular programme learning intentions can be set against trade-offs made elsewhere.

We illustrate this assessment problem with comments on the assessment of workplace learning, bearing in mind that employers and many postgraduate departments are impressed by evidence of workplace learning that has been integrated with academic and personal development. We add that there are considerable variations in the practice of work-based learning: in its length, type and quality, and in what students say they have got from work placements (Blackwell *et al.* 2001). We also appreciate that low-stakes, mainly formative, assessment may be the most appropriate for some learning intentions. The Engineering Professors' Council (2002), for example, recognizes that, for some outcomes of learning, evidence of suitable experiences is more appropriate than summative assessment evidence, and 'apprenticeship' approaches to learning (for example, Guile and Young 1998), put more emphasis on coaching and other formative assessment activities.

Figure 8.3 shows some of the conceptual distinctions we find it helpful to make. It indicates that different learning intentions (that learning happens *in*, *through* or *for* the workplace) and modes (*informal*, *non-formal* and *formal*) imply different workplace learning practices and, by extension, different approaches to assessment. Formative assessment, for example, would be particularly appropriate for informal learning *through* the workplace. Summative assessments, of the sort needed when work-based learning is assessed in order to certify achievement or competence, go more easily with formal learning *in* or *for* the workplace. Given the concern in this chapter for reliability, we shall concentrate upon summative assessment purposes and learning *in* the workplace.

Recall that reliability is related to the number and diversity of performances judged by more than one trained observer by reference to common criteria that are understood by learners and assessors alike. For certification purposes, work-based learning would need to be judged several times during any one placement and judgements from several placements would be reviewed before warranting competence. There are four main areas that assessment can explore:

- *Information.* Recall of facts, formulae.
- *Understanding.* Can the learner apply information appropriately, analyse it, evaluate and appraise it?
- *Performance.* Direct observation of learner's performance in the workplace, through computer simulation, in an artificial situation.

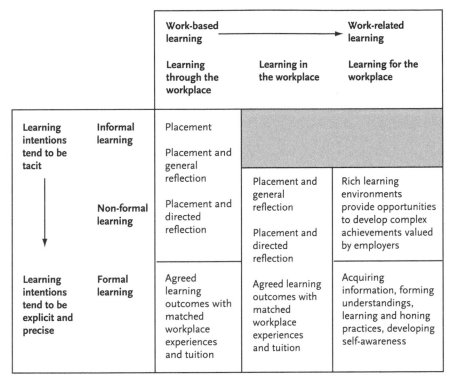

		Work-based learning ——————————→ Work-related learning		
		Learning through the workplace	Learning in the workplace	Learning for the workplace
Learning intentions tend to be tacit ↓	Informal learning	Placement Placement and general reflection		
	Non-formal learning	Placement and directed reflection	Placement and general reflection Placement and directed reflection	Rich learning environments provide opportunities to develop complex achievements valued by employers
Learning intentions tend to be explicit and precise	Formal learning	Agreed learning outcomes with matched workplace experiences and tuition	Agreed learning outcomes with matched workplace experiences and tuition	Acquiring information, forming understandings, learning and honing practices, developing self-awareness

Figure 8.3 Activities contributing to work-related and work-based learning

- *Impact on clients.* Are clients satisfied? Have they gained from, or been helped by, engagement with the learner?

Information is cheap to assess reliably but the architects of the English vocational education system of the 1990s were adamant that it is not a good proxy for appraisal of performance (Jessup 1991), although it may reassure assessors that a learner has enough information for far transfer. *Understanding* is cheap to assess reliably but paper-and-pencil tests of understanding may not be very authentic, although simulations, case studies and other simulacra of work situations can be. Attention is drawn to the tension between validity and usefulness, on the one hand, and reliability and cost on the other. Information and understanding can be cheaply and reliably assessed but there are doubts about whether the findings are useful as predictors of performance in the workplace.

Direct observations of performance are expensive if done by university tutors, who may also be criticized for being out of touch with the 'real' world. The costs of training workplace mentors/assessors are significant and the costs of trying to maintain some common understandings of standards and criteria in their judgements of performance in their own, local settings are also appreciable and recurrent. Such costs should not be underestimated because observation of

performance tends to be a high-inference activity. When the purposes are summative and the stakes are high, considerable care has to be taken to ensure that
assessors follow similar standards in looking at things that matter in a way that is
equitable and not discriminatory. In teacher education, where there is a long history
of work-based learning, the difficulties are generally recognized, although that does
not prevent government from implying that the quality of serving teachers' classroom work can be judged on the basis of occasional observations using ill-defined
criteria. Expenditure on training and monitoring will not necessarily secure
acceptable levels of consistency, especially where it is imperative to get students
a placement, with questions about quality of mentoring and assessment being
treated as secondary issues. Writers on social research methods have a lot to say
about the inherent unreliability of observational methods and the loss of validity
that can accompany attempts to increase reliability by using checklists (for example,
Knight 2002d).

There are understandable attractions, then, for following the principle that, 'by
their fruits ye shall know them' and judging work-based learning by its *impact on the
students themselves or on their clients*. This principle lies behind student satisfaction and
student feedback surveys in higher education, is present in the English government's performance-related pay scheme for schoolteachers, and underpins all
attempts to measure school effectiveness (Goldstein and Woodhouse 2000).

Although any assessment evidence of impact on clients can be compelling when
the results are extreme and a cue for concern when they are less dramatic, it is not
always appreciated that there are serious technical issues to resolve before this
approach can be fairly applied. Arguments about performance-related pay for
teachers (Richardson 1999) highlighted the danger that the professional can get
blamed (or occasionally praised) for outcomes that are not directly and reliably
attributable to what they have done. There are also serious issues to address when
the intention is not to identify outliers – the stars and disasters – but to rank
everyone.

In terms of the assessment of work-related learning, there are other serious
problems with measuring impact. Three of the most pressing are:

- What could we define as impact? How could it be described precisely enough for
  high-stakes assessment?
- What would count as fair assessment devices?
- How can we make high-stakes judgements on the basis of responses of a few
  clients and a short placement in one setting?

With observation and impact we have approaches to the assessment of work-
based learning that have high usefulness and validity. However, these approaches
bring with them problems regarding affordability and reliability. It is hard to see
how any accommodation can be reached unless it is planned at programme
level, so that judgements of competence can be based on more than one work-
based learning episode, generating all different types of evidence across a series of
varied settings.

Reliability in the assessment of portfolios

Baume and Yorke (2002) investigated interrater reliability[7] in the assessment of portfolios that were used for summative purposes in an Open University post-graduate programme. The structure of the portfolio was complex, involving 74 components and a final, overall, assessment. The 74 components, subsumed under seven course outcomes, included a number of technical requirements, a range of course elements and underpinning values, and a judgement regarding the achievement of each course outcome. Notice the priority given to ecological validity.

There were four grading categories for elements and values[8]: well achieved; just achieved; not quite achieved; and not achieved. Whilst the assessors tended strongly to agree regarding the fulfilment of technical requirements (as one would expect), the level of agreement was weaker where the assessors' judgement was called into play. The hard criterion of agreement is an exact match between assessors' judgements: here agreement was found on roughly 60 per cent of occasions where elements and values were concerned, and at 39 per cent on course outcomes (where there is a 'snowballing' of the effects of the judgements relating to requirements, elements and values). Relaxing the agreement criterion to one grade leeway produced agreement percentages in the upper 80s. These figures are broadly consistent with a varied set of studies of inter-rater reliability in portfolio assessment (Herman *et al.* 1993; Koretz *et al.* 1993; Nystrand *et al.* 1993; LeMahieu *et al.* 1995; Wolfe 1996; Supovitz *et al.* 1997; Heller *et al.* 1998; Pitts *et al.* 1999).[9]

An analysis of the scores from raters of the 53 portfolios used in this study showed clearly that interrater variability tended to be greatest where there was – when one looked back at the curriculum – the greatest scope for interpretation. This should occasion little surprise.

The value of the analysis, summarized in Table 8.2, was that it demonstrated to the course team where it needed to concentrate its efforts on improving shared understandings of what was being assessed. The programme's underpinning values of 'concern for equality of opportunity' and 'continued reflection on professional practice' were highlighted as being the aspects more vulnerable to variability in assessment. Equality of opportunity is clearly problematical in a practice-oriented course, since course participants will be faced with varying amounts of challenge in their work: one may have to deal with fairly straightforward matters of physical access to sites, whereas another may have to focus on the complexities of sex or race. The problems for the course designers, and hence the assessors, are to specify the extent to which equal opportunities issues need to be addressed by participants, and what the criteria for success actually are. As a result of this study, the course team did review its expectations in this aspect of the course. In the case of 'continued reflection on professional practice', the most difficult issue was that of planning the future development of practice. What the requirement actually meant was not as transparent as the course designers thought it was, and further work was needed by the course team to elaborate what was expected and to share this with the various interested parties. It should be noted that the amount of staff preparation for assessing portfolios was, for this course, probably at the upper end of the

Table 8.2   Discrepancy rates for underpinning values from assessments of 53 portfolios, set against course outcomes

	Course outcome							
Underpinning value	*1*	*2*	*3*	*4*	*5*	*6*	*7*	*Mean*
1 How students learn	5	4	5	5			12	6.2
2 Concern for student development	7	7	5	5			14	7.6
3 Scholarship				5			8	6.5
4 Equal opportunities	9	9	11	15			12	11.2
5 Colleagueship				5		6	10	7.0
6 Reflection		12	9	6	10	8	8	8.8
Mean	7.0	8.0	7.5	6.8	10.0	7.0	10.7	8.2

Notes:
1. The course outcomes are: (1) Plan teaching sessions; (2) Teach; (3) Assess student work; (4) Monitor and evaluate teaching; (5) Keep records; (6) Cope; (7) Continue your professional development.
2. Differences counted in this table are those exceeding one grade.
3. There are blank cells in the table because not all course outcomes are required to be underpinned by all values.

Source: data from Baume and Yorke 2002: 18

spectrum. The lower end would be represented where staff are supposed to pick up, without much preparation for the role of assessor of portfolios in which reflective commentary is expected, an understanding of what is expected of them.

Further work by Baume *et al.* (forthcoming) involved the experimental re-assessment of ten portfolios (each by two trained and paid Open University assessors). The assessors were asked to record the considerations they had borne in mind whilst coming to their judgements. Although, as in the previous study, technicalities were relatively unproblematical, there were instances of assessors relaxing the 'letter of the law' in the interests of what they saw as the spirit. When it came to the elements and values, they exercised their professional judgement to a greater extent. Some of the difficulties in reaching judgements are exemplified in Table 8.3.

Table 8.3 points clearly to some problems associated with the assessment of complex achievements such as portfolios. Many items in portfolios cannot be assigned unproblematically to an assessment category – judgement often has to be exercised regarding the level of performance. Sometimes the judgement can be cross-referenced to other aspects of the portfolio where the required evidence can be found: should the misplacing of evidence constitute a fatal mistake on the part of the compiler?

More of an inferential leap is made when the student is given the benefit of the doubt, or when the criteria are not well understood. Sometimes, as illustrated in Table 8.3, the leap seems to extend well beyond the evidence. As with conformity to

Table 8.3 Examples of assessors' comments when grading portfolios

Difficulty	Example
Benefit of the doubt	'I am taking him on trust, and giving him the benefit of the doubt . . . as I think that the methods in the module descriptors in his evidence save him.'
Having to dig for relevant material	'A difficult mark. The information is available but needs to be hunted – links to the reflection. But essential information seems to be there.'
Possible misperception of criteria	'Aspects of e.g. gender, race, age not discussed. "Provision" was appropriately considered' (for the award of WA [Well Achieved] in respect of Equal Opportunities)
Possible misapplication of criteria	'No evidence of reflection, just assertion' (for the award of JA [Just Achieved] in respect of Reflection)
Uncertainty about the judgement	'I have to take a leap in the dark here, as I am not sure what other technology is available to deliver the subject matter, i.e. videos etc. But an OHP to distil issues to a few focus words and a flipchart to list issues raised in debate etc. may have been enough. It depends also on the style of use of these.'
Sticking to the rules, albeit uncomfortably	'Seems unfair to be borderline [Bare Pass] – because with the exception of 3g [Equal Opportunities] the rest is quite good – but rules are rules.'
Rule-bending	'Now I have to look it up in the rules of assessment again and I know that I am not going to like the rules. The rules say with one NA [Not Achieved] the element cannot be passed at all. So once again as I regard this as plainly unjust with so many objectives and values all of which have a WA [Well Achieved] but one, I will change the NA to a NQ [Not Quite Achieved] so that at least I can have a CP [Clear Pass]. Well, I may be wrong, but she is a very good candidate. A debate with her about the NQ would be good in order to understand it, and resolve it, but this is not part of the game is it?'

'the rules', the key is that the criteria and how they are to be applied are widely understood. This takes the discussion into the realm of the 'community of practice' (Wenger 1998), in that course designers, students and assessors (both internal and external) – and perhaps quality assurers as well – share the fullest understanding possible regarding what is being expected of the students. As noted earlier, the discussion of exemplars of performances is important to the development of understandings regarding what is expected. In the Open University course at the focus of the two studies used to illustrate this chapter, considerable effort is made to share understandings of what is expected; despite this, analysis showed that, for some course components, it had proved insufficient to narrow the range of possible interpretations to an acceptable level, and that further work was needed in this respect.

A similar issue arises where the rules for combining assessments are concerned. In the Open University course the final pass/fail grade is derived from grades on the seven course outcomes which in turn are derived from gradings of the technicalities, elements and underpinning values. There is an implicit equivalence of weighting of each of the components, though there must be some doubt that failure regarding a technicality like word length is as significant as one relating to teaching ability. The examples in Table 8.3 suggest that some assessors do colour their judgements with their own, rather than the course's, perceptions of acceptability of an overall performance. These assessors are probably overriding the cumulation of component assessments with holistic judgements regarding the calibre of the portfolio.

This raises an issue which is ever present in assessment, and that cannot be resolved here: whether the most appropriate approach is to build up from components to an overall assessment, or to start from a perspective that is closer to the holistic. Advocates can be found for both general propositions. The purpose of the assessment is a significant consideration. For some purposes it may be sufficient to say that the student has reached an acceptable level of attainment – as is the case with a master's or doctoral thesis – where strengths are adjudged to outweigh weaknesses. For other purposes the 'compensation' inherent in holistic judgements may need to be suspended for some components of an assessment – safe medical practice, proper behaviour towards students, and respect for confidentiality are three areas of action in which unsatisfactory practice might be a sufficient condition for failure even though the rest of a student's performance was above threshold level.

For staff who are new to the use of portfolio-based assessment, there is a need for developmental work to help them to come to terms with a mode of assessment that will differ considerably from traditional approaches in which the level of connection between theoretical constructs and the learner's actual performance is relatively easy to discern.

It will be seen that the Open University has succeeded in the summative use of programme portfolios with good ecological validity and has secured acceptable levels of reliability by the procedures described above. However, in a personal communication, the current programme leader reports that:

> In the two years since this research was undertaken . . . feedback from participants, tutors, University systems and external examiners have made it clear that the costs of such standards are not sustainable. The assessment of the programme has changed its focus, in line with the rest of the sector, to place a greater emphasis on learning and the environment for learning, rather than evidence of individual competence. The current challenge for the programme team is to develop assessment processes for portfolio work that appreciate the complex roles of [higher education] teachers in their diverse situations.

How much reliability?

There is no shortage of ways of increasing the reliability of high-stakes assessment and the principles can be extended to formative assessment purposes, where they can encourage honesty and care. The problems are not technical – we know exactly what high-reliable assessments look like; the problems are moral. Do we value complexity, validity and usefulness? Are assessment decisions essentially economic ones? How much reliability do we need?

Notes

1. Some HE systems equate year of study with level of study (year 1 = level 1). Those using levels have various ways of describing them. A numerical system is used in England (NICATS 2002).
2. Exam jockeys, a Malaysian term, are syndicates who obtain examination papers and dictate the correct answers over the mobile phone to students doing the exams.
3. The internet also hosts a number of plagiarism detection services, most of which are available by subscription. We are not convinced that they are refined, cheap and robust enough to be routine adjuncts to the marking process in humanities, arts and social sciences. For further details of UK work on plagiarism, visit the JISC-sponsored Plagiarism Advisory Service website at www.northumbria.ac.uk/jiscpas
4. Bespoke essay-writing businesses and the like cannot be thwarted by setting good questions, although they may put up the price of plagiarism.
5. Reducing the risk of plagiarism in this way may strengthen another source of unreliability. The fresh tasks may be more divergent (stimulating a greater range of acceptable responses) or make greater inferential demands on assessors.
6. There are other assessment trade-offs, for example those between high-fidelity, in-depth assessments and broader, less thorough ones.
7. The validity of the assessment was assumed, for the purpose of this exercise.
8. There were only two for technical requirements.
9. There are various technical considerations that need to be borne in mind when dealing with the issue of interrater reliability. Correlation coefficients, such as the Pearson r are insensitive to level, so it is possible for a high coefficient to arise from two similarly shaped distributions of grades which are nevertheless differentiated by grade level. The nature of the data suggests that the non-parametric Spearman ρ would be preferable to the Pearson r. Percentage agreement, frequently used in studies, is on its own a poor measure since no allowance is made for chance agreement. The kappa (κ) statistic (Davies and Fleiss 1982) which was used by Pitts *et al.* (1999) and Baume and Yorke (2002) is probably less susceptible to distortion than the other statistics mentioned.

9

Making Better Use of Formative Assessment

Capitalizing on the potential

A major challenge for higher education is to respond to the main 'message' from Black and Wiliam (1998) and from Mentkowski and Associates (2000) – that good formative assessment encourages good learning. The use of the word 'encourages' implies that formative assessment might not be effective, perhaps because of a breakdown in the formative signalling system (Chapter 3). It is also possible that formative assessment could simply be serving modest learning intentions or could fail to mesh with what we know about human learning processes. The stance taken in Chapter 1 was that higher education is associated with ambitious learning intentions, so attention needs to turn to theories of learning that are consistent with them.[1]

Complex achievements take time. This implies practice but it also implies feedback on practice, whether it be self-generated, or comes from other learners or experts. Without feedback, the learner is like someone learning to play chess blindfolded, wearing earmuffs and beyond any helpful tactile contact. When achievements are complex, careful thought is needed about the nature of the feedback. When the aim is improving future performances, the most useful feedback is about improvement strategies: what are the most important two or three things on which to work if performance on a similar task is to be improved? Unless there is a requirement that learners master particular detail, there is the danger that too much correction of specific detail will take attention away from improvement strategies.

The assumption so far has been that learning is something that happens in proportion to teaching. This is true at some stages of learning (early), on some materials (unfamiliar and simpler ones), and for some purposes (orientation). However, learning also happens through study and metacognition, by application, through interchanges with others and by engagement with tasks that pose problems. It does not necessarily follow a predictable and progressive course: understandings may come quickly or slowly. Much learning is informal, which is to say it does not arise through direct response to teaching, or, to a lesser extent, in direct response to tasks. It comes from participation in 'communities of practice', workgroups and cultures that create lots of feedback on achievements as part of the normal way of working (Wenger 1998; Brown and Duguid 2000). Where the group, community and culture face new challenges, either from internal tensions or from outside forces calling for fresh responses and perhaps exacerbating tensions, then the individual learns within a 'learning organization' (Easterby-Smith 1997; Engeström 2001). However, as those who point out that experience does not equate with learning (let alone with the formation of expertise) know, complex learning is neither guaranteed nor predictable (Guile and Young 1998). With such unpredictability in mind, Goodyear (2002) describes the design of study sequences in terms of the provision of opportunities for engagements that are likely to lead to the sort of learning that is intended.[2]

If this is a fair account of understandings of ways in which complex learning tends to take place, then:

- it provides conceptual substantiation for the meta-analysis of studies of formative feedback (Black and Wiliam 1998);
- it draws attention to the importance of feedback from peers and, by extension, to self-assessment as well;
- it raises significant issues regarding the design of learning, such as how learning environments[3] should be designed to stimulate informal learning with uncertain outcomes.

It is partly against this background that discussion of ways of capitalizing on the potential of formative assessment should be understood. That such discussion is needed can be inferred from the consistent criticisms emerging from the process of subject review in UK higher education (see Chapter 3).

The significance of students' backgrounds

The characteristics of students entering higher education have a bearing on their success. In the UK, the 'new' universities and the colleges tend to enrol more students from lower socio-economic groups and more 'mature' students than do the 'old' universities. These characteristics are strongly associated, at institution level, with higher levels of attrition and non-completion (Yorke 2001b), with entry qualifications a highly probable mediator.[4] It is well-known that the A-level qualifications[5] of those entering the new universities and colleges are in most subject areas lower than those of entrants to the old universities.

The data relating to school performances in England show that in all regions of the UK, high A-level points scores tend to be negatively associated with social deprivation (measured by proxy as the proportion of pupils entitled to receive free school meals). Taking the local educational authority as the unit of analysis, the association for the whole of England is −0.54 (Pearson *r*), with the range being from −0.76 in the north-east to −0.06 in the south-west. The largest negative correlations are to be found in those areas dominated by large cities, and a more fine-grained analysis would probably show that the effect was even more marked in the inner city areas. In other words, where pupils go on to study A-levels (a measure that is itself class-biased), pupils who do not get free school meals, i.e. those from the higher social classes, perform better.

Students from lower socio-economic groups and mature students, for different reasons, probably have less awareness on entry than others about what higher education will expect of them. This is a reflection of their generally lower levels of conventional cultural and social capital (Bourdieu and Passeron 1977). The performance indicators for all UK institutions that are published annually by the Higher Education Funding Council for England (see, for example, HEFCE 2002) show that those institutions that attract the highest proportions of disadvantaged students tend to have the highest rates of non-completion. About two-thirds of those who leave an institution do so during or at the end of the first year of full-time study. The need for significant adjustment in a short time may be a barrier to learning and an influence towards learned helplessness and discontinuation of study. The cognitive and cultural jumps may simply be too large. Bandura advises against demanding large cognitive jumps, since it can be demoralizing not to make good progress towards a distant goal:

> The less individuals believe in themselves, the more they need explicit, proximal, and frequent feedback of progress that provides repeated affirmations of their growing capabilities.
>
> (Bandura 1997: 217)

There are significant implications for curriculum design here, especially in the first year. Perhaps driven more by the publication of the indicators (and some 'naming and shaming' in the press) than by an educational rationale such as that advanced by Yorke (2001a), a number of institutions have moved away from a practice of giving summative assessments at the end of the first semester (i.e. in December) in favour of formative feedback. The first year of study in almost all full-time UK programmes is in fact merely a qualifying year for those that follow: students merely have to pass in order to progress. The intention of a formatively oriented first semester is that students will feel more supported and not disheartened – with beneficial effect on both students and the institution (whose income is affected by non-completion). There are counterarguments, including concerns that students (particularly if under pressure from part-time employment) might do the minimum to get by and hence not take proper advantage of the learning potential unlocked by the formative orientation, and that this might merely postpone for a further semester the revelation of students' performance in summative assessment.

However, supportive feedback sometimes cannot overcome a student's self-doubt, as is vividly shown by the following quotation from a survey of students who had left before completing their programmes in higher education:

> I didn't have enough confidence to take part in the tutorials, and I spoke to my teachers and they were all easier with me but I didn't like voicing my opinions in case everyone thought I was stupid, and I became very unhappy. . . . I just lost all confidence in myself even though my teachers told me I was a really good student, I didn't believe them. I thought they were lying.
>
> (Student reading joint arts; from Yorke 1999b: 15)

This student did not accept an offer of counselling, and left the institution concerned.

How might students respond to feedback?

Critical to the success of formative assessment (and, broadly, to the student's 'emancipation') is how the student interprets and deals with feedback. Involved here are also their psychological state and disposition towards subsequent action. Academics can often be heard to say that students look at the grades given for an assignment, and then put the assignment away in order to get on with other work. In such circumstances, the value of the feedback is clearly limited, however much information may have been provided by comments on the script or on a covering feedback pro-forma.

Lack of success is likely to discourage performance-oriented students, whereas those who are learning-oriented are stimulated to further effort. The teacher is in a critically important position. If the teacher can detect the nature of the student's goal orientation, then they have a chance to influence a shift in orientation away from self-presentation and towards learning. The need is to promote a climate in which the student sees feedback as an opportunity for learning – to encourage an orientation towards 'learning goals', in Dweck's (1999) terms. Explicit requirements may speak louder than exhortations, so one way round the difficulty of getting students to reflect on feedback is to not release the grade until the student has commented on the feedback that has been provided (Gibbs 1999).

The greatest problem is arguably with weak or failing performance. Research on children by Dweck and co-workers (e.g. Dweck and Leggett 1988; Elliott and Dweck 1988) has shown that children vary considerably in the way that they face up to difficulty and failure. Children who are 'mastery-oriented' are positive and resilient when faced with problems, seeing them as challenges from which learning might stem. Children who are 'helpless', in contrast, have a negative orientation, seeing failure as a reflection on their (perceived low) ability, and giving up easily. The differences between the two types are related to personality and not to intelligence. However, Dweck (1999) has shown that self-perception of the extent to which intelligence is malleable (the student's self-theory about intelligence) does play a part in determining outcomes, for both schoolchildren and college students. As an example of the point, about one-third of a group of students in a study reported by Ecclestone and Swann (1999: 383) seemed to have a view of their ability (measured by A-level examination scores) as immutable, and because of this did not expect to be able to improve their work. The proportion of believers in a 'fixed' intelligence is similar to that found by Yorke and Knight (2003) in a sample of 2269 first- and final-year undergraduates across a wide range of subject disciplines.

There are two points here for the teacher: to be aware of fixedness and malleability in students' (and their own) self-theories, and to encourage 'fixed' students in the direction of malleability. A discussion of the educational implications of the four pairings derived from fixed/malleable and teacher/student can be found in Knight and Yorke (2003).

We argued in Chapter 3 that the goal which the individual is pursuing is important, since this provides a framework for interpreting and responding to events that occur. The response to feedback is likely to be different according to whether the student is driven by a 'performance goal' (where the key question is, 'Will I look good [or, not look bad]?') and 'learning goals' (where the central question is, 'What is the best way to increase my skill?'). Elliot and Dweck's (1988) research with children showed that failure produced different effects: for those working to learning goals, it was merely task information to be assimilated or accommodated (using Piagetian terminology), whereas for those working to performance goals it was a crushing blow.[6] Brunson and Matthews (1981) observed similar effects in 'Type A' undergraduates (whose characteristics included extreme competitiveness, aggression and a sense of time-urgency) who, when faced with repeated failure in respect of the challenges in front of them, would lapse into helplessness and give up responding.

As students move through their programmes of study the tasks facing them (ought to) become more demanding.[7] A final-year undergraduate project ought to be more than a routine exercise – it ought to have some of the features of a research-based higher degree, but on a much smaller scale. Developmentally, students will be expected to become increasingly able to solve complex problems, since, from the point of view of employability and lifelong learning, it is an advantage to be able to deal successfully with the 'messy', uncircumscribed problems that work and life throw up. The potential for things to go wrong increases with the complexity of the problem, and the successful learner has a capacity to cope with disconfirming evidence (i.e. negative feedback on the work put in) and move on. Hence we reiterate the importance of the student having an orientation towards Dweck's 'learning goals', rather than 'performance goals', and a strong belief in self-efficacy.

There is an implicit tension in much of undergraduate education, and in some taught master's programmes, between the expectation that students will attain specified learning outcomes and a desire that they should be encouraged to succeed in more open-ended tasks – even to the point of breaking new ground in exceptional cases. This provides a reminder of a point we made in Chapter 3: the desirability of including opportunities for 'divergent assessment' (Torrance and Pryor 1998: 2001), in which attention is given to the student's imagination and creativity in dealing with the challenges they are required to face.

Speed of feedback

To be useful, the provision of feedback has to match the needs of the situation. Some feedback needs to be instantaneous, such as when the student is inadvertently about to throw away a needed chemical solution, or is placing themself in a position of danger when undertaking fieldwork. As Eraut (1994: 149ff) notes, the assessor recognizes immediately, from his or her repertoire of understanding, that there is a need for rapid action and does not need to deliberate regarding the appropriateness of that action – it is professionally 'obvious' what has to be done. At other times, the assessor has to make a fairly quick, but not instantaneous, decision about the performance – for example, in judging the merits of a drama student's delivery of a speech from Shakespeare,[8] or of a team presentation in a business studies programme. These kinds of feedback share features with Laurillard's (1993) 'intrinsic feedback', i.e. comments provided in the context of the action (for example, rapid, informal feedback on what the students are doing in a geological field trip or a drama studio). At the 'slow' end of Eraut's spectrum of response rates, feedback is often deliberative (in Laurillard's terms 'extrinsic'), such as when the need to comment on an essay-type assignment requires the assessor to analyse what the student has said and how well it has been said, what they have not said, and so on.

Equity in formative assessment

An issue that is – apparently unwittingly – raised by Sadler (1998: 82) is that of equity in giving feedback. This can be posed as a question: 'Is feedback which is differentiated with reference to the student's level of performance and/or personal circumstances inequitable, or is it appropriate for the development of learning?'

Although her attention is directed more towards summative than towards formative assessment, Stowell's (2001) comments on equity have some relevance here. Stowell argues that 'fairness' and 'sameness' should not be confused when thinking about equity. 'Unfairness', she points out, 'may arise from treating unequals equally as much as from treating equals unequally' (p. 2). Stowell pursues the issue with reference to the decision-making of examination boards regarding student performances. Where formative assessment is concerned, the issue is much less contentious. Formative assessment is concerned with maximizing the learning of each individual student. In theory, each student should receive feedback that is most appropriate to their learning needs. Feedback should therefore be differentiated. The problem occurs on the assessor's side when time and resources are constrained. The assessor then has to make choices regarding the amount of feedback that should be given to each individual. The choices they make will reflect personal value judgements about the purposes of education: some teachers will opt for 'levelling up' in the interests of social justice, whereas others will give priority to 'high flyers', seeing their actions in Darwinian 'survival of the fittest' terms.

Self- and peer assessment

Formative assessment can be expected to help a student to become familiar with expected standards, but if the student relies on the teacher to demonstrate strengths and weaknesses, their own capacity for self-diagnosis may be prejudiced. Less use is made of peer and self-assessment than is warranted by a commitment to the development of students' capacity for self-regulation. Boud and Falchikov (1989), reviewing half a century of research, noted that weaker students were likely to overvalue, and stronger students to undervalue, their efforts. Dochy *et al.* (1999) concluded from a more recent review that self-assessments could correlate reasonably well with teacher assessments (the relationship being strengthened by positive motivation), and that it promoted learning. The findings regarding the accuracy (relative to tutors) of peer assessment were varied. Such assessments were likely to be affected by social considerations such as friendship, social dominance and race (and we would add that the picture becomes cloudier when groupwork is the focus). Despite the difficulties, Dochy *et al.* (1999: 345) indicated that students' engagement in assessment could assist learning, and listed a number of positive effects, amongst them being:

- increased student confidence in the ability to perform;
- increased awareness of the quality of the student's own work;
- increased reflection on the student's own behaviour and/or performance;
- improvement in the products of learning;
- greater independence in learning;
- increased student satisfaction;
- better learning climate.

The argument that peer assessment can stimulate learning has been set out in Chapter 4 and earlier in this chapter. Gibbs (1999: 43–7) gives an interesting example. During a second-year module in engineering, students were required, on six occasions, to grade their peers' work on specified problems an hour after its submission, using guidance sheets provided by the staff. Feedback to the students was immediate, and was provided on an anonymous basis. A very marked improvement in students' end-of-course performances was found. The improvement can be interpreted in terms of practices that support good learning. Relevant to this chapter are the promptness of the feedback, the significance of knowing that others have given some careful thought to what one has produced, and the stimulus the whole exercise gave to self-regulation regarding expected standards. These are, of course, actions that are shared by good teachers, although the lack of a power differential in the peer assessment might have been an additional contributory factor to the observed success.

The implementation of self- and peer assessment requires that students be given a coherent rationale, lest they interpret these approaches as the teacher abrogating their responsibilities. For many students entering higher education, assessment is the teacher's job, not theirs (after all, the earlier stages of education are likely to have socialized the students to expect this). A developmental approach is desirable, perhaps staged along the lines suggested by Adams and King (1995): students initially discussing what is required in an assessment, with examples of good and poor work; then identifying appropriate criteria for an assessed task; and subsequently moving on to undertake actual self- and peer assessments.

Risks of collateral damage

Student vulnerability

Some students are particularly vulnerable to a sense of personal failure. For instance, the student who has entered higher education via an access course in which teachers have provided ongoing supportive encouragement and feedback may need more support than a teacher might appreciate. Tutorial support (probably dominated by informal formative feedback) may, in such cases, be vital to success, as is exemplified by the following comment.

> I completed an Access course prior to attending [university] where the staff were really helpful and knew you on a 1 to 1 basis. At university this wasn't the case and . . . I couldn't cope with the workload with no tutorial support.
> (Student reading for a diploma in higher education; from Yorke 1999d: 21)

Students unsure of themselves may see a poor grading as reflecting adversely on their ability. The result may be a loss of confidence: 'I am a failure' may come to dominate over a more reasonable interpretation, such as 'I didn't understand what was expected of me', and edge the student towards learned helplessness. Few academic staff, other than those whose subject disciplines call upon it, have much more than a lay understanding of how students' psychological states can influence the way(s) in which they respond to feedback. An awareness of what comments and commentaries can do could help academics to make formative assessment more of a supportive act, even when serious criticisms of the work have to be made.

Dealing with student vulnerability is primarily a matter for groups of teachers, especially those sharing an engagement in a programme. The ethos of a programme contributes significantly to the quality of the student experience: dissatisfaction with tutorial support is implicated in the decision of some students to withdraw from their programme (Yorke 1999b). This is the kind of issue on which a programme – perhaps a departmental – team can work as a collective developmental activity.

Learned dependence

The process of assessment (both formative and summative) can discourage students from developing to their full potential. Discouragement may occur as a result of failings on the part of the teacher and/or the student. Although discouraged students may not develop 'learned helplessness' (Peterson *et al.* 1993), they may develop 'learned dependence'. Boud picks up the point when he writes:

> Too often staff-driven assessment encourages students to be dependent on the teacher or the examiners to make decisions about what they know and they do not effectively learn to be able to do this for themselves.
> (Boud 1995: 39)

Learned dependence is present when the student relies on the teacher to say what has to be done and does not seek to go beyond the boundaries that they believe to be circumscribing the task. The construction of curricula around explicit learning outcomes risks the inadvertent building-in of circumscriptions or, for the 'strategic' student seeking to balance study and part-time employment, a welcome 'limitation' to what they have to do. Formal and informal feedback can be interrogated for what it can tell about what is expected, and can become part of a vicious spiralling-in towards 'playing it safe', basing action on perceptions of the implicit – as well as the explicit – expectations. It is a paradox that active 'cue-seekers' (Miller and Parlett 1974) can exhibit a form of learned dependence, through 'playing it clever' (at least, superficially) by hunting for hints that will help them to maximize the grade received for their investment of effort. Over-reliance on the teacher can thus give achievements a meretricious ring: these may look worthier than they actually are, in respect of the needs of employment, where problems do not come ready-defined but require the employee come up with a response, often on the basis of incomplete information. An analysis undertaken by Naylor and Smith (2002) of performances of students graduating from UK universities in 1993 showed that pupils from fee-paying schools, when compared with those with equivalent qualifications from state schools, obtained on average a *lower* class of degree.[9] We speculate that this perhaps unexpected finding may, in part, be attributable to independent school pupils being better prepared by their teachers for the A-level examinations (or, more crudely, being better taught to the test), but not necessarily better prepared for the learning experience of higher education – a minor version of 'learned dependence'.

The curricular need is for opportunities for students to develop their autonomy to A-level that fits the expectations likely to be laid upon them. Expected learning outcomes that are essentially 'closed' (in that the student can succeed by, in effect, giving 'the right answer'), are not optimally supportive of employability.

Interim feedback

Where pressures permit, feedback is sometimes given on a draft of work in the interest of assisting the student towards fulfilling the aims set for the assignment by achieving a 'maximum performance' (Wood 1987). Wood, drawing on Vygotsky's notion of the 'zone of proximal development' suggests that 'the teacher/tester and student *collaborate* actively to produce a best performance' (Wood 1987: 242, emphasis in original). This has its drawbacks. First, and obviously, the student could be privileged against peers if all do not have the same opportunity for support. Second, whose is the 'best performance'? The student may be seduced into believing that they can now achieve the same standard without support when in fact this is not the case, and the 'scaffolding' of support is still needed. This is particularly an issue when a qualifying assignment is passed on the strength of a feedback-enhanced performance and the student is subsequently expected to achieve on their own: a case in point would be a taught doctoral programme where the 'capstone' dissertation rests upon the learning achieved in earlier programme components.

The necessary autonomy may not have been fully developed in the student. Failure, or a bare pass, in the ultimate assessment may be an unwelcome consequence.

Judging the effectiveness of formative assessment
Formative assessment can clearly be said to have 'worked' if the student demonstrates having learned as a result of the feedback provided. This requires that the student has a concept of learning that allows them to take in what the assessor has sought to convey and that they then act on the basis of this developed understanding. This demanding criterion for empirical verification is favoured by Harlen and James (1997).

A less demanding, but nevertheless useful, evaluative question focuses on what the assessor does: 'Is what the assessor has done regarding feedback the best that could have been done (or – more weakly – reasonable in the circumstances)?' An assessor could plausibly argue that the feedback they give regarding a student's work is formative in intention, even though the student perhaps merely notes the grade and ignores the comments. For the assessor, the intention is the important thing. Hence the level of success depends on the quality[10] of the proffered feedback, but not on the student's response.

Both the teacher-centred and the student-centred perspectives have validity, but it is important to be clear as to which is being adopted when formative assessment is under discussion or being researched. The perspective adopted needs to be geared to the evaluative question. If the evaluative focus is about what the member of staff does when faced with student work, then the less demanding question should prevail; if it is about student learning, then primacy has to be given to the more demanding question.

Enhancing formative assessment

Realizing the need

As the establishment of the UK quality enhancement agency[11] for higher education shows, in recent years the development of academic staff as educators as well as subject specialists has become a focus of attention in a number of national systems. Scrutiny of educational quality is a commonplace, reports of formal appraisals are published, as are the outcomes of surveys of Australian graduates regarding their experiences of higher education (see, for example, GCCA 2002). 'In-house' developmental programmes have burgeoned as a consequence, in which reflection relating to formative assessment is one component.

Although they assess their learners formatively, teachers may simply not recognize some of their actions as comprising formative assessment (Cowie and Bell (1999) noted this in the context of schools), or they may be missing opportunities to maximize formative impact. Heightening teachers' awareness of the relationship between what they are doing and student learning can contribute to their development as educators: for example, Swann and Ecclestone (1999: 76) showed that getting staff to work reflectively on the provision of more effective feedback to students spilled over into improvements in their ability to grade work.

Theorizing about formative assessment

It is surprising that an activity of such importance for student development is so weakly theorized. Yorke (2003a) points out some of the problems with the current state of theory, and implies that its underdevelopment is connected with the multiplicity of perspectives that need to be brought to bear. He offers the following as the beginnings of a theory of formative assessment, acknowledging that it needs considerable further development.

A theory of formative assessment that extends existing theory[12] should include the following:

- The epistemological structure of the relevant subject discipline(s).
- The ontology of students (subsuming both psychopathology and development).
- Theoretical constructs relating to learning and assessment.
- The professional knowledge of the educator/assessor (which will subsume not only their disciplinary knowledge but also their knowledge of student development at the generic and specific levels, and, further, knowledge of assessment methodology and of the psychology of giving and receiving feedback).
- Theory relating to communication and interpretation.

This theoretical perspective is captured to some extent in Box 9.1 which, as a subset of Laurillard's (1993: 102ff) 'conversational framework' for teacher/student interaction, lists the events that characterize effective formative assessment. Box 9.1 suggests a set of pragmatic starting points for the development of an enhanced theoretical appreciation of formative assessment.

Box 9.1 could form the basis of staff workshops aimed at improving the effectiveness of student learning. Many of the listed components could be the subject of an audit process set up by a programme or module team committed to better understanding of its practices in assessment. Others, such as the student response to formative assessment, could be the subject of action research. Whatever enhancement activities are set in train, it is preferable that they are grounded in prior reflection on both the nature of formative assessment and current assessment practice.

Assessors are learners too

The act of assessing has an effect on assessors as well as on students. First, assessors learn about the extent to which students have developed expertise, and should tailor their teaching accordingly. This is part of the cycle of effective teaching–learning described by a number of researchers, often using the idea of reflective practice, which has become widely known in higher education (Brockbank and McGill 1998; Moon 1999).

Box 9.1 Components of effective formative assessment

TEACHERS . . .

- are aware of:

  - the epistemology of the discipline;
  - stages of student intellectual and moral development;
  - the individual student's knowledge and stage of intellectual development;
  - the psychology of giving and receiving feedback.

- provide:

  - tasks sufficient in number to create opportunities for giving feedback on all *key* module/programme learning outcomes;
  - tasks of progressively graded difficulty, appropriate to the students;
  - criteria against which performance(s) will be judged.

- communicate with students:

  - clearly regarding the standards expected of students;
  - in a timely manner;
  - highlighting the strengths and weaknesses of presented work (and not of the students themselves);
  - indicating how the students' work might subsequently develop.

STUDENTS . . .

- understand what is expected of them (with reference, *inter alia*, to the assessment criteria);
- elicit the meaning from formative comment;
- act on the basis of their developed understandings.

Source: developed from Knight 2002a: 155–7; Gibbs and Simpson 2002; and Yorke 2003a

Secondly, the act of assessing may stimulate teachers to see new pedagogical possibilities, particularly when a task specification and accompanying grade indicators are deliberately written to encourage 'divergent' responses. The teacher can be challenged, for example, when an 'expressive objective' (Eisner 1985) leads to the production of work whose nature could not be predicted at the outset – the writing of a poem, the creation of a work of fine art, or a new critical slant on a writer's *oeuvre* are cases in point. The assessor may have to reconstrue the artefact in the light of further information (or, possibly, of an academic appeal).

Thirdly, assessors may extend their disciplinary and/or pedagogical repertoires after a period of reflection (perhaps supported by a staff development programme), with the effect that the revised repertoires become available for subsequent cohorts of students.

Collectivity in enhancing formative assessment

One of the problems of higher education, faced by the education system as a whole, is that it is alleged not to be good at bringing findings together to give clear guidance regarding 'what works'. Whilst the concept of cumulation is problematic,[13] there is a strong argument for working collectively to develop formative assessment theory and practice. To work collectively on a research question contrasts with the retrospective mining of research findings, many of which will have arisen in response to different research questions posed at different times.

The immediate need is for greater understanding of the effectiveness of formative assessment. How can teachers maximize the likelihood that their feedback to students will be taken and acted upon? What perceptions of formative assessment exist in both teachers and students? These questions point towards qualitative investigations, perhaps in the form of action research, which, *if handled programmatically* rather than as a number of disconnected studies, offer the prospect of deepening the understanding of, and hence strengthening the practice of, formative assessment. Torrance and Pryor (1998, 2001) have developed an action research methodology that could be developed to fit the higher education context. Through examining the complexity of classroom interactions and teachers' interpretations, broad understandings can emerge about where formative assessment might promote student learning, and where it might do the opposite.

The programmatic approach would need to combine both subject discipline and generic angles. In the UK, the most appropriate vehicle for dealing with the issue at a level beyond the institution is the Learning and Teaching Support Network (LTSN) with its 24 subject centres and its generic centre. Within institutions, a similar approach could be organized through the educational development unit (or similar) working in partnership with academic departments.

A challenge to pedagogical culture

Formative assessment is under threat from the widely felt pressures on higher education. Yet formative assessment is vital to student learning. Teacher 'contact time' is a costly institutional resource. If student learning is a primary institutional aim, then it makes sense to use 'contact time' in a manner most likely to achieve this. Teaching that involves students in active learning, and provides good opportunities for formative assessment, is likely to fulfil expectations of both effectiveness and efficiency. We reiterate here the importance of feedback that is developmentally useful (Boud 1995; Knight 2002b), and that the 'consequential validity' of feedback is high when there is a positive deferred effect on learning. The 'consequential validity' is low if the feedback encourages, say, narrowly focused instrumental learning that runs counter to that really desired in the curriculum.

The argument for more (and better) formative assessment rather than less[14] is non-trivial. It implies the radical reconstruction of many curricula, because increasing the attention given to formative assessment will require offsetting decreases elsewhere. One candidate for reduction is that staple of higher education, the lecture, which Bligh (1998) has for a long time shown not to be particularly effective in enhancing student learning. The increasing availability of web-based materials makes much, but by no means all, lecturing an expensive luxury. Where students are undertaking a substantial amount of part-time work in order to support themselves through their studies, there are advantages in having material available when students are in a position to access it, and not when the staff want to present it.

Sadler (1998: 77) observes that, 'Substantial modification to the learning environment through changes to regular classroom practice involves turning the learning culture around.' Bringing formative assessment to the fore in curriculum design and delivery can be expected to involve a cultural shift of some magnitude.

Notes

1. There is no shortage of theories of the ways in which people learn well-defined and limited things in highly structured settings.
2. This is a summary of an analysis that is more fully developed in Knight (2002a).
3. North American research, notably that reported by Astin (1997), concludes that the quality of the whole environment in which students learn contributes to the outcomes of the college years. The formal curriculum is a part of it.
4. Data protection and confidentiality considerations preclude access to the raw data that would enable the connection to be explored more fully.
5. Students can, of course, enter higher education with a range of qualifications. However, the most widely used index of 'entrant quality' is a score derived from students' profiles of A-level results.
6. Summaries of this work can be found in Sylva (1994) and in Dweck (1999).
7. It is often assumed that we make tasks more demanding by using more complex criteria with which to assess performance. Such is certainly the message contained in the plethora of scales, taxonomies, schemes and other tabular matter that are proffered as reference points. An alternative is that the tasks should be less well-defined and 'wilder' – less scaffolded – with the criteria remaining the same.
8. If video-recorded for later and more deliberative assessment, then the task moves towards the 'slow' end of the dimension.
9. The scatter in the results showed that, in respect of a few schools, pupils from independent schools outperformed their state-educated counterparts.
10. The *way* in which the feedback is given may be as important to student acceptance as the feedback comments themselves, so 'quality of feedback' is more complex than might appear at first sight.
11. Bringing the Learning and Teaching Support Network, the Institute for Learning and Teaching in Higher Education and the Higher Education Staff Development Agency into a single organization.
12. See, for instance, Gipps (1994); Brown and Knight (1994); Black (1998).
13. See Rudduck and McIntyre (1998), a series of articles in the *British Educational Research Journal* 27 (5), and Yorke (2000a) on cumulation in respect of higher education.
14. See Knight (2000) for a fuller discussion.

10

Progression

Development and curriculum

The underlying presumption of a degree curriculum is that the programme is developmental. It follows that assessment arrangements should support developments within programmes that are designed to support progression from lesser attainments to greater ones. This was intended when modular curricula were introduced in the UK, with successive years of study being described in terms of ascending levels.[1] Subsequently, 'level descriptors' were formalized in the Framework for Higher Education Qualifications in England, Wales and Northern Ireland[2] (QAA 2001c). However, the concept of 'level', like the levels in Bloom's (1956) *Taxonomy of Educational Objectives*, is not straightforward (see Winter 1993b, 1994; Anderson and Sosniak 1994; Anderson and Krathwohl 2001).

A commitment to progression implicitly acknowledges that some learning is necessarily 'slow learning' (Claxton 1998). An advantage of monodisciplinary programmes is that, almost without the need for curriculum planning, some of the learning can take place over the full span of the programme. The advent of unitized curricula means that opportunities for slow learning have to be deliberately planned at programme level, since the individual study units are likely to be too short in duration to permit it to happen, and hence for assessment to capture it. Indeed, unless deliberate effort has been made to encourage slow learning, there may be no locus at which its development can be formally recognized save, perhaps, by means of a culminating 'capstone' project or dissertation.

Development is not always positive

If there is a need for caution regarding 'level', there is also, as Squires notes, a need to be cautious about the notion of 'development', for

> 'Development' is one of those halo words which tends to disarm our critical faculties. . . . It implies that there is something to be developed; that the

development of something can be at least partly planned and influenced; and
that such development is, by definition, for the better.

(Squires 1990: 123)

Later in his book, Squires warns against assuming too easily that the development induced by higher education is automatically beneficial to students:

> We tend to assume a little too easily that higher education is a positive affair.
> But it could have effects or side-effects on its students which are unwanted and
> undesirable, which limit them as individuals, misfit them for society, disequip
> them for their jobs and undermine their development as lifelong learners.
> Such effects could come from, for example, overcrowded curricula which
> induce 'surface' learning, methods of assessment which encourage 'strategic'
> learning, curricular or teaching functions which have become dysfunctions, or
> the transmission of closed or complacent attitudes towards continuing
> education.

(Squires 1990: 146)

He goes on to note that higher education can be a disturbing experience for some
students. 'Unlearning' what has been learned at school, and having to start again
can be dispiriting, particularly if coupled with insensitive teaching. The higher
education experience can also be disruptive of personal relationships. Partners can
be threatened by the various impacts of the learner's entry into new cognitive
territory, as is instanced in this comment which is reminiscent of Rita's domestic
situation in Willy Russell's play *Educating Rita*:

> Things have altered over the last couple of years and I have got more, I
> suppose some people would say it's bolshie but I think I've decided I've got
> opinions, but even then I always had opinions, but I suppose it's scary for him,
> it's scary that this person he's been married to all these years has suddenly
> altered.

(Wakeford 1994: 244)

Further, the learner's membership of social groupings may be compromised by
the latter's perception that the learner has moved away from being 'one of us'.
Tinto (1993), in formulating a theory with reference to Durkheim's theory of
suicide, refers to the higher education experience in terms of a rite of passage from
one environment to another. For many, the transition will not be extreme – the
learner may simply be doing what generations of the family have done beforehand
with, behind them, all the cultural capital that is needed to ease them into the new
situation. For others, and particularly those from disadvantaged backgrounds, the
transition may be much more stressful as they seek to come to terms with an
environment very different from that with which they are familiar. Higher education can have serious impact on the learner's construction of the self, in that the
opening-up to new ways of thinking can break apart an apparently well-formed
personal construct system – in the most extreme instances, to the point of (real)
suicide.[3]

Progression is multidimensional

Development is not the same as change. Development is teleological; it is headed somewhere. A major issue in child psychology is whether changes should be regarded as developmental or not, particularly given that the path of development is not a smooth upward slope and that deteriorations in performance precede structural improvements (van Geert 1994).

Whereas child development has been heavily studied and remains controversial, the development of young adults has been less examined, partly because of an assumption that once formal operational thinking, say, has been established in late adolescence, development stops. A consequence is that our understanding of development and progression in the undergraduate years is not as well-related to research as, for example, it is in science in early adolescence (Adey and Shayer 1994). In Figure 10.1 we identify eight inter-related lines of thought about adult development. Others could be added. Our aim here is not completeness; rather, it is to make the point that different accounts of progression have quite different curriculum and assessment implications.

Progression is personal

In programmes such as modular schemes, in which the student has choice as to the study units followed, development in the subject disciplines may be less structured than in a single-subject programme, as that choice is exercised. A degree programme, Richards observed,[4]

> is not a matter of initiation into a well-defined intellectual and social space, but is a series of encounters with an increasingly wide range of discourses, techniques and people. The administrative groupings needed to give students a home base . . . may still be tied to subject disciplines or intellectual areas, but cannot have the circumscribing effects on students' outlooks which tend to be exercised by traditional departments.
>
> (Richards 1993: 10)

The implication is that, to some extent, development in respect of knowledge and understanding has to be interpreted from the perspective of the learner. Robertson (1993) developed the student-centred perspective. Pointing out that the 'supply-side' definition of learning needs was being challenged by the introduction of credit accumulation systems coupled with modular programmes, he wrote:

> . . . it is likely that students-as-learners will be invited to exercise substantially greater control over definitions of personal learning needs, less constrained by the historic judgements of their academic tutors.
>
> (Robertson 1993: 73)

This has important consequences for assessment, since if students exercise significant choice in respect of their learning programmes they are to some extent

From	To	Comment
1. Understanding of simple substantive concepts	Understanding of complex substantive concepts	These are common views of progression, especially in well-ordered, cumulative subjects, such as the natural sciences. Some doubt whether this logic of epistemology matches psychological reality (Hoyles 1990). Others note that problem-based learning programmes challenge it
2. Little sense of the nature and structure of the subject	Epistemological awareness	
3. Low-level intellectual operations	High-level intellectual operations, with an emphasis on metacognition	Commonly associated with Bloom's *Taxonomy* – often in ignorance of the work itself (Anderson and Sosniak 1994). The new version (Anderson and Krathwohl 2001) *is* worth taking seriously, though
4. Reception and repetition of information	Application of understanding	Most clearly seen in programmes that require students to do a final-year project or *practicum*
5. Working on 'tame', well-defined problems set by teachers, often with help from others	Working 'in the wild' and with a high degree of autonomy over inquiry methods and, sometimes, inquiry topics	The idea that development involves working with less scaffolding and more autonomously is taken from Vygotsky. The implied distinction between problem-solving and problem-*working* is less commonly appreciated (Boud and Feletti 1997)
6. Slow, stepwise approach to problems	Fast, automated approaches to problems, drawing on cases-in-memory and intuition	One form of expertise is working faster and more automatedly. Eraut (1994) shows that experts do not usually address problems in the stepwise manner that novices are taught
7. Emphasis on IQ	Development of practical intelligence	Two things are involved here. One is the displacement of an 'entity theory' that holds that one is born smart or not and that achievement is conditional on being smart. The other is the development in many programmes, especially professional ones, of an ability to act wisely
8. Development of a stronger sense of self		We include here the work of Kohlberg (1964) on the development of moral reasoning, and Perry on ethical and intellectual development (1998/1970). We note that Kohlberg's taxonomy is not reckoned to be secure (Moshman 1999)

Figure 10.1   Some trajectories in adult development that are relevant to higher education

undercutting the disciplinary rock on which traditional academic standards have been founded – the notion of standards changes when multidisciplinarity replaces monodisciplinarity. 'Multidisciplinary students' are having to draw upon knowledge and understanding from a range of disciplines in a way that their monodisciplinary peers probably do not. So some of the 'standard' that they reach derives from the *integration* of what they learned. A lack of immersion in the subject might mean that multidisciplinary students would not do as well in that subject as their monodisciplinary peers. The question then arises as to whether the algorithm for the grading of the overall award (if this is computed) contains an inherent bias against the multidisciplinary student.

Students will need (perhaps, want) to develop in different ways, reflecting their varied starting points. In other language, the 'value added' – conceptually, the gain made by the student – by engaging in higher education will vary amongst students even where they are enrolled on the same programme. For example, the profile of students embarking on a first degree in the UK is very varied. The norm is often taken to be the school leaver with a clutch of A-level examination results. However, many students enter on the basis of vocational qualifications gained through further education colleges, or as a consequence of success on access courses run in these institutions. Yet others who have gained the necessary qualifications whilst at school enter higher education after a break, perhaps to make a significant career change, or perhaps to bolster their self-esteem. Cutting across these variables is that of social class, and the need for some students to move towards the acquisition of a level of cultural capital that is already possessed by others.

Moreover, there is an issue where students are faced with learning in a second language, as is the case with some communities in the UK. In Australia, the student body includes many from other Pacific Rim countries, which brings in its train the issue of learning in English as a second language. In the USA, the growth in the use of Spanish in some southern states due to a rise in the Hispanic population has implications for student learning where resources exist in English. Many students, then, are implicitly adding the study of a language to their formal academic studies.

The development of autonomy

In general, academics are more attuned to the structure and progression of their subject discipline than to conceptions of student development. We noted in Chapter 3 that writers on student development have in common a conception of development running from acquiescence to autonomy. It is surprising, therefore, that this line of thinking figures so little – even implicitly – in higher education curricula. However, the Framework for Higher Education Qualifications in England, Wales and Northern Ireland (QAA 2001c) hints at their relevance when outlining its expectations regarding students performance *outside the realm of their particular subject discipline(s)*. Table 10.1 hints at a movement from acquiescence to autonomy as students progress through to a bachelor's degree with honours (and there is further movement as they progress through the master's degree to the doctoral level). The movement was more pronounced in an earlier draft of the Framework (QAA

Table 10.1 The expectations, relating to qualities and skills outside the subject discipline, stated for the first three levels of the Framework for Higher Education Qualifications in England, Wales and Northern Ireland

Level in FHEQ	Description and approximate duration	Expectation (emphases added)
C (Certificate)	Certificate of Higher Education (1 year's full-time study)	. . . qualities and transferable skills necessary for employment requiring *the exercise of some personal responsibility*
I (Intermediate)	Bachelor's degree without honours (2 years' full-time study)	. . . qualities and transferable skills necessary for employment requiring *the exercise of personal responsibility and decision-making*
H (Honours)	Bachelor's degree with honours (3–4 years' full-time study)	. . . qualities and transferable skills necessary for employment requiring: the exercise of initiative and personal responsibility; decision-making in complex and unpredictable contexts; and the learning ability needed to undertake appropriate further training of a professional or equivalent nature

2000b)[5] in which, at the first level (Certificate), it added that the criteria for decision-making were largely set by superiors.

However, the development of autonomy, as with other developments, is often not ordered as tidily as the Framework suggests it might be. For one thing, the Framework implicitly assumes that entrants will be school leavers continuing an educational trajectory. Those who enter higher education after a break in which they have engaged with the world in one way or another may have developed qualities and skilful practices appropriate to employment: their needs on entry may be markedly different from those of an 18-year-old.

Secondly, recall that, even for 18-year-olds, development is rarely linear. People often have to go back to relearn things they have not kept refreshed through practice. Learning in one area may be considerably advanced compared with that in another.

Thirdly, 'development' can be resisted. Perry (1998/1970) identifies three alternatives to growth, which are of increasing severity: 'temporizing', 'retreat' and 'escape'.

Fourthly, there is ambiguity in the meanings to be inferred from the terminology of the Framework. The phrases used offer the interpreter considerable latitude, almost to the point of Humpty Dumpty's contention that 'When *I* use a word . . . it means just what I choose it to mean – neither more nor less'.[6] Wolf's (1995b) study of the way in which precepts of the UK NVQ specifications were understood by teachers in further education showed that exemplars of practice were necessary for the intentions of the precepts to be understood.

Moving on

The poet Robert Browning wrote: '. . . a man's reach should exceed his grasp,/Or what's a heaven for?'[7] Vygotsky (1978) made something of a similar point, albeit more prosaically, in his description of the 'zone of proximal development' (ZPD). The ZPD, broadly stated, is the region between the student's existing problem-solving ability and the ability to solve, with help, more complex problems. It implies that a person's current performances can be enhanced with 'scaffolding' (Wood *et al.* 1976; Bruner 1985) and the support of others possessing greater skill. With practice, the new achievements, which have been secured because of the support provided, should become incorporated into the repertoire of things that can be done unaided. The student will develop the ability to operate autonomously in the original ZPD. With more practice, performances will become faster, more accurate and automated. By then the original ZPD no longer exists, and a new ZPD is now available further up the developmental gradient (Figure 10.2). The combination of support and practice ought to lead the student towards the development of independence, and hence move the ZPD up the developmental slope.

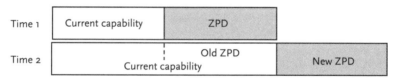

Figure 10.2   The assimilation of the original ZPD into a student's current capability and the development of a new ZPD

There are three key assumptions in operation. The first is that the teacher and programme team have a secure account of that which the ZPD might embrace (i.e. 'what comes next'). The second is closely related. Ausubel put it succinctly in a well-known dictum:

> If I had to reduce all of educational psychology to just one principle, I would say this: The most important single factor influencing learning is what the learner already knows. Ascertain this and teach him [*sic*] accordingly.
>
> (Ausubel 1968: vi)

The third is that students are motivated to exceed their current grasp.

Practical intelligence

There is, here, a connection with the concept of practical intelligence which we introduced in Chapter 3. Sternberg and Grigorenko (2000: 216) suggest that practical intelligence includes the following: recognizing problems; defining problems;

allocating resources to solving problems; mentally representing problems; formulating strategies for solving problems; monitoring solutions of problems; and evaluating solutions of problems. Reviewing the evidence relating to practical and academic intelligence, they conclude that, despite some fluctuation in the detail of the evidence from different studies, these have different trajectories. Academic intelligence tends to reach a peak in a person's early twenties, then declines relatively slowly (and perhaps rapidly later on). Practical intelligence, on the other hand, tends to grow throughout adult life (though it, too, is susceptible to sharp deterioration with senility or if a condition such as Alzheimer's disease strikes). Like expertise, its development is associated with the growth in tacit knowledge and operational competence that is often associated with work placements.

Curriculum design

There is no all-encompassing theory that will underpin either the variety of demands made of a student in higher education, or the diversity of entrants to programmes. The development of students involves too complex a mix for that. Curriculum design is, therefore, necessarily a pragmatic activity. It may be informed by theories from various domains of knowledge, but in the end it has to steer an optimal course through the theoretical swirl whilst taking account of the students who are expected to pursue it. In statistical language, the espoused curriculum is 'the line of best fit' through the data points. A line of best fit implies that some students will be well suited by the programme, but others less well so.

Consideration of curricular coherence and progression has shifted in focus in the UK during the past 30 years or so. Initially, coherence and progression were seen in terms of disciplinary structures – and particularly so in the case of science-based subjects where there was a tradition of building up from basic blocks of learning, analogously to the way that many school chemistry syllabi started with the structure of the atom. This could be represented as a 'supply-side' perspective. In the 1980s, the argument for modular schemes was accepted by the higher education community, and these were introduced with differentiation between 'levels' corresponding to years of full-time enrolment. Progression was thereby inbuilt, but there had been a shift of perspective regarding coherence which was now seen to reside – at least in part – in the mind of the student. To some extent, then, a 'demand-side' perspective could be said to have evolved. As employability has emerged as a major governmental policy concern, the construction of curricula has been shifted back towards the supply side, as institutions have responded. The enhancement of employability requires that 'slow learning' be acknowledged in programme structures, and in the assessment expectations. In the UK, the political interest in employability has caught a tide that was already running in the higher education sector: the interest in programme specifications that had been restimulated by a policy document issued by the QAA (1999).

Coherence becomes a more complicated matter when learning from different areas is combined, such as when the programme is made up from more than one subject discipline, when learning from work experience is integrated with academic learning, or when a problem-based curriculum requires a multidisciplinary approach of the kind depicted by Gibbons *et al.* (1994).

Whereas coherence is, to some extent, a matter for the individual learner in curricula of all kinds (although the extent will vary with the nature of the programme), progression can be identified in terms of the learner's capacity to handle different sorts of complexity (see Figure 10.1). For some, complexity will be addressed primarily in terms of subject discipline; for others it will be addressed primarily in terms of the capacity to integrate (justifiably) material from a number of areas of endeavour. This is perhaps another way of approaching the tension between depth and breadth: in order to attain the award sought, the learner has to demonstrate a threshold level of performance, which could be represented by the vector diagram of Figure 10.3.

The closer the student's programme lies towards the 'depth' vector, the greater the discipline-specific content. There is, if the programme has been properly validated, a good fit between each programme component and the programme as a whole. Coherence and progression are almost automatically built in. Assessment – both formative and summative – will tie in with disciplinary norms. Within a discipline there is an accumulated appreciation of what is implied in greater complexity, the kinds of assignment that should be set for students to demonstrate this progressively, and how feedback might be used to enhance students' disciplinary capacities. This is not to suggest that discipline-specific assessment has few problems (as Chapter 2 showed, it has many), but to lead towards the suggestion that it is when the programme vector swings towards breadth that the greater problems are likely to be encountered.

The more the programme is characterized by breadth, the less likely it is that the programme components (or modules) will mesh well – even after validation, since the validation of such programmes is likely to have to make compromises because many modules will be serving a variety of curricular ends. Whereas assessment at the module level can reflect the expected learning outcomes, a programme-wide approach to assessment is more difficult to sustain. Formative and summative assessments will reflect curriculum *parts* (which can be substantial in the case of joint honours degrees). When the aim of fostering employability is made explicit, it

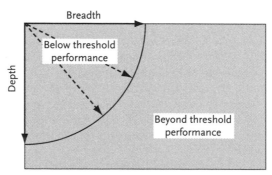

Figure 10.3   Threshold performance as a vector combining breadth and depth in proportions which will vary with the student's programme

swings the vector in Figure 10.3 towards the 'breadth' axis, and hard assessment issues (notably problems in warranting achievement reliably) cannot be avoided.

Assessment and progression

The preceding commentary raises a number of issues that are connected with progression:

- Encouraging learners to move outside their cognitive 'comfort zones' without stressing them to the point of giving up their studies.
- Encouraging deep, rather than surface, learning.
- Encouraging learners to take risks with their learning, and not to play safe.
- Devising assessment procedures that can support progression, even though there are competing views of the concept . . .
- . . . and different starting points amongst learners.
- Recognizing learners' capacity to integrate knowledge from different disciplinary sources (particularly relevant in modularized curricula).
- Valuing 'practical intelligence'.
- Catering for 'slow learning' across a whole programme.
- Supporting the development of autonomy in learners.

These issues, which are interlinked in various ways, return attention to the trajectories listed in Figure 10.1. Rather than treat them as separated, we make some broad comments in response.

There is a need for teachers/assessors to remind themselves from time to time that learners enter higher education with different collections of experience and expertise, and that this has implications for the way that both parties think about progression. If progression is seen in (qualitative) value-added terms, then where the learner starts from is as important as where they end up. It is unlikely that someone entering higher education direct from school will share a developmental trajectory with someone entering after a period in full-time employment: their learning needs and their stressors will probably differ. Progression, for these two individuals, is likely to look very different. Most study units make implicit assumptions of commonality regarding students' cognitive starting points, and the assessments at the end are, to a first approximation, homogeneous. Some students will fit the prescribed curricular model (and the associated assessment demands) quite well, others less so. Further, whilst the learner may exhibit a generally positive developmental gradient, there are times when they may temporarily regress.

A progressive or developmental curriculum needs to emphasize 'learning', as opposed to 'performance' goals. Unless there is a strong contribution to student learning via formative assessment, there is a real risk that students will decode the tacit message regarding assessment in terms of performance, rather than of learning, in their study units. This could lead them to use surface learning approaches, to limit their attention to the listed learning outcomes, and to avoid divergence and risk-taking in their learning. They may do well on summative assessments, but this success could be relatively short-term. The potential problems will be mitigated where the learning engagements incorporate opportunities for formative assessment: the use of 'transmission' teaching sessions should be limited and judicious.

Integration of material from more than a single discipline is often supported by 'capstone' assignments, projects and dissertations which are usually to be found in final-year undergraduate study. Problem-based learning (PBL), now widely used in medicine and spreading into other disciplines such as engineering, requires integration from the start, and also exploits the potential of the approach to develop 'soft skills' such as teamworking. The assessment of groupwork in PBL and elsewhere is acknowledged as problematic where individuals have to be graded: arguments abound regarding the respective merits of differentiating individuals' performances and of awarding the same mark to each group member.

Problem-working, in the institution or in a work placement, offers particular opportunities for the integration of understandings from different disciplines and for the development and demonstration of practical intelligence. It also has the potential to contribute to the development of autonomy, as do any assessment demands that require the student to do more than repeat the knowledge and practices of others. Autonomy, for those learners who have yet to develop it, is one of the characteristics that could be subsumed under 'slow learning'. This is where a whole-programme perspective – the longer assessment view – has value, since it can establish in broad terms the kind of developmental trajectory that is featured in Table 10.1. We note, again, the value of cognitive 'scaffolding' and its progressive removal, and the desirability of presenting assessment tasks of progressively greater scope and/or complexity as the curriculum is followed through.

There is an unavoidable tension between two educational desires: the legitimizing of the individual developmental growth and the need to certify that the learner has reached the standard expected in respect of the sought award. Where external accreditation (such as that of a professional body) is an issue, the balance lies towards the second. However, there are many curricula where 'degree-worthy performance' (say) can be identified in a variety of configurations *without compromising on the overall standard of attainment* – a point we elaborate in Chapter 11. There is, however, a real difficulty when a complex, multidimensional performance has to be captured in a single grading, such as a grade-point average (GPA) or an honours degree classification.

The multidimensionality of employability

The multidimensionality of employability is illustrated in Box 10.1, which reproduces 39 aspects of employability that were identified pragmatically, and in addition to discipline-specific achievements, in the Skills *plus* project. The point here is not the precise number of aspects of employability – a case can be made for coalescing some, or for adding others such as managing in an ethnically diverse work environment – but the sheer complexity of employability and, implicitly, the difficulty of grading (summatively) learners' performances.

It was noted earlier that learners will be unlikely to develop evenly across such a broad front. Some aspects might not be fully covered during the learner's time in

Box 10.1   Aspects of employability

The acquisition of disciplinary understanding and skills is assumed: note that their application is listed at 30.

A. PERSONAL QUALITIES

1. **Malleable self-theory**: belief that attributes (e.g. intelligence) are not fixed and can be developed.
2. **Self-awareness**: awareness of own strengths and weaknesses, aims and values.
3. **Self-confidence**: confidence in dealing with the challenges that employment and life throw up.
4. **Independence**: ability to work without supervision.
5. **Emotional intelligence**: sensitivity to others' emotions and the effects that they can have.
6. **Adaptability**: ability to respond positively to changing circumstances and new challenges.
7. **Stress tolerance**: ability to retain effectiveness under pressure.
8. **Initiative**: ability to take action unprompted.
9. **Willingness to learn**: commitment to ongoing learning to meet the needs of employment and life.
10. **Reflectiveness**: the disposition to reflect evaluatively on the performance of oneself and others.

B. CORE SKILLS

11. **Reading effectiveness**: the recognition and retention of key points.
12. **Numeracy**: ability to use numbers at an appropriate level of accuracy.
13. **Information retrieval**: ability to access different sources.
14. **Language skills**: possession of more than a single language.
15. **Self-management**: ability to work in an efficient and structured manner.
16. **Critical analysis**: ability to 'deconstruct' a problem or situation.
17. **Creativity**: ability to be original or inventive and to apply lateral thinking.
18. **Listening**: focused attention in which key points are recognized.
19. **Written communication**: clear reports, letters etc. written specifically for the reader.
20. **Oral presentations**: clear and confident presentation of information to a group (see also 21, 35).
21. **Explaining**: orally and in writing (see also 20, 35).
22. **Global awareness**: in terms both of cultures and of economics.

Box 10.1   continued

C. PROCESS SKILLS

23. **Computer literacy**: ability to use a range of software.
24. **Commercial awareness**: understanding of business issues and priorities.
25. **Political sensitivity**: appreciates how organizations work and acts accordingly.
26. **Ability to work cross-culturally**: both within and beyond the UK.
27. **Ethical sensitivity**: appreciates ethical aspects of employment and acts accordingly.
28. **Prioritizing**: ability to rank tasks according to importance.
29. **Planning**: setting of achievable goals and structuring action.
30. **Applying subject understanding**: use of disciplinary understanding from the higher education programme.
31. **Acting morally**: has a moral code and acts accordingly.
32. **Coping with ambiguity and complexity**: ability to handle ambiguous and complex situations.
33. **Problem-solving**: selection and use of appropriate methods to find solutions.
34. **Influencing**: convincing others of the validity of one's point of view.
35. **Arguing for and/or justifying a point of view or a course of action** (see also 20, 21).
36. **Resolving conflict**: both intrapersonally and in relationships with others.
37. **Decision making**: choice of the best option from a range of alternatives.
38. **Negotiating**: discussion to achieve mutually satisfactory resolution of contentious issues.
39. **Teamwork**: can work constructively with others on a common task.

---

higher education, which may or may not be a matter of importance. It was also recognized that there are likely to be further problems stemming from assessors' lack of depth in understanding what standards of performance should be accepted, and so on. The Skills *plus* project concluded that, if progress was to be made in encouraging employability throughout a programme, then, especially in highly modularized programmes, it is necessary to look away from summative assessment practices with their often unrealistic demands for reliability, and towards other ways of providing developmental feedback and helping students to make claims to achievements. This theme is introduced here and continued in the next chapter.

It also became appreciated that assessment arrangements could be more considerate of beginning students. The initial demands of higher education are difficult for many students (especially those who have a limited amount of cultural capital or who have entered higher education by a route other than the tradi-tional[8]). From the perspective of learning (and also from that of student retention), it is desirable for institutions to allow students time to make the transition to higher education. This has implications for the assessment process. Summative and 'route-critical' assessments early on may result in failure that would not have happened had the student had longer to make the transition. The consequence, particularly in semesterized modular schemes, is often 'failing and trailing' of modules – which places an extra burden on those who are struggling hardest to come to terms with the expectations laid upon them.

Some departments may need to have summative assessments early on, but the weightings for these assessments can be sufficiently low that a poor performance at this stage can be redeemed without unnecessary difficulty by the end of the module, or even year. The first summative assessment in a module could, for example, be weighted at zero, as happens in at least one institution: the student *must* undertake the assignment, but the emphasis is on the learning that can be derived from the performance (in Chapter 2 we referred to this as 'ticketing'). The key point we make here is the need to be creative in balancing the needs of the students with those of the institution and (where relevant) external interests.

A department is for ever having to juggle in order to make the best use of the resources available to it. Attention has to be given to resourcing the whole curric-ulum, of which assessment forms an important part. The corollary is that assess-ment should not be considered in isolation, perhaps as a separate, concluding component of a study unit. Instead, a 'whole curriculum' perspective (one fairly radical version of which is the 'capability envelope' described in Chapter 7) offers the department the opportunity to reflect on the balance of learning activities and summative assessment, and also what the most effective and efficient learning activ-ities are likely to be. In a time of constrained resources, and where the cost of academic staff is high, it makes obvious sense to optimize the way in which staff are deployed.

Rebalancing of resources is not to be undertaken lightly, and the implications could be of quite radical change. The change could be too great for a single leap, but a department with a commitment to enhancement might achieve it incre-mentally through reflection on its practices. Knight and Trowler (2001, esp. 91ff) offer a number of prompts towards reflection. Amongst their suggestions are the following.

- Assessment audits, examining matters such as the way in which the various demands on students build progressively (or do not), whether the assessment methods used exhibit adequate variety, and the balance between formative and summative assessment.
- Looking at the feedback that students are given, and the use to which this is put, from the point of view of asking, 'Is the feedback system effective (and, if not, what can be done to improve it)?'
- Organizing professional development sessions on the theme of assessment, from the perspective of the discipline, drawing in expertise from outside the department where necessary.

- Networking with other departments and benchmarking through a mutual commitment to improving practice (Yorke (2000b: 68) refers to this as 'developmental benchmarking' in marked contrast to compliance-oriented 'regulatory benchmarking'[9]).

A further point which might be added to their list is:

- Checking whether, in the various programmes run by (or supported by) the department, the assessment demands are broadly comparable.

Identifying and recording progress

Many 'graduate jobs' require the graduate employee to draw on a wide range of academic and practical learning, even when they have focused their studies on a single discipline. If growth in the graduate job were construed in terms of depth and breadth as in Figure 10.3, it is quite likely to veer towards the 'breadth' axis of the figure as the employee develops. There are many in employment who have made the transition from subject specialist to a more broadly based engagement: switching into a managerial role is a typical example. It is often left to the individual in employment to make sense of what they experience, and to engage in self-evaluation regarding their performance. If, in the interest of enhancing employability, the curriculum is to foster abilities on the lines delineated in Box 10.1, it follows that the individual should be encouraged through appropriate curricular expectations to be reflective regarding their past performance, during their current performance, and for their future performance. Learning logs and portfolios are the kinds of vehicle through which progress(ion) can be charted. More than many ways of assessing the learner's performance, they offer to the learner the prospect of a positive spin-off: in Boud's (1995) terms, they have 'consequential validity'.

The *Report of the Steering Group* charged with reviewing the national record of achievement (NRA) in the UK, noting that self-management would be a key capacity, went on to point to the need for continuing self-development:

> In the place of a one-off preparation for employment, which many expected to last a lifetime, we need to encourage the idea of continuous qualifying, a more flexible approach in which continuing, rather than completing, our learning becomes the norm.
>
> This changing world will thus place much greater emphasis on individuals taking responsibility for reflecting on what they have already experienced, setting future learning goals and preparing plans for how these will be achieved in order to improve their contribution and their employability.
>
> (Steering Group for the NRA Review 1997: paras 1.9, 1.10)

Reflection is at the heart of personal development planning (PDP).[10] PDP involves the learner in reviewing achievements to date, identifying new learning needs and making plans to meet the identified needs. The outcomes of cycles of activity of this sort are to be recorded in progress files, which may encompass the production of a portfolio of achievements which can be drawn upon for a range of purposes.

The relationship of PDP to part-time study is problematical, since part-time students will often engage in higher education for reasons that differ from those of their full-time peers – for example, seeking discipline-based achievements to set alongside more general employability-related achievements that they already have to their names.

As Box 10.2 indicates, PDP activity can take a variety of forms.

Whichever model is adopted, there are five key issues that have to be addressed if PDP is to deliver the anticipated benefits:

- The curriculum design has to be coherent with the notion of PDP.
- Staff have to be willing to assist the PDP process to work.
- The level of guidance to learners has to be adequate.
- The support provision has to be coordinated.
- The learners have to believe that their engagement in PDP will be worthwhile.

The first four issues offer some formidable challenges that cannot be discussed in detail here. Suffice it to say that the first requires thoughtful design. The second cannot be taken for granted, since many academic staff will feel a greater allegiance to their subject discipline than to something that might be perceived as general. The third and fourth are clearly related. Many learners will need quite a lot of guidance as to what PDP will imply for them in higher education – for example, in identifying reasonable targets – especially if their previous education has not given them any experience of this kind of activity. Since the range of potential targets is wide, individual members of staff may not possess all of the expertise needed by the learner. A coordinated approach is needed to deal with such circumstances, which poses obvious logistical problems.

From the point of view of assessment, the fifth is critically important. If learners construe PDP as non-essential then, with other things competing for their attention, they will not engage meaningfully with it. Although students' transcripts will be able to show whether they have participated in PDP, experience in the school sector suggests that this will not be enough. Another tack is to integrate PDP into the awards made by higher education but, given the assessment difficulties and cost, this is unlikely to be workable in practice. The most promising approach is to design PDP into programmes so that reflection and claims-making are integral parts of learning, as they are at Alverno College, for example. However, few universities or colleges are constructing their programmes along such integrated lines.

One way in which the attractiveness of PDP may be enhanced is to see it in terms of a process of developing and updating a curriculum vitae. The point of the exercise could be set out at the beginning of the programme and a 'progress check' made at the end of the first year of full-time study. The second year might give greater emphasis to drawing material together since soon after the end of that year many students will be wanting to test the labour market. Making the major effort in the final year may be to leave it too late for maximum benefit, not least because students are likely to be engaged in final-year projects and in preparation for final examinations. Given a clear (instrumental) purpose such as this, PDP might obtain a greater degree of acceptance than if it is seen as a mere chore.

The discussion of PDP and of the progressive enhancement of the complex

Box 10.2 Models for personal development planning

PDP model	Description	Comment	Provider roles	Examples	Implications
A. Additive	Separate guidance, skill-building and portfolio-making modules available to students. Level 1 provision likely to be compulsory, optional thereafter. Usually offered university- or faculty-wide	Convenient for institutions but (a) students tend not to opt into things, (b) there is little educational justification for additive models which imply that complex learning outcomes can be achieved through short, separate provision	Enthusiasts can offer modules without getting bogged down in negotiations with other colleagues. May work well as a part of the personal tutor system	PADSHE (Nottingham), York Award, Essex Skills Award	Strengthen personal tutor or other pastoral system. Develop, staff and publicize free-standing option.
B. Integrative – making the implicit explicit to create 'knowing students'	Guidance, skill-building and portfolio-making modules or other sequences are designed into a programme of study. Level 1 provision likely to be compulsory; less likely at levels 2 and 3	The integrated design is a major advance on model A, especially if guidance, careers and teaching staff have jointly planned the sequence. But students tend not to opt into things	This implies that the key colleagues will be programme teams who will negotiate with other groups to achieve adequate provision	Lancaster BA (Educational Studies), Universities of Surrey and Leeds	Workable and reasonably affordable. Harder to do in highly modularized, high-choice programmes

Box 10.2 continued

PDP *model*	*Description*	*Comment*	*Provider roles*	*Examples*	*Implications*
C. Integrative – as above but reinforced through the curriculum	There is a scheduled pattern of PDP activity throughout the programme and, if it is not compulsory, it is certainly treated as very important. The PDP framework is tailored to reflect the learning outcomes valued in particular programmes	This is probably the ideal. Difficult to design, although easier when new programmes are being devised than when it is a case of reworking established programmes. Harder with highly modularized, high-choice programmes	Programme team orchestrates an all-through programme involving carers and guidance colleagues in the design and delivery of the programme	Alverno, some foundation degrees, Lancaster Learning Sciences and Technology BSc, Newcastle (medicine), Luton	Demands a more integrative approach to curriculum design than has been usual
D. A personal curriculum	Rather than PDP centring on a coherent programme, this proposes that students use the PDP process to make sense of and integrate the learning choices they have made	Preserves student choice and flexibility. Depends on individual tutor–(employer) student–(employer) negotiation, which may not be affordable outside of premium rate programmes and courses. Hard to see how it could be compulsory (as in C) – might degenerate into A	Not clear who would take the lead here. Those staff negotiating with students and employers would need to be good on curriculum, guidance and employment issues	Ufi learning through work scheme	Demands skilled staff and resources to support an individualized process

achievements that make for employability raises again fundamental issues, such as the purposes of higher education and the role that assessment plays in determining what learners actually commit themselves to doing. Broadfoot, although coming at these issues more from the standpoint of school education, comments in terms that are relevant to higher education:

> Existing approaches to assessment are almost exclusively concerned with explicit learning, with measuring what has been consciously learned and reproduced in a formal setting. However the goals of learning are likely in the future to centre increasingly on the acquisition of attitudes, skills, and personal qualities since the acquisition of knowledge, formerly the core of the curriculum, is likely to become more irrelevant by its universal availability at the push of a button. It is the ability to know what knowledge is needed, to know how to look for it and to be able to apply it, that is likely to become central.
>
> (Broadfoot 2000: 212)

She questions traditional approaches to assessment, concerned that these have drawn attention away from aspects of learning that are valuable. The more that the focus turns to individuals and their progression, the stronger the pressure to rethink the role of assessment in higher education.

Notes

1. UK institutions typically distinguish between Part 1, the first year of full-time undergraduate study which, if passed, qualifies the student (full-time or part-time) to enter the rest of the programme (Part 2). Some differentiate Part 2 into distinct levels, whereas others do not. For part-time study the year/level connection is necessarily less clear cut – in the Open University students can move between levels as they choose.
2. A separate framework document was subsequently issued in respect of Scotland, whose higher education system differs from those of England, Wales and Northern Ireland (see www.qaa.ac.uk).
3. In the UK there were 1482 student suicides in further and higher education during the 1990s (UUK 2002: 9). The proportion attributable to personal perturbation deriving from the changed educational environment is unknown.
4. Richards was, at the time of writing, on the staff of the University of East London which had a strong commitment to degree programmes based on independent study.
5. See www.qaa.ac.uk/crntwork/nqf/pospaper/contents_textonly.htm (accessed 22 January 2003).
6. Lewis Carroll, *Through the Looking Glass*, chapter 6.
7. In the poem *Andrea del Sarto* (1855), lines 97–8.
8. In England, Wales and Northern Ireland, the traditional entry route is via A-levels; in Scotland, via Scottish Highers.
9. A variety of approaches to benchmarking can be found in Jackson and Lund (2000).
10. PDP may not be a familiar term outside the UK and there may be no requirement elsewhere for PDP to be required of students. However, there is increasing international interest in portfolios as a means to stimulate development and record achievement and it is clear that systematic reflection, whether it is called PDP or not, is involved (Cambridge 2001).

11

Claims-making

The complexity of standards

The argument has been built that whereas universities and colleges may choose to warrant some achievements, students will have to establish their own claims to others. Before addressing the ways in which this might be done, it is necessary to consider the standards to which both warrants and claims refer.

Standards in higher education are complex. It is relatively straightforward (although not as straightforward as some believe) to identify standards for some educational activities, whether academic or vocational: for example, competence in grammar or arithmetic, or – where there is greater potential hazard to life – competence in the repair of faulty electrical equipment or in driving a motor vehicle. However, standards in many higher education activities reflect the integration of knowledge, understanding and skills.

The complexity of standards allows commentators to be selective in the evidence they use – one has only to note the annual arguments in the UK about school standards to appreciate the way in which modest rises in pass rates are treated as signalling either rising standards of attainment in the school population or the consequences of setting the criterion grades at lower levels. A similar argument is made with respect to first degrees in the UK. Whilst there was a rise in the modal honours degree classification over the period 1973–1993 (largely in the then university sector, before the removal of the binary distinction with the polytechnics) (HEQC 1996), the overall rise has latterly been more modest. However, that overall rise has masked considerable variation between subject areas, with the trend in some being essentially 'flat' whereas in others it is quite steeply upward (Yorke 2002a).

Relatively little analysis has been undertaken into what the subject area is requiring nowadays of students. An exception is the investigation by Kahn and Hoyles (1997) of the single honours degree in mathematics which showed that the level of demand of the content had declined, and that there was a trend away from pure to applied mathematics. These authors concluded that there were 'pointers to an overall reduction in rigour and abstraction' (Kahn and Hoyles 1997: 355). It has to be stressed that the study was centred on mathematics, and that little allusion was made to the broader expectations laid upon higher education. What cannot be inferred, therefore, is the extent to which the reduction in rigour and abstraction is counterbalanced by the giving of attention to the broader, more generic skills that could be expected to be of value to students in the labour market and elsewhere.

The tension between commonality and individuality

Assessment in higher education has to reconcile a tension between a desire for demonstrable commonality of standards and the need to accommodate the learning achieved by individual students. National quality assurance systems have a particular interest in assuring their publics that awards reflect students' merits and cannot be gained by dubious methods: the strong concern in some countries is that awards should reflect broadly comparable performances. Whilst broad commonality would be an advantage to employers, there is a belief amongst some that graduates from particular institutions are, *ceteris paribus*, more suitable for their needs (Hesketh 2000). Further, and as we have noted earlier, the preferences of employers often include achievements that are difficult to pin down in marks and grades – employers are interested in what the individual is able to claim, often over and above the possession of a degree (Brown *et al.* 2002).

Shaw (1996) reported that some institutions with commitments to 'capability' (see Chapter 1 and Stephenson (1998)) were nevertheless stronger on the rhetoric of capability than they were in actually developing appropriate methods of assessment for it. Given what was said in Chapter 2, this is not surprising. However, if employability is to be taken seriously as an aim of higher education, it is necessary to think about assessment methodologies that can make reasonable claim to capture it: we suggest in this chapter that 'claims-making' can make a useful contribution.

'Graduateness'

In the UK the drive towards formalizing a commonality of standards followed a visit by the then Minister for Higher Education to east Asia in the early 1990s, where it was impressed on him that there was no single 'gold standard' of the UK honours degree despite the official protestations that it existed. The erstwhile Higher Education Quality Council (HEQC) was subsequently asked to investigate the issue and in 1997 issued the final report of its Graduate Standards Programme (HEQC 1997). This report drew attention to the many aspects of 'graduateness' which, in pilot work, it summarized in the matrix shown in Figure 11.1.

The Graduate Attributes Profile (GAP) suffers from a number of weaknesses:

- It is an ad hoc compilation that lacks a theoretical underpinning.
- Performances in respect of a number of the attributes are not amenable to grading (and the graded attributes are likely to weigh more heavily in an honours degree classification or a grade-point average).

Subject mastery	Intellectual/ cognitive	Practical	Self/individual	Social/people
Development of knowledge and understanding of:	*Development of the following attributes:*	*Development of the following attributes:*	*Development of the following attributes:*	*Development of the following attributes:*
Subject content and range	Critical reasoning	Investigative skills/methods of inquiry	Independence/ autonomy	Teamwork
Subject paradigms	Analysis	Laboratory skills/fieldcraft	Emotional resilience	Client focus
Subject methodology/ies	Conceptualization	Data/ information processing	Time management	Communication
Subject's conceptual basis	Reflection/ evaluation	Context/textual analysis	Ethical principles and value base	Negotiation/ micropolitics
Subject's limitations and boundaries	Flexibility	Performance skills	Enterprise	Empathy
Subject's relation to other frameworks	Imagination	Creating products	Self-presentation	Social/ environmental impact
Context in which subject is used	Originality	Professional skills	Self-criticism	Networking
	Synthesis	Spatial awareness		Ethical practice

Figure 11.1   The Graduate Attributes Profile (HEQC 1997, vol. 2: 86)

- The 'Self/individual' column probably does not sufficiently emphasize the significance of efficacy beliefs and related matters.
- Metacognition is absent, despite its influence on modern accounts of learning and achievement: it is an important category in Anderson and Krathwohl's (2001) revision of Bloom's (1956) *Taxonomy*, for example.

Further, the GAP indicates that 'graduateness' can be demonstrated in a variety of ways, reflecting different weightings of cells in the matrix. Put another way, the GAP reveals how difficult it is to demonstrate commonality of standards.

On the positive side, the GAP implies the possibility of students negotiating the emphases that they wish to give to their particular degree: a person desiring a career as a researcher, say, might wish to emphasize the subject-specific cells, whereas someone seeking a career requiring a high level of 'people skills' might wish to focus on the last two columns. This leads directly into the theme of this chapter: claims-making.

Towards claims-making

Assignments set for students are rarely unidimensional: instead they typically require students to draw upon a number of attributes from their repertoire. Although students are often provided with lists of the criteria against which their work will be graded (and sometimes with the way in which these criteria will be weighted), there is always a considerable degree of professional judgement on the part of the assessor regarding the standard attained.

The identification of standards is undertaken at a number of levels, which adds further complexity to the argument about what can be accepted as appropriate. In the UK, many institutions organize their undergraduate programmes within a modular framework, and so the issue of standards can be approached at the levels of the individual assignment, the module, the intermediate award[1] and the final award. Whereas an individual assignment may not be regarded as particularly demanding, the *totality* of the collection of demands made upon a student may nevertheless be deemed to be of an appropriate standard.

As regards the totality of a student's performance, most would see threshold standards in terms of achieving acceptable grades on the various components of their programmes, with some compensation being allowable for marginal failure in a few components. It is possible to look at this issue from a different perspective – that of asking whether the degree-seeking student, say, can make a credible claim for graduate status – this would allow students to argue for 'graduateness' on the basis of their profiles of achievement which are always multivalent and can vary according to the student's own purposes and learning trajectory. One student may wish to become a research historian, for instance, and concentrate on forensic analysis of texts, whereas another may be interested in a career in business and concentrate a considerable amount of effort on learning about social interaction in various practical settings. As Figure 11.2 suggests schematically, the two may both be well worthy of an honours degree but for very different weightings of reasons.

Hence a statement that a person has an upper second class honours degree in subject X is not very informative, and could lead the impercipient to read more into

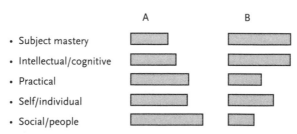

Figure 11.2   A schematic illustration that differing profiles of achievement can be consistent with recognition of graduate status

this than is warranted. An example (from an institution which should have known better) is the appointment, some time ago, of a lecturer in the field of business studies. It was only after the person had joined the institution that it emerged that he was not equipped to teach quantitative methods (a key consideration in the appointment) since his degree had, atypically, not required him to have undertaken any quantitative work. How much better the appointment process would have been had the institution been provided at the outset with a transcript of what the applicant had studied whilst at his university[2] (and, of course, had the institution concerned had the wit to ask the applicant the critical question).

Contrast the above example with that of the selection process adopted by the consultancy and accounting company KPMG, which claims to have received over 8000 applications for 650 vacancies in 2000–01 (Purcell *et al.* 2002). This company acknowledges the need for a profile of the graduate at the commencement of the selection process, in order to filter out those least likely to fit the designated needs. Candidates are asked to profile themselves by completing a questionnaire on screen. Purcell *et al.* comment:

> This provides them with more standardized competency-based data and it also encourages inappropriate candidates to realize that they don't have the qualifications or experience that are required, so to screen themselves out rather than proceed with the application.
>
> (Purcell *et al.* 2002: 10)

Those whose profiles offer the best fit with the company's needs proceed to a challenging series of interviews and assessment centre exercises that are decisive in the appointments.

Self-generated profiles clearly have a place. Some of a graduate's achievements can be signalled through the outcomes of summative assessments, problematic as these may be (Chapter 2). The possession of the 'soft skills' that are valued in the world beyond academe is more difficult for an awarding institution to 'measure' in terms of percentages or grade-points, and to certify. A self-profiling approach, 'claims-making', may have a greater utility.

What is 'claims-making'?

The principle of claims-making is straightforward. The student makes claims against the expectations set for the programme, and justifies these with evidence. Where the curriculum designers decide that claims-making should cover only part of a programme, then the process is limited to that part. Apart from some technical considerations (discussed below), claims-making has one drawback that might disconcert those who are committed to an award that is graded, for it does not lend itself to the apparent precision of overall gradings such as the classification of the UK honours degree or the US grade-point average.

In the UK there has, in recent years, been a recommitment to the programme as the 'unit of analysis' for student performances, and the subordination of the study unit to it. This can be seen in the publication by the QAA of descriptors for levels of award (QAA 2001c) and the agency's advocacy of 'programme specifications'. The latter represents a return to the approach to curriculum that was adopted in the then 'public sector of higher education' (i.e. the polytechnics and colleges) by the Council for National Academic Awards.[3]

The focus on programmes fits well with Claxton's (1998) notion of 'slow learning'. Much that students learn during their time in higher education cannot be 'boxed off' into particular modules: it develops throughout the programme, influenced not only by the overt signals from it, but also by cues and clues picked up in less formal settings (some well beyond the programme's boundaries). Skills such as those of working collaboratively and of constructing an argument (to select two very different examples) are typically developed progressively through the time spent in higher education, and often outside the specified curricular activities. They need to be refined through experience and reflection and, where transfer is expected, in a variety of situations. Providing disconnected, 'bolt-on' modules of, say, study skills is a comparatively weak approach to their development, since the student may 'bracket off' much of the value of the experience on the grounds that the module has been completed.

The more subdivided a student's programme is, the more difficult it is for anyone outside the immediate academic milieu to interpret the student's performance. Transcripts can attest to what the student has studied, and can give a broad assessment of their level of achievement, but can do little in a relatively short document to convey what the student has learned. Nor would the production of a transcript necessarily require the student to reflect on their learning in order to identify where they had strengths, and where weaknesses, so that they could judge where they might contribute in some future activity or employment.

There is a further argument in favour of claims-making. Particularly when the programme is modular, and covering more than a single subject discipline, the only person who can really make sense of the student's performance is the student. The argument can be extended to encompass learning not specifically derived from the programme itself, by adopting an approach analogous to APEL (the accreditation of prior experiential learning), which has proved generally acceptable for the purposes of student entry into higher education. This would allow students to draw on their learning from part-time employment outside the programme, and to offset any lack of breadth in their on-programme learning occasioned by the need to support themselves financially through higher education. (This would swap one kind of learning for another, make a virtue out of what for many students is a necessity, and potentially make some shift in an individual's personal profile. The corollary is that the degree-awarding process would need to recognize the learning that took place outside the programme: some would see such a suggestion as contentious.)

An advantage of the claims-making approach is that its very nature encourages students to be reflective and evaluative about their learning. This coheres, too, with the introduction of progress files and personal development planning into UK higher education. If the student is being encouraged to be self-evaluative and future-oriented, it would be consistent to have an assessment approach that overtly valued these. Osborne *et al.* (1998) note that a student's reflective analysis of performance opens up the assessment process to some self-assessment. Showing how a setback was turned from a potential disaster to advantage in terms of learning, and justifying why certain avenues were not pursued, are examples here.

Claims-making, self-evaluation and self-regulation will probably not come naturally to most students, and will have to be fostered through the curriculum. As Osborne *et al.* (1998) note, and as is further evidenced by McLeman and Smith (1998), some students have difficulty in recognizing what they have achieved and in going beyond presenting in a descriptive narrative what they have recognized about their personal development. Guidelines can help, but for some students they may simply induce a series of point-by-point, checklist-type, responses. The problem may best be attacked at programme level, as is the case at Alverno College in the USA, where self-evaluation and self-regulation are key components of the learning experience. Students at the College do not receive grades for their work, but they are expected to take good note of feedback and learn from it. Mentkowski and Associates (2000) note that older adult learners realized more quickly than their younger classmates that the strongly formative assessment regimen at the College enabled them to judge their progress. One older student (who appears to have come to privilege learning goals over performance goals) wrote:

> But the whole ability thing has been good for me, partially because I feel the competition is with self, and I also don't feel the need to strive for an A. If I'm giving it my best, then, for me, that's enough. . . . I think I get sufficient feedback to know what I'm doing well and what I'm not doing well. I'm more my own measure.
>
> (Mentkowski and Associates 2000: 90)

The claims-making approach shifts the assessment from – at its most extreme – an expectation that the learner will achieve a set of precisely specified outcomes (as in various post-compulsory vocational curricula in the UK and New Zealand), to a post hoc recognition that what they have achieved is consistent with general expectations for the award. The overall assessment challenge is switched from something like, 'Can you do this set of things?', to, 'How have you satisfied, through your work, the aims stated for your particular programme of study?' (Yorke 1998a). The latter challenge, of course, offers the prospect of a greater diversity of acceptable responses.

Claims-making via portfolio

Employability is not an attribute for which detailed criteria can be set up in advance and performances assessed against them.[4] As with 'graduateness', the construct has many components which are expressed with varying amounts of fuzziness. Different people will be 'employable' by virtue of different concatenations of qualities, understanding and skills – just as 'graduateness' is multivalent. The assessments typically used in higher education do not have the scope to cover all the dimensions of employability, and, as argued earlier, it is not sensible to try to pin down all possible components of assessment in advance.

Claims-making can be done through the construction of a portfolio, as we noted in Chapter 7. This is best seen as an organized collection of evidence coupled with claims (and justifications for them) cross-referenced to that evidence. Conceptually, the principle is little different from the production of an empirically grounded research thesis where the argument (i.e. the claims and justifications) appears in the text, but the candidate keeps raw data and other artefacts in a box for the examiners to explore if they should wish. The practice also has similarities with the portfolios produced by academic staff in the UK who are seeking to become accredited as teachers through courses validated by the Institute of Learning and Teaching in Higher Education.[5] A precursor to this form of accreditation was implemented at the Open University, in which applicants had strict limits on what they could submit in their portfolios – with the implication that they had to be very selective in their choice of material to support their claims (Baume and Yorke 2002).

Winter and Maisch (1996: 99ff) make a case for the higher validity of portfolio assessment over the approaches typical of higher education. They note that candidates on the ASSET programme had to organize material effectively and to present it clearly. The challenge was that organization and presentation might be overvalued in relation to the learning achieved and the performances represented (one might be reminded here of politicians' concern with presentation of policy, to the detriment of policy itself). An external examiner commented that

> she thought that what differentiated candidates who had been awarded a high grade was their superior ability to organise a complex *text*, which does not seem, at first, to be central to the criteria of the programme.
>
> (Winter and Maisch 1996: 99, emphasis in original)

Winter and Maisch responded that, if this were the case, it would indeed be an unfortunate displacement of attention: however, the displacement would be higher if the candidates were expected to write an essay on their performance, or to produce conventional coursework. In other words, compared with typical approaches to assessing performance in practice, the relative validity of the portfolio assessment would be higher.

The ASSET programme was set up with competence statements and core assessment criteria (and these are 'tighter' than could be written for a more generalized construct such as 'employability'). The idea was that good practice would generate evidence and commentary much more readily than would poor practice. Hence there would be a strong likelihood that performances in the field and in the production of a portfolio would be correlated.

The issue of authenticity of portfolios was a significant one for Winter and Maisch, since – as would be the case with employability – there was little direct observation of practice. Candidates on the ASSET programme were required to obtain evidence to corroborate their claims, which in turn raises the question of the authenticity of the corroboration. As the authors intimate, there is a limit beyond which one cannot reasonably go in authenticating a student's claims – in the end one is left with the need to take a view on the plausibility of what has been put forward. The more that an assessor can 'triangulate' a claim, the greater can be the confidence placed in it. This comes very close to Hirsch's (1967) qualitatively probabilistic approach to validation in respect of the interpretation of literary texts: the most valid interpretation is that which is most likely to be true (i.e. is the most plausible) on the evidence available.

Validity and reliability

The preceding section points to the need to examine the extent to which traditional psychometric concepts such as validity and reliability can be applied to claims-making. A key question is whether a claims-making portfolio 'tests' what the curriculum designers expect it to 'test' – a matter of 'construct validity'.[6] It is necessary for the curriculum designers to be very clear regarding the assessment purposes the portfolio is intended to serve. Also, the criteria for assessment are necessarily fuzzy, and subject to interpretation by curriculum designers, students and assessors alike. Assessment is unavoidably a matter of professional judgement as to whether the criteria have been met. It is a process that is at least moderately inferential. For the level of inference to be kept as low as possible, it becomes vital that all parties to the assessment have as clear an idea as possible of what is likely to 'count' as success. As we have already noted, it is not enough to state expectations: for these to be maximally understood, they need to be supported by exemplars (as was done in the Open University course described in Baume and Yorke (2002a)). Note that, for most assessment tasks that are non-trivial, it is necessary for the assessor(s) to exercise professional judgement. Even in public examinations at GCSE and A-level, the examination is underpinned by the intersubjective understanding of the panel of examiners (Black and Wiliam 2002).

An issue in portfolio production is whether the portfolio should include only the best work of the student (across the range of outcomes it is expected to cover) or a representative sample. A case can be made for each, and there is no unequivocal 'best buy'. However, if the student is expected to be self-evaluative and reflective, it should be appropriate to include some weaker performances coupled with evidence that the student has learned from them. It is probably not enough simply to say that a performance was not particularly good, and that it could have been improved in such-and-such a way; rather, the student should show that they have developed their practice to a higher level as a result (perhaps in respect of the same expected outcome, or perhaps in relation to another for which the improvement was relevant). Validity, then (and the emphasis is on content validity here), can only be interpreted with reference to the expectations stated for the portfolio. Further, validity is influenced by the extent to which the assessment, or self-judgement, of a portfolio component identifies how innovatory the student's work has been: for example, was it in essence the replication of a well-understood routine or an engagement with something unfamiliar?[7]

Psychometricians also speak of 'concurrent validity', which refers to the extent that the results of a test correlate with those of another, better established, test. Concurrent validity has little relevance to assessment via portfolio, since there is no comparable test to which reference can be made. Further, the portfolio is a derivative of the outcomes of other assessment procedures, and cannot be seen as some kind of parallel form of assessment.

More important for the purposes of this book is the issue of predictive validity. Does the outcome of the assessment predict, even roughly, how the person will perform in life? This is a notoriously difficult problem. Degree outcomes are widely believed to have predictive value, even though the evidence for this is sketchy. Where the 'before' and 'after' realms are closer together, such as A-level and degree performances, the correlations between the two have been consistently low, with the possible exception of science-based subject disciplines, where a moderate relationship has been found.[8] Even with various forms of work-related study incorporated in higher education programmes, the 'realm difference' is probably greater. The conclusion has to be that the use of portfolios may be 'better' in predictive terms than some forms of academic assessment, since it does require the student to be self-aware regarding their personal qualities, skills and understanding – but it cannot generally be taken as strongly predictive. That said, the portfolio (and any preceding progress files kept by the student) provide the student with the raw material from which they can communicate to any prospective employer what they have to offer.

The assessing of portfolios is not without its disagreements, as we demonstrated in Chapter 8. It seems to require some adjustment to standard psychometric concepts such as validity and reliability, along the lines shown in Box 11.1. Some other

---

Box 11.1   Validity and reliability, in the context of claims-making via portfolio.

Concept	Question(s)	Comment
Validity	Does the portfolio cover those outcomes of the programme that it is expected to cover?	It should 'test' what it is supposed to test (construct validity)
	Does it go beyond them: (a) to include evidence from life in general, analogous to the APEL?	As above, if APEL-like evidence is admissible
	(b) to evidence learning that goes beyond what is expected?	Validity as revealing what the tester did not (or could not) know beforehand[1]
	Can the experiences in it be judged to be authentic? And does the compiler adequately justify the authenticity?	Determining authenticity comes down to 'triangulation', and the concept of reasonable plausibility. It is up to the constructor of the profile to be aware of the need for justification and hence to provide suitable evidence[2]
	What evidence is there that this is representative of the student's achievements?	The assessment requirements will have determined whether the student is expected to put forward their best work or a representative sample. In that sense, this is a content validity issue

Box 11.1 continued

Concept	Question(s)	Comment
Consistency (the distinction between validity and reliability gets blurred here)	Is the portfolio internally consistent?	If it is not, then questions as to its validity arise
	Is it consistent with any other assessments?	A hint of concurrent validity here, but the portfolio should draw upon other assessment evidence, as appropriate. Hence this is more of a reliability issue
	What evidence is there that learning is not tied to a particular context?	A hint of content validity here, since the issue will be the narrowness of the experiential base. Multiple contexts hint at greater transfer value and hence at predictive validity
Reliability	Do assessors broadly agree in their judgements regarding the portfolio?	Interassessor reliability can be determined where there is more than a single assessor assessing completely independently (i.e. 'blind')
		Test/retest reliability determination in respect of both profiles and assessors is infeasible
Consequential validity	Boud (1995) defines consequential validity in terms of the positive or negative impacts of the assessment	This can be treated in terms of predictive validity – does the portfolio provide reasonable grounds for inferring that the person can transfer the learning represented in the portfolio to other contexts? More in line with Boud, what is the likelihood that the student has learned something useful as a result of compiling the portfolio?

1. Validity is hardly ever construed in terms of enlightenment, perhaps because testing tends to refer to some preordained criterion or criteria, and hence becomes bounded. Fransella and Adams (1966) provide – perhaps unwittingly – an example of a repertory grid test providing information about an arsonist's rationale for behaviour that broke new ground for the clinician involved. Here the validity of the test can be interpreted in terms of its capacity to reveal what the tester *did not know* at the outset (Yorke 1985: 384).

2. Winter and Maisch (1996: 100ff) document the difficulties that can be experienced in the provision of authenticating evidence.

aspects of portfolios and claims-making that bear on validity with varying amounts of weight are shown in Box 11.2.

The effect of pressure on students' study time

The more that students are under pressure to provide for themselves financially as they follow their programmes of study, the likelier it is that they will be 'strategic' (perhaps a better word is 'instrumental') regarding the way in which they allocate their time. They are likely to have to become skilled at time-management (and those with responsibilities for others will need to develop time-management skills to a high level). This is of significance for employment, yet students do not always appreciate that this counts as an asset.

The specification of learning outcomes, together with the associated assessment requirements and criteria, gives a strong indication of what is necessary to gain an adequate grade. This is an advantage: the student generally has a reasonable amount of information as to the kind of performance that is expected, and so the likelihood of a response that is wildly off-key is relatively low. However, if the time made available for study is limited, the student may well concentrate on the essentials as designated in (or inferred from) the assessment schedule, to the detriment of the wider reading that is held to be desirable in a higher education programme.

The pressure on a student's study time potentially has a more insidious effect. There is an understandable desire on the part of a student to do well in their studies, from the standpoints of both achievement satisfaction and the value of the performance for improving their position in the world. The desirability of getting a good grade militates against the taking of risk. In systems in which performances are cumulated arithmetically, as when grade-point averages or mean percentages are calculated, getting a good score may be the dominant consideration. This, in turn, may encourage students towards the 'performance' or 'mastery' goals described by Dweck (1999), though here the performance is more concerned with getting the grade than with besting peers or with wanting to avoid appearing intellectually weak. 'Learning goals' could be given less attention than they might be under conditions of lesser time constraint. Put in other terms, the pressure on students might tip the balance a little towards surface learning at the expense of deep learning. Lessening the assessment weighting on curricular components and increasing the weighting to overall achievements could help to shift the balance away from surface learning and towards deep learning. Claims-making could make a significant contribution in this regard.

Box 11.2   Some other matters that bear on validity

Aspect	Questions	Comment
Truthfulness	Is the portfolio truly authentic, i.e. is it wholly the student's work, and is it an accurate representation of their learning, or does it contain the unacknowledged work of others, or fictions?	Heywood (2000: 342) provides a reminder of the danger of an assessor not recognizing the support given by others, including teachers. Misrepresentation of a student's experience cannot be picked up with certainty – attention to the actual evidence, and the coherence of the content of the portfolio can mitigate the risk
Learning	Does the portfolio demonstrate the compiler's learning, even from apparent failure? What evidence is there that the student has acted on formative feedback?	Reflective students ought to be able to evidence the reflection in the portfolio, by pointing to the way in which their learning has been influenced by feedback and by the application of self-awareness. Some failures may be turned to positive account (successes even), if the students give evidence that the reasons for the failures are understood, and appropriate remedial action has been undertaken
Usefulness	Does the portfolio contain information that will be useful to the student – and, possibly, to others?	The portfolio ought to act as a 'resource bank' when students are constructing applications for jobs or presenting themselves for interview or in other contexts. It is in those derivative forms that the portfolio will be useful to others, since few will have the time to go through a portfolio in detail
Cost	How is the portfolio process to be afforded?	Assessing portfolios takes time, and implies some redistribution of curricular resources if it is to be done properly
Ethics	Have any sensitive components been dealt with appropriately? If so, how, and how can the reader know?	The need is for students to demonstrate ethical awareness and sensitivity, and to buttress this with evidence. As noted above, with reference to the ASSET programme, there is a limit to the extent that the authenticity of a claim can be pursued

Notes

1. For full-time students, the opportunity often exists to leave with a Certificate in Higher Education after year 1, and a Diploma of Higher Education after year 2. These so-called intermediate awards are, for the students receiving them, sometimes final awards.
2. We note, though, that the claims for the virtue of transcripts need to be treated cautiously. Adelman (1990) found that many transcripts in the USA did not make clear what the students had learned.
3. The CNAA ceased to exist in 1992, and for some time prior to that had operated accreditation at the level of the institution, having begun its work with a strong focus on individual curricula.
4. Holmes (1996) made the point with reference to 'capability'.
5. To be subsumed under the new UK quality enhancement agency.
6. See Cronbach and Meehl (1955) for discussion of different approaches to validity.
7. See Knight (2002c: 282) for notes on this point.
8. See Black and Wiliam (2002) for a recent account.

12

Assessment Systems in Academic Departments

Assessment systems

We need assessment plans to keep track of the diversity that is necessary if assessment is to reach the range of learning intentions that stems from a concern to enhance student employability. By 'plans' we mean all the arrangements that need to be orchestrated if students are to get feedback, including tolerably reliable grades, on the work they do, and if others are to get feedout on students' achievements. We have argued that module assessment plans are necessary but, because employability develops across a programme, then we need *programme* assessment plans. Since assessment plans touch teaching, learning, curriculum, record-keeping, communication and professional development arrangements, we end up thinking about assessment *systems*. We have already identified some of their features – consistency of assessment with programme learning intentions, teaching and learning practices; coherence; progression; differentiation by task, purpose, level and audience; communication; and fitness for purpose. Figure 2.1 in Chapter 2 described six elements of the summative assessment systems that provide feedout. Figure 2.2 did the same for feedback systems.

This coordinated or systemic approach is directly opposite to common ways of dealing with assessment, which have more of a cottage industry feel about them.[1] Although we appreciate that there are countries, subject areas and institutions that think about curriculum in terms of the design of individual modules, rather than in terms of programme architectures, we echo the conclusion reached by Pellegrino *et al.*, who said that

> A multitude of different assessments are already being conducted in schools. It is not surprising that users are often frustrated when such assessments have conflicting achievement goals and results . . . [that] cause much confusion for educators, students and parents. In this section we describe a *coordinated system* of multiple assessments that work together, along with curriculum and instruction, to promote learning.
>
> (Pellegrino *et al.* 2001: 252)

Systemic approaches and coordination are elusive. The practical grounds are apparent to practitioners, but there are less obvious theoretical difficulties. Checkland (1981), the inventor of 'soft systems methodology', argued that the 'hard' systems thinking he learned in industry might have suited the world of matter but did not suit human systems. He said that the systems analyst tackling a problem to do with human systems would have difficulty in deciding what the system was *for* and what it comprised. Furthermore, different participants and stakeholders in the system would be likely to give different answers to those questions. The analyst would also find that even systems that were presumed to be simple could turn out to be an extensive and changing network of connections between people, tools, rules, goals and other systems. Therefore, notwithstanding any inferences that might be drawn from the neatness of Figures 2.1 and 2.2 (Chapter 2), we argue that assessment systems and the others that are contiguous with them, are networks of fluctuating communication – webs of relationships – between the elements under varying conditions. System boundaries are unclear, not least because what can be seen as part of a system depends on the observer, task and context. As with social systems in general (Checkland 1981; Luhmann 1995), assessment systems are 'soft', 'fuzzy' and 'loosely coupled'.

It follows that any definition of an assessment system is just one possible definition, an idea previewed in Table 4.2 (Chapter 4). Consequently, we cannot then think about changing it in the same way as we might change a mechanical system because we do not have the same certainty about what the system is. Nor are we clear about the interactions between elements of the system – indeed, analysts are likely to hear different accounts of what those elements are and how they interact. So, we argue that when it comes to designing new assessment systems, especially systems that have to process the complexities of enhancing student claims to employability, then some established assumptions about curriculum design will need to be displaced (Ganesan *et al.* 2002), with less emphasis on rationally planning to deliver clearly defined learning outcomes and more on coordinating learning opportunities, teaching and assessment practices across a programme in the belief that students who engage with them are more likely[2] to show the sorts of achievements described by the programme's learning intentions.

Not everyone would agree, though, that programmes, departments and higher education institutions need to have assessment systems.

The case against assessment and other systems

As a student, you could go to university in the 1960s and 1970s without being exposed to panoptic assessment systems. Many of us throve on worthwhile material and tasks whilst having enough space to make mistakes and enjoy being at university. We might feel that nowadays things are over-regulated and believe that students learn a lot just from the experience of three or four years at university. In some countries, especially in North America, there are traditions of academic freedom that seem to privilege the module and its teacher against the programme and its team (Bercuson *et al.* 1997).

Unease about assessment systems can stem from more pragmatic concerns. For example, there are analyses suggesting that people do not plan teaching sequences 'rationally', nor do they make decisions in a similar logical and linear way (Clark and Peterson 1986; Weick 1995). We may try to represent the outcomes of their 'unsystematic', somewhat intuitive, creative processes on standard validation forms but we delude ourselves if we imagine that planning proceeds in that way. We might get some impressive assessment systems on paper but there could be questions to ask about the fit with assessment practices.

A second objection is seen in a common response to our view that there are good reasons to grade less and trust formative and low-stakes assessment more. The objection is that, however good our case is, students will not get the message. When generalized, we have the claim that impressive-looking systems are not understood by their participants, and are, at best, paper systems. It is a good point and inescapable. Transmission and understanding (or 'broadcasting' and 'receiving') are different and there are usually slippages between what is planned, what is created and what is understood. The implication is that a carefully planned assessment system may be invisible to students and, more seriously, have no practical effect on assessment, learning and teaching practices. Few higher education institutions are able to sustain the level of coordination needed to ensure that students generally believe that they are working within coherent programme assessment, learning and teaching arrangements. However, the transmission–understanding gap can be narrowed. In our notes on actor network thinking in Chapter 4, we described some of the 'moments' involved and talked about the importance of establishing programme learning cultures. Later in this chapter we will emphasize the importance of communications that highlight the degree of coordination between modules and between learning, teaching, assessment and programme goals.

A third objection is that universities and colleges are intrinsically unsystematic. They are distinguished by their commitment to academic freedom and creativity, their tendency to cell-like architectures, their valuing of collegiality, and their attachment to diverse and sometime contradictory values. They are not managed and systematized but look more like 'organized anarchies'. It might be pleasing to imagine that good managers could align human resource policies; recruitment and communication practices; timetabling; team leadership; and research, teaching and reward structures. The doubt is whether that is realistic. This objection could be extended to most organizations engaged in non-routine, complex business with people as their prime concern – schools, social services, legal practices, health care practices. They are all to some degree 'loosely coupled', which is to say that, unlike the production line – the underlying metaphor in Taylorism, Fordism and managerialism – they are systems where outputs are not directly predictable from inputs and process specifications. 'Command and control strategies' have limited sway because the tasks are complex and cannot be tightly specified in the ways that managerialism needs. The result is that high levels of autonomy have to be delegated to workers who make non-routine decisions about what to do.

These workers – those who teach in higher education – can appear unbiddable in professional matters because they have allegiances to at least three 'communities of practice'[3]: networks of colleagues teaching the same subject elsewhere, connections with others in the university, and participation in a subject department, sub-unit or programme team. These departments, sub-units or teams resonate with the con-tradictions and misunderstandings of the networks within which their members operate and are rippled or riven by the flows of power within them. Yet they have shared tasks to do, they are accountable as groups and they create their own local interpretations of what it is to work as a teacher in higher education. They are the basic organizational unit in higher education institutions and, as owners of the programmes which students follow, they shape the students' learning experiences. Departments and programme teams provide a matrix in which students learn and well-designed programmes can stimulate robust, complex achievements, whereas haphazard arrays of uncoordinated modules leave students with information in bits. A well-designed programme has assessment arrangements that are coherent and which support complex learning intentions. However, academics' different allegiances and complex roles combine to make departmental leadership problem-atical (Knight and Trowler 2001) and there is reason to wonder how often academic staff can be induced to take teaching seriously *and* to do so within a departmental or team approach. This does not mean that we should do nothing. It does suggest that systemic action is difficult and invites us to recognize that we need 'soft systems methodology', not the false certainties of 'hard systems' theory (Checkland and Scholes 1990).

These objections to our claim that good assessment practice needs assessment systems suggest that we should not claim too much for them but, informed by soft systems thinking, see them as sets of arrangements that make certain sorts of outcome more likely. They also imply that communication and the development of a shared learning, assessment and teaching culture are central issues in the design of departmental assessment systems.

Tensions

Assessment systems have two purposes which are not entirely compatible: enhancing learning and warranting achievement. There are other sources of tension.

- Several groups of people – teachers, students, employers, higher education managers – participate in assessment systems. They are not recipients of infor-mation. They create meanings. The more that an assessment system helps participants to share similar meanings, the more useful it ought to be for them. Good systems have plenty of processes and other opportunities that, for example, help employers to appreciate what a 2:1 degree might signify; teachers to realize that some learners understand an argument to be a collection of notes; and students to see why formative assessment matters.

  Different consumers will also create different meanings because they have different purposes. Employers may only need to know that someone is a 'good' graduate. University managers may be happy with a system that translates 'A' or

'First Class' into '6', 'F' or 'Fail' into '1' and in which a mean departmental score of 4.8 is acceptable, with anything below that triggering sanctions. Students, though, need to know what each teacher means by 'an A grade' or by 'an argument'. The more fortunate students will work in departments where tutors' meanings are broadly similar and they use a common language to convey them.

- They are systems for selective communication. A system is a selection from the environment (Luhmann 1995) and assessments are selections of information about the system or elements of it. Consequently, we should be concerned that assessments contain the most important information possible. The meaning of 'important' relates to purpose and audience. Suppose that assessment has two main purposes (to promote learning and to warrant achievement) and four audiences (learners, teachers, higher education managers, employers). Table 12.1 suggests some of the major communicative preoccupations that a good assessment system would have. The tensions are easily seen.

Assessment systems are about *communicating* these selections of information and they can be judged by how well their audiences understand the systems, with their contradictions, their purposes, and the intended meanings of the information they offer. We have suggested that audiences often do not share these understandings.

We also expect that the information is useful and used, which is not always the case. For example, some employers ignore grades from some colleges and universities because they are the 'wrong sort' of institution, or from some groups of graduates because they have particular preferences for age, sex and so on.

- Assessment systems are not tightly coupled but are shot through with 'disrupted meanings'. In higher education, ambiguity is a major feature of the information they generate.

We identified some sources of mis-meaning in the previous point. There are others. For example, however hard we try to explain the relationship between the formative and summative purposes of assessment, they are still two systems that happen to share the same students, courses and programmes. Considerate assessment planning can moderate the ambiguities but not eradicate them. Likewise, teachers can explain what they take to be 'an academic argument' and students may believe they understand it and have acted accordingly, but there will still be mismatches where a student's argument looks like a description to a tutor.

- There are many things that can be done to improve the probabilities that people in assessment systems will create similar sorts of meanings and none that will ensure that they do.

We identify some ways of improving departmental assessment systems later in this chapter and of improving institutional ones in the next. However, some of the evidence that experts may speak the same language and yet still judge differently was reported in Chapter 2, where it was said that the more complex the objects of judgement the greater the likely disagreement. We may hope to reduce the range of disagreements but, as O'Donovan *et al.* (2000) found, even when markers use the same marking grid, differences in understanding and application persist.

Table 12.1   Communication priorities for a simplified assessment system

| | *Purpose* | |
Audience	*To stimulate learning*	*To warrant achievement*
Learners	*Priority*. Getting feedback that really does help students to do better next time	*A common priority*. Getting good grades/marks *Espoused priority*. Good grades, knowing what they signify and getting information about how to do better next time
Teachers	*A common priority*. Teachers identifying student misconceptions and other shortcomings *Espoused priority*. Giving feedback that helps learners to do better	Although teachers spend a lot of time grading, it is not at all clear that they make much use of grades: they are more producers than consumers. We lack evidence of the extent to which teachers are concerned about the meanings that are associated with their marks
Managers	*Priority*. Having trustworthy marks or grades to use in resource allocation decisions and for performance management purposes	*Priority*. Having trustworthy marks or grades to use as evidence of department and institutional achievements
Employers	Employers value complex learning and would certainly agree that anything that promotes it is desirable. They seldom directly intervene to get it	*Priority*. Having trustworthy marks or grades to use as evidence of student achievements

Note: Shaded cells denote non-priorities

- There is no one point of leverage in assessment systems. Power is dispersed and change can hardly be managed.

  Just as there is a tendency to see assessment problems as technical problems (the right method will cure all ills), so there is a tendency to attribute difficulties in making change happen to a lack of power (get the powerful people on-side and change will happen). Ironically, powerful people, such as vice-presidents and pro vice-chancellors, often feel that they do not have the power, and works on leadership are likely to say that their job is to articulate the organization's vision, not to impose one upon it (Birnbaum 1992; Barach and Eckhardt 1996; Leithwood *et al.* 1999).

Assessment system processes

This section looks at departmental assessment systems in terms of component processes, highlighting features that foster assessment practices that have the best chances of communicating useful information about complex achievements.

Making purposes, expectations and demands explicit

Purposes, expectations and demands need to be known by teachers, students and those, such as employers, who are interested in what students understand and can do, not just in the numbers or letters that universities affix to those achievements. We comment here on four areas.

Students and their teachers need to know what assessment is supposed to do in a programme of study, which means understanding the respective roles of activities with formative and summative purposes, as well as the significance of tutor, peer and self-assessment. These distinctions should be mapped on to the ways in which achievements are publicly represented, partly through certification and partly through student claims to achievement supported by evidence which will often be drawn from a portfolio. At first sight this is not an assessment standards issue. Many colleagues have found otherwise because students, especially those who believe that teachers provide the answers and that learning involves stockpiling information, can assume that formative feedback and peer or self-assessment are shabby substitutes for summative tutor grading. Differentiated approaches to assessment invite the charge of low standards unless students, teachers, external examiners and accrediting bodies are helped to see the good sense of the standards that the approaches incorporate.

'Assessment messages' are a way of being explicit about the impact we are trying to make on students with all assessment tasks. Our ideal is that assessment should: provide useful information for improvement; say that achievements are not limited by supposedly fixed attributes such as intelligence; reinforce the value of the meta-cognition–effort combination; and praise real achievements (sham praise is not helpful – Dweck 1999). The standard is that teachers should embody these ideals in their practices and that students should know the ideals and expect them to watermark the assessment tasks within the department's programme of study.

At departmental level it is desirable to have a set of grade indicators that will be used to guide assessment throughout the programme. A history department, for example, would have 'fuzzy' indicators pointing towards typical features of essays of different quality (excellent through to fail), at different levels (entry through to honours level). Other departments have standard grade indicators for other sorts of task – laboratory reports, fieldwork, presentations, exhibitions. Not all elements of the descriptions would be appropriate for all essay tasks, say, but teachers would identify in the task specification those that were likely to be relevant. In the case of tasks such as essays (which often require students to locate and evaluate information, synthesize, analyse, criticize and then express the conclusions in good style), grade descriptors will span several criteria (see Chapter 2). An alternative is to try to develop indicators for each level and grade of each learning outcome. We fear that this can become a long and wearisome exercise that produces unwieldy documents. However it is done, departmental assessment systems need to centre upon some agreed standards so that student learning can be cumulative, rather than the discontinuous experience of unsystematic assessment practices.

Process standards (introduced in Chapter 4) describe the scaffolding associated with the performance so that users of assessment information know if a student succeeded in using industry-standard software to analyse the accounts of a small business with or without a lot of guidance. Following the thrust of Chapter 10, we suggest that process standards be arranged so that students face 'wilder' and more complex tasks and receive less up-front support as they progress through a programme. Students will need to appreciate the reasoning behind this reduction of support, because otherwise some may consider that that it is symptomatic of laziness and slack standards.

Communicating

In Chapter 4 we raised the issue of how judgements could be communicated so that they were useful to outsiders. Employers know that information about degree classes or grades is available. They rarely know what it *means* because transcripts seldom say what the new graduate should understand or be able to do and rarely refer to the process standards associated with these achievements. Some appreciate that the information about achievement they do get is relatively unhelpful[4] but do not understand enough to see where it is unhelpful and how they might make efficient use of alternatives, such as the claims to achievement in a CV and supporting portfolio.

Higher education and government have an interest in helping employers to get more information and have a better sense of what it means, what it cannot signify and how they might go about identifying graduates who are likely to match their job specifications. Reciprocally, higher education needs to understand better what employers want of new graduates. We have suggested that employers and academic staff seem to agree on many of the achievements they would like to associate with higher education and suggest that the problem may be more one of translation than, as is often assumed, of opposed agendas. This can be done through print, face-to-face and consultancy work. Apart from governmental bodies, in the UK there are organizations, such as the Council for Industry and Higher Education, the Higher Education Careers Service Unit, the Careers Research and Advisory Centre, and the Association of Graduate Recruiters that stimulate dialogue, but assessment issues have not been properly explored.

We have repeatedly said that students need to be 'knowing students' who understand the reasoning behind assessment patterns which some may find strange. They will not benefit, for example, if they think that formative assessment is a cue for them to treat the task lightly (and students will tend to treat marginal tasks lightly) and an excuse for teachers to save marking time (and it does save marking time). Under this circumstance of false belief, there is little chance of formative assessment fulfilling its potential. Again, if students do not appreciate the significance of assessment messages about themselves as learners, messages encouraging reflection, metacognitive development and malleable self-theories, then advice in these areas is likely to be screened out as noise that interferes with the 'really important' message, which is carried by a letter or number.

Explanations of 'how we assess round here and why' need to be full and frequent. There is a hope in England that programme specifications, which describe learning intentions and their connections with teaching, learning and assessment arrangements, will be public documents, available on the web. This can contribute to student understanding but there is a case for plenty of reinforcement through placing extracts in all module and stage/level/year handbooks. When it comes to personal development planning and work on portfolios, it is particularly important that students are reminded of what is valued in the programme and that their attention is drawn to the sorts of summative and formative assessment evidence they might use to substantiate their claims to achievement.

Paper and web-based communication are necessary but far from sufficient for helping students to understand what the assessment language and criteria *mean*. Teachers and students alike also need face-to-face conversations about their experiences and expectations of assessment, leading to explorations of the reasoning expressed in the programme's differentiated approach to it. Practical work helps to develop meanings, as when students practise using grade indicators to judge pieces of work, comparing their judgements and reasoning. This is a common seminar exercise which can usefully be repeated several times in the first year and revisited later in the programme. Notice the assumption that the programme has some core or common grade indicators. Notice too that this work lays the foundations of peer assessment, which complements self-assessment and is a preoccupation in the approach to assessment we have been developing in this book, which has been emphasizing assessment as an aid to self-regulated learning.

Then there is communication as feedback on performance. There is evidence that, where the importance of feedback is stressed and appreciated as a contributor to learning and achievement, feedback gets taken seriously by students (Mentkowski and Associates 2000). However, Chanock's (2000) findings may describe a more common situation. Nearly half of his 76 history and politics students did not understand what was meant by tutor calls for more analysis and less description. We suspect that the main problem with tutor feedback is not so much that tutors often clutter it up with comments on second- and third-order points, nor that students skip to the grade and skim the comments, but that we do not create lots of space for learning about assessment purposes, expectations and demands. Had Chanock's students been in a programme that took time to develop peer and self-assessment in the ways we have recommended, they would have been led to understand what 'analysis' meant in that community of practice.

Module evaluations can be used as opportunities to ask students, anonymously, whether they understand the meanings of the programme grade indicators used in the module. Their views show where further conversations are needed.

This section is ostensibly about communication but has reached beyond the transmission of messages to the development of shared understandings and practices. These processes might be variously described as the formation of a learning culture, analysed in terms of actor network thinking and understood as recruitment into a community of practice by participation in its discourse and practices. Whatever the theoretical frame, the point is that assessment systems assume effective communication.

Stimulating learning and teaching

Given our premises that assessment is primarily *for* learning and that assessing shapes learning, this theme can be treated quite sharply. Biggs (1999), the Higher Education Quality Council (HEQC 1996) and the Quality Assurance Agency (QAA 1999) have all commended coherent curricula in which learning, teaching and assessment arrangements dovetail to support the programme's intended outcomes. This invites us to think less of teaching arrangements and assessment arrangements and to consider, instead, the LTAC system, the symbiosis of learning, teaching and assessment in the curriculum. Let us illustrate this by returning to work done by Pellegrino and colleagues. They recommend that

> *Developers of assessment instruments for classroom or large-scale use should pay explicit attention to all three elements of the assessment triangle (cognition, observation and interpretation) and their coordination.* All three elements should be based on modern knowledge of how students learn and how such learning is best measured. Considerable time and effort should be devoted to theory-driven design and validation processes.
>
> (Pellegrino *et al.* 2001: 13, emphasis in original)

Their position is that modern cognitive research is providing accounts of learning that differ quite markedly from assumptions that have traditionally been made. We have used some of these ideas: metacognition, self-theories, the importance of context, progression, slow learning, zone of proximal development and social learning. Assessment practices should, they say, be consistent with these research accounts, directing students' attention to metacognition, say, or to peer assessment, or to tackling task sequences with progressively less scaffolding. 'Observation' refers to the ways in which evidence of achievement is collected and 'interpretation' to ways in which inferences are made. Not only should they be coordinated with the areas highlighted by cognitive research, they too should be founded on good research accounts, as with measurement theory and modern thinking about the provisional and context-related nature of interpretations. Apart from calls for integration of systems with research, there are three main views of how coherence might be achieved. We examine each and add a fourth.

The student constructs coherence

Derived from constructivist psychology, this view, commonly associated with high-choice modular programmes, holds that integration is ultimately done by the student. However, integration is not automatic and we appreciate better now that there are many areas in which people hold disjointed and contradictory ideas. Furthermore, meaning-making can be quite quixotic and may bear scant relationship to the meanings that academic staff might have wished to promote. Students certainly construct coherence but they can be helped to identify the themes and achievements that the programme promotes, as well as those of a more personal nature. The 'participative appropriation' version of constructivism is preferred to an 'anything goes' version.

A focus on assessment

This is a view that coherence comes from programme learning outcomes. Begin by writing programme aims, then objectives. Then imagine assessments which should create information of sufficient reliability and validity for each outcome and its likely audiences. Now sketch variants of those core assessment tasks that would suit students at different stages of the programme. Consider which modules will be offered and begin to associate assessments with them. Taking account of the content and provisional assessment arrangements, devise teaching and learning methods.

Start with the subject area

Here coherence is seen as a property of a subject area. Identify the modules to be taught, always preferring more central topics over more marginal ones. Devise tasks that engage learners with important issues and which represent the subject's characteristic inquiry procedures. Consider how task performance might be judged and arrange assessments accordingly. Identify the outcomes that are therefore likely to be promoted and write the programme specification. Check it against suitable points of reference – subject benchmarks in England, government requirements (as in the case of teacher education, for example), and professional standards. There are often shortfalls. In some cases they arise because some of the learning outcomes listed in benchmark statements are covered by the programme but had not been distinctly highlighted, along with their associated learning, teaching and assessment arrangements. In other cases, there is a gap. One option is to contest the legitimacy of the missing outcomes and another is to look for ways of 'tuning' the plans to accommodate the extra learning goals.

Orchestrate what is already there

'Tune' existing practices to get more harmony. Consider existing programme learning outcomes and extend them if necessary. (It is necessary anyway when policy priorities have changed since the programme was created. The addition of employability as a priority in the UK means many programmes need to extend their declared aims.) Now audit the modules that contribute to the programme to establish whether:

- they provide a sufficient range of teaching and learning activities to stimulate the desired learning;
- assessment arrangements are differentiated enough to support the teaching and learning methods and the goals they are intended to advance;
- some learning, teaching and assessment methods are over- or underused;
- they are distributed across the programme in a pattern that will encourage sustained learning and progression.

When the audits are done, a series of negotiations with colleagues should follow in order to orchestrate these arrangements to encourage symbiosis and growth. In these negotiations it is often useful to refer to a principle advanced by Gibbs and Simpson (2002: 5): 'the trick when designing assessment regimes is to generate engagement with learning tasks without generating piles of marking.'

Use subsequent programme reviews to establish how much coherence students see and fine-tune accordingly.

However coherence is achieved, it is important to make the cohesive principles as explicit as possible to all concerned. Our programmes may stimulate that learning, but it is little credit to us and less use to our students if students are not aware of what it is they understand and can do. Telling them what they are learning, how and why, helps. Conversations help more. Repetition is necessary.

Quality assurance

Quality assurance has been a preoccupation with higher education institutions as, in many countries, they have increasingly been called to account by managers and elected representatives anxious to establish that the public gets value for money (see Harvey (2002) for a review of this external quality monitoring). Good assessment systems are often assumed to generate summative assessment data that are treated as indicators of teacher, departmental and institutional performance. Depressed scores are reckoned to indicate poor teaching. High scores are sometimes allowed to indicate superb teaching but may less charitably be taken as evidence of slipshod standards. This view of good assessment systems is challenged here. With few exceptions, summative assessment data are quite unsuited to this quality assurance purpose because, whilst they may indicate that some things are out of line, they cannot pinpoint the cause, nor do we know whether to attribute the difference to a measurement artefact or to a real learning failure (or success).

Suppose we wanted to know how well a teacher or a department was doing and that assessment was criteria-related. (Norm-referencing is not fit for this purpose.) We might assume that we could compare the marks achieved by students following the teacher's module with the marks gained by students taking other modules. Suppose that we do find a mean difference of a couple of marks. Relatively small differences are not statistically significant until we have quite large numbers of students involved. In this case the difference could just be a chance variation. Even if statistical significance is found, the size of the difference is well within the range of legitimate difference between markers – we have suggested that it is unrealistic to expect pinpoint consensus and that a piece receiving a mark of 68 could plausibly be given 66 or 70: perhaps 64 or 72. For the sake of argument, let us say that the difference between one module and the department mean is quite marked. This does suggest something is going on but we cannot infer that it is poor teaching – in other words, the signal that there is a quality (or, perhaps, standards) issue does not indicate how it is to be addressed. The module might contain material that students find difficult (statistics fox many arts and social science students), or have an unusual assessment pattern (we said earlier that examination marks tend to be lower than coursework marks), or attract atypical students (it might be the timetable alternative to a difficult course that attracts the most poised students), or be marked more severely than other modules (new teachers tend to mark harder than older ones). None of these four explanations points to a teaching deficiency, although there might be one of consistency in marking standards.

When it comes to comparing one department with another in the same institution the main problem is differences in student intake. If we compare just raw exit scores we are not comparing like with like, partly because of differences in the qualifications of students on different programmes. We can make some allowance for variations in entry qualifications, but there is a range of technical problems with 'value-added' calculations (McPherson 1997; Yorke 1998c). More importantly, even if we identify differences between the value-added scores of students graduating from different programmes in the same institution, we have little idea about the causes. For example, there are established national differences in the patterns of exit scores, with some subjects regularly awarding higher grades than others (Yorke *et al.*, 2000b). This is compounded by legitimate variations in assessment practices, with some subjects and departments taking more account of coursework, presentations and other methods associated with higher scores than traditional examinations. Others will be struggling to get students through packed programmes leading to professional qualification and see levels of performance depressed by overwork. The variations that will be found in departments and universities will be attributable to legitimate differences in curriculum aims, organization and operation, as well as to different institutional practices – we remarked earlier that a profile getting an upper second class degree under one institution's combination rules could get a lower second under another's.

There are also limits to the validity of monitoring standards by comparing criteria-referenced exit grades in a department over several years, even using value-added methods. Curricula change ceaselessly and there are usually subtle ways in which the assessment regime experienced by one cohort is different from that experienced by its successor. There will certainly be variations in the difficulty of the summative assessments done by students. Desforges (1989) explains in some detail why this is a doomed enterprise even when working with large numbers of students taking high-reliability public examinations.

The use of assessment data for quality assurance purposes is understandable because managers have to be seen to monitor quality, and assessment data seem, at first sight, to be valid and reliable indicators. However, the data are seldom of the quality required by measurement theory, which means that whilst they can be useful for raising questions, great care needs to be taken when trying to use the data to get answers.

Quality enhancement

This does not mean that summative assessment data have nothing to contribute to quality. Unusual patterns ought to stimulate inquiries about their cause, either so that things that seem to work well can be tried out elsewhere, or so that practices that depress performance can be investigated. Assessment numbers can be treated as quality signs, always on the semiotic principle that signs get meanings from those who see them: meanings are not inbuilt.

Figure 12.1 lists ten departmental quality-enhancement practices and relates them to assessment, our premise being that assessment systems contribute to quality enhancement but do not determine it, because many drivers for improvement are not assessment-driven.

We have already said a great deal about enhancing learning quality through assessment that has formative intentions and will say nothing more about it here, where we concentrate on other ways in which departments go about continually reviewing the quality of what they do. However, good formative assessment practices may contribute more to the quality of learning than any of the measures in Figure 12.1.

Coherence requires a programmatic approach

A systemic approach to the assessment of student learning has coherence as its guiding principle and requires teams to look at their own professional learning, communication, pedagogies and quality-enhancement practices. Figure 12.2 re-presents the main themes of Figure 3.2 (Chapter 3) and adds connections between assessment activities and quality enhancement. The suggestion is that quality enhancement involves constructively aligning or orchestrating a range of activities and standards in order to increase the chances that assessment comes as close as possible to delivering its potential. It requires a mindset that sees assessment as a collective issue that intermingles with all the other arrangements that are made to evoke good student learning. However, coordination will never be perfect and good assessment systems will not be static, not least because of the 'bottom-up' changes that come from teachers adjusting their courses and assessment tasks.

Seen like this, a task for those trying to induce good assessment systems is to encourage this dynamism, put in place things that support good assessment practices, and to stimulate colleagues to see assessment and the concerns that attach to it as departmental or team matters, not as 'my module' issues. This, though, does not sit easily with the dominant discourses about management and change in

Quality-enhancement practice	Relationships with assessment
1. Peer reviews of modules	Colleagues review module quality, perhaps once every three years. In the UK, programmes are usually formally monitored each year
2. Annual programme review	
	Reviewers will be interested in summative assessment data and are in a good position to explore the reasons for any marked difference between particular modules and others in the programme. Assessment contributes to quality enhancement by providing signs for reviewers to consider
	Reviewers will examine the arrangements for enhancing learning by means of assessment
3. Staff-student committees	Students may raise assessment concerns, often arising from their direct learning experiences, but they will be treating assessment as an object of attention, not as a contributor to improvement
4. Student focus groups (possibly run by student unions)	
5. Student evaluations of modules	Assessment systems do not directly contribute to this aspect of quality enhancement
	(There is an enormous literature on this topic which raises some interesting, fundamental questions about how module quality may be assessed and how the results can spur quality enhancement)
6. Departmental 'what works' seminars for teachers	These quality-enhancement practices may arise from a sense that formative or summative intentions could be better worked out, but in committed departments it is usual for teachers to be always tweaking what they do. They may be responding to their own dissatisfaction with aspects of assessment but the assessment system has no privileged role as a contributor to action
7. Tinkering and other normal module improvement activities	
8. Alumni feedback	
9. Courses, workshops and events organized by an educational development unit	These stimuli for quality enhancement are likely to raise assessment issues throughout the life of a programme. However, that is no guarantee that fundamental changes will be made. Programmatic changes are the most complex and therefore the most resistant to these outside stimuli
10. Responses to external pressures – to highlight key skills development or employability	

Figure 12.1   Assessment and quality-enhancement practices

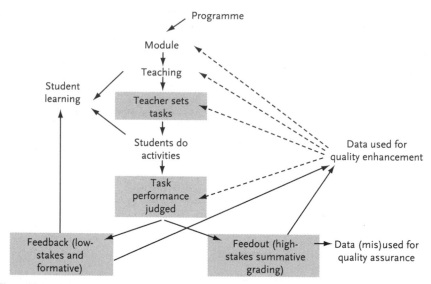

Figure 12.2 An assessment system (principal assessment activities are in the shaded cells)

some states, universities, colleges and departments, where an attachment to 'commonsense' change strategies can limit the potential to improve learning, teaching, assessment and curriculum in general (Trowler *et al.* 2003).

Notes

1. We mean that assessment is often treated as a craft involving the deployment of correct tools (assessment methods) to solve problems. Our position is that the problems are often 'wicked problems', which means they may be attenuated but not solved; that technique is not enough; that there are theoretical issues of importance to be addressed; and that the focus must be on the programme and its elements, not simply on the module or course.
2. Sometimes when we present the Skills *plus* USEM description of employability and say that programmes should be designed to promote such achievements, we are asked whether those programmes will transform shy students into barnstormers. Probably not. Programmes can improve the odds that groups of learners will have better USEM profiles. Improved probabilities make no promises about any individual.
3. Useful, because its intentions are easily grasped, the phrase 'communities of practice' has become a cliché. It implies that consensus is the norm and downplays discord (Knight and Trowler 2001).
4. It is not clear that producing transcripts showing the courses students have taken and the marks received adds a great deal, or that replacing degree classifications with mark or grade profiles would overcome fundamental difficulties with using numbers to represent diverse and complex achievements.

13

Developing the Institutional Assessment System

Expectations from beyond the academy

With the exception of a relatively small number of specialist institutions, higher education consists of complex, loosely coupled institutions (Weick 1976) held together, it is sometimes sardonically said, by nothing more than a central heating system or a common concern with car parking. Where governments have greater sway over what institutions do, the list of internal ties can be extended to include the need to deal collectively with policy initiatives, expectations and the like. Amongst these can be counted, in countries around the world,

- the assurance of quality and standards of curricula;
- the need to prepare students for the world of work;
- a requirement to demonstrate equality of opportunity across a diverse potential and actual student body;
- the development and implementation of strategies that optimize retention and completion;

although the amount of pressure varies.

Governments are influenced by supranational considerations. Higher education everywhere is being affected by globalization,[1] whether it be by the movement of students and institutions across national boundaries, the availability of resources on a worldwide basis, or the desire for harmonization of qualifications. In Europe, the Bologna Declaration of EU ministers and its successors from the Salamanca and Prague conferences are set to have considerable influence on the way in which higher education qualifications can be 'translated' across the EU member states. There are indirect implications for assessment that will stem from the impetus in the EU to promote employability (Haug and Tauch 2001).

All four of the governmental desires noted above feed through into the way in which an institution approaches the task of assessing its students, though to these must be added the expectations of others with a legitimate interest in assessment, such as professional and statutory bodies. The power of such bodies to influence institutional practice varies considerably with the discipline: medicine, engineering and law are three disciplinary areas in which assessment practice is greatly influenced by professional interests.[2]

However they are structured, institutions cannot now avoid the need to respond corporately to the pressures of the 'outside world', even though it might have been possible to do so in the past. The implications of this are far-reaching, and require a *systemic* approach to assessment, even though this may be coloured differently in different disciplinary areas because of their cultures and norms.

Influences on assessment in contemporary higher education

We noted in Chapter 3 the concern in the UK regarding assessment. The Learning and Teaching Support Network, aware of these developments, commissioned a series of briefing papers on the subject, some targeting particular readerships, and some focusing on specific aspects of assessment.[3] A similar concern has arisen in Australia. The Assessing Learning in Australian Universities project, commissioned by the Australian Universities Teaching Committee, took a broad look at contemporary practice in assessment (James *et al.* 2002).[4] The project team suggested that a number of influences, which have a worldwide resonance, were converging and challenging conventional thinking. The project team identified the following considerations, the first three focusing primarily on students and the last three focusing more on institutional issues:

- The changing nature of the student body and its engagement with the learning process.
- The significance of assessment requirements in establishing expectations and guiding student learning.
- The prominence attached to the development of 'generic skills' (or, in other language, 'employability').
- The need for staff to find assessment methods that are time- and cost-effective, and applicable to cohorts of increasing size and diversity.
- The emergence of new technological possibilities for assessment.
- The threat of plagiarism.

These and other issues are discussed below. The division between issues relating to students and those relating to institutional implementation of curricula is to some extent arbitrary, and does not acknowledge the fuzziness of the boundary.

Predominantly student-related issues

Changes in the student body

In some countries (for example, the USA), students have for a long time been expected to fund themselves through higher education, and hence for many of them part-time work has been a necessity. The widening of participation in countries such as the UK and Australia has only recently given rise to a similar situation for the student body. Minimizing and/or alleviating debt (and, in some cases, supporting a lifestyle above the basic[5]) have drawn students into part-time work of varying kinds. This has influenced the pattern of their engagement with study.

The diversity of enrolments has also had its impact. In the UK, the government commitment to widening participation is bringing into higher education more students who, for various socio-cultural reasons, have little background knowledge of what higher education will demand of them. We also noted in Chapter 10 that in some ostensibly English-speaking countries there are significant numbers of students for whom English is not their first language. Moon (2003) notes that some languages do not have a word for 'reflection', and that teachers will need to explain to some students for whom English is not their first language what this concept implies for their learning: the relevance of Moon's point for employability is clear.

It is well understood that assessment expectations (as perceived by students) influence learning behaviour. Hence, following Resnick and Resnick (1992), it makes sense to design assessments so as to encourage the learning that is desired. If that learning is to encompass 'employability', then there have to be clear curricular signals via the assessment specifications that employability figures significantly, and is not relegated to the margin of a student's attention. We have shown in earlier chapters that a lot of what is subsumed by the term 'employability' presents problems as regards grading, and that the implications of encompassing employability in the assessment scheme are more profound than some might suppose.

Students in consumer-like roles

The popular phrase is 'students as consumers', but this implies the purchasing of a product by, or on behalf of, the student. What the phrase misses is that the student is necessarily an active participant in the process. There is, undoubtedly, a consumer aspect to the situation in that the student enters into a quasi-contract with the institution for the provision of services. Where 'the deal' is not honoured by the institution, the student has the option of seeking restitution through institutional procedures or ultimately through recourse to the law.[6]

Where a student pays directly for participation in an educational programme, rather than simply benefits from a 'free' provision, the assertion of rights in respect of all aspects of provision becomes potentially more powerful. In the area of assessment, the student voice is strengthened in a number of respects, and the institution has to anticipate where student dissatisfaction might emerge, and make appropriate preparation. Box 13.1 gives some examples of expectations to which an institution may have to give attention.

Provision for students with disabilities, a human rights concern in most advanced economies, brings into particularly sharp focus the issue of student rights in higher education. The Special Educational Needs and Disability Act (SENDA) came into force in England, Scotland and Wales in September 2002, and requires institutions to make reasonable adjustments to their assessment arrangements to ensure that those with disabilities have an equivalent opportunity to demonstrate their achievements.[7] Institutions are charged with the responsibility, under SENDA, of

---

Box 13.1   Some student expectations of their higher education institutions

- Assessment regulations and practices that do not disadvantage certain students.
- Clarity in assessment specifications, as expressed in student handbooks, module templates and the like.
- Timely and informative formative feedback on work.
- Assessment tasks, including examinations, not 'bunched' unreasonably.
- Opportunities to retrieve failing performances, through resit or other arrangements.
- An appeals procedure through which, when performance might have been adversely affected, personal mitigating circumstances or allegations of institutional maladministration can be considered. (Although appeals against academic judgements are typically not permitted, the issue of assessor bias may be admissible for consideration.[1])

1. For example, racism or personal animus could be raised as grounds for appealing against an assessment outcome. Some appeals fall on the borderline. One example is where two appellants in the field of art and design argued in an initial hearing that a Eurocentric perspective had been brought to bear on artefacts which had their bases in African culture, and that they had been marked down as a result. In the event, the appeals were not pursued – but the issue of cultural bias remains one that could erupt dramatically, and a defence that academic judgements cannot be challenged might prove inadequate in the court of public opinion.

---

anticipating the needs of their students. Students with apparently similar disabilities may have different preferences regarding provision: as McCarthy and Hurst (2001) point out, some blind students prefer materials to be available in braille, others prefer audio-recordings. These authors offer a number of practical suggestions for ensuring equitability of opportunity for students with disabilities, and go on to point out the desirability of having a 'whole institution' strategy in contrast to expecting everything to be handled by a single Disabled Students Officer. Under such a strategy, for example, an examinations section would need to develop its capacity to deal with the anticipated need. The broader point is that it requires an institution-wide commitment (implying a senior member of staff to take responsibility for it) if fair treatment is to be assured.

Formative and summative assessment

In Chapters 2 and 3 we scrutinized the arguments surrounding summative and formative assessment, and in this chapter we discuss how an institution might seek to deal with the tension that exists between the two. It is now widely understood that the first-year experience of full-time study is of critical importance to students' success (and, although there has been far less research into part-time study, the same probably applies). A negative experience in the early stages, and the student may be discouraged from further engagement – perhaps even for life. The following quotation illustrates particularly vividly how formative assessment can be destructive of a student's engagement:

The course was taught very loosely, the tutors were never around to help, and when they were, they were very unhelpful. They were critical of your work to the point of being rude, not constructive criticism, if your work was not the best, average, then you were ignored in favour of the best students. . . . The way one tutor spoke to me . . . has put me off higher education and will take a long time in considering ever going back.

(Student from a programme in art and design; from Yorke 1999d: 18)

Some students make the transition into higher education with little difficulty, often because their previous education has provided sufficient of an academic base. Such students will also tend to have the advantage of the experience of other members of the family in higher education as a resource. In contrast, those who enter higher education from disadvantaged backgrounds may lack adequate educational experience even if they have the capacity to benefit from higher education. They may also lack the 'cultural capital' that would enable them to attune relatively easily to the new environment. This is not to suggest that standards be lowered so that people not really suited to higher education 'succeed'. We have suggested that there be variety in assessment methods and modes (Chapters 4 and 5) and that a whole-programme view be taken, so that assessments early in their careers give learners a chance to turn their potential into actual performance. We stress that being more sensitive to student diversity in early assessments does not imply abandoning the standards expected on graduation.

Our view is that it is desirable to give strong emphasis to formative assessment, especially in the early stages of a higher education programme. The first year of full-time study is often a qualifying year for the final stages. A requirement to pass summative assessments at the end of the first semester becomes unnecessary if the educational aim is that the student should reach a level appropriate for progression by the end of the first year as a whole. In fact, early formative assessment is good educational practice anyway – one that is being collaterally encouraged in the UK by the publication of institutional retention data that show that nearly two in three withdrawals occur during, or at the end of, the first year of full-time study (see, for example, HEFCE 2002).

Issues predominantly related to institutional curricular practices

Pressure on institutional resources

Summative assessment inevitably involves compromise between what is desirable and what is affordable. As noted in Chapter 2, it is impossible to assess, rigorously and affordably, a number of aspects of a student's capability within the time and resources available to an institution. Four courses of action are available, singly or in combination:

• Limit summative assessments to what can be done with defensible rigour.

(Rigour here includes both affordability and dealing with cheating, of which plagiarism is a prominent contemporary concern.)

- Use technological approaches where they can satisfy, but will not distort, assessment aims.
- Introduce methods through which students can make – and justify – claims to attainments.
- Reconfigure the whole 'curriculum package' in order to allow more time and resources to be devoted to stimulating good learning through assessment.

The introduction of semesterized modular schemes in many UK higher education institutions sharply increased the amount of summative assessment compared with that for programmes that ran the length of the full-time year. The major loss, under modularity, was in the amount of formative assessment that took place (Chapter 3). Further, modular curricula were expressed in terms of 'expected learning outcomes', which provided the students with clear indications of the learning that was being encouraged. However, the list of learning outcomes in many modules was far too lengthy for the module-end summative assessment to cover. Some of the outcomes were, on the argument of Chapter 2, unassessable because of problems with rigour and/or cost. The learning intentions may have been reasonable, but the assessment system could not cope.

Institutions are faced with the interrelated questions – not easy to answer – of how much summative assessment is really needed for the multiple purposes that assessment serves (Atkins *et al.* 1993; Yorke 1998a), and how much of the current summative assessment diet could be discarded without an unacceptable loss of information. The questions are difficult at module level, since each module leader is likely to assert the importance of their particular component of the assessment. They are also difficult at programme level, since they imply some coalescence of assessments across modules, which would be affected by the particular combination of modules selected by the individual student. The picture is complicated further in respect of intermediate awards or credit for individual modules. Some adjustments to existing assessment systems are no doubt possible, but a desire to assess employability may need to be preceded by a more far-reaching review of assessment intentions and practices.

Assessment generally is a time-consuming process, if done 'by hand'. For many assessment purposes, there is no substitute available for the involvement of 'live' assessors, although there now some multimedia systems capable of assessing student performance in a manner analogous to the simulation training machines used for aircraft pilots. Where the costs – and risks – of real-life performance assessment are unacceptably high (as in some aspects of medicine), there is an obvious attraction in pursuing technologically-based assessment methods. At the other end of the scale, it is reasonably easy to undertake the assessment of a student's capacity to identify a correct answer from a number of 'distractor' answers using computer-based methods, although the costs of writing a bank of good multiple choice questions is usually underestimated. Computer-mediated conferencing, asynchronous online discussions and electronic drafting all have assessment potential (Palloff and Pratt 1999; Salmon 2000), although it is likely that the electronic communication medium will not have much, if any, effect on the processes of judgement. Online systems have great potential for just-in-time and flexible learning and can encourage new learning and teaching approaches – though some learners appear to need support of a more directly personal nature.

With the exceptions mentioned above (simulations and testing), it is not evident that electronic media will make a lot of difference to the processes of judgement, except in so far as programme teams may wish to assess skill in computer-mediated conferencing, skill at searching the web and evaluating results, or facility in database analysis.

However the curriculum might be developed to enhance employability, there are likely to be implications for both the distribution of time between curricular components and staff time. If, as is likely, more time is needed for assessment, then, in a 'zero-sum game', this has to be gained at the expense of other curricular components. Put another way, assessment cannot be treated in isolation.

Rethinking curricular structure

Whilst assessment within an institution can be tweaked to accommodate some employability expectations, a broader institutional commitment to employability might require some more radical thinking about the curriculum and the related assessment. We described the 'capability envelope' in Chapter 7 as representing one way of restructuring a whole or part curriculum that could be used in some disciplinary areas (in others, the requirements of professional and statutory bodies could make its use problematic).

Students' part-time employment can be construed as a learning opportunity, rather than as a threat to learning. This employment could provide an experiential base for the academic study of employment-related disciplines, such as individual psychology, organizational sociology, management, finance, and so on. This, as in the 'capability envelope' could be assessed by a variant of the portfolio approach. Some students, particularly those whose subject disciplines are less obviously employment-oriented, might welcome a joint honours programme involving a specific subject discipline and what might be termed 'employment-related studies'. A lifelong learning perspective would encourage such students to extend their studies of the subject discipline (and of matters more directly related to employment, for that matter) beyond the boundary of the first degree.[8]

Matters of institutional policy that 'wrap around' the curriculum

Centralization and decentralization

Where there is a whole-institution strategy in respect of assessment, then, following the line taken in Chapter 12, loose coupling of the institution's component departments implies that they will need to interpret and implement the overall strategy with reference to the disciplinary culture and particular contextual conditions. The challenge is to resolve the inevitable tension between centralization and decentralization: too tight central direction, and departments will jib; too loose, and anarchy beckons. At minimum, a department should be able to justify its own assessment practices with reference to the overall institutional policy. From the perspective of external quality scrutiny, to err on the side of centralization may be safer, because scrutineers then have less scope to challenge that the divergences from central policy are leading to significant disparities in standards.

This tension is part of a larger issue relating to centralization – the extent to which an institution actually works on the basis of command and control. There is some anecdotal evidence of senior managers in institutions issuing commands to subordinates to little effect – as if a signaller on a railway were trying to send a train down a different track, but with a break in the connection between the signal box and the track control mechanism. Successful institutions strike a judicious (and widely understood) balance between central control and delegated powers.

Doing things right, or doing the right things?

The institutional perspective involves consideration of two important questions. First, is the approach to assessment ('approach' might, in some institutions, be better expressed in the plural) being implemented properly: are things 'being done right'? Second, is the approach to assessment suitable for the outcomes it is intended to achieve: are 'the right things being done'?

Doing things right

External quality scrutiny has focused institutional attention on coherence and consistency in curriculum delivery, in which assessment is prominent. Questions are asked, for example, as to whether the assessments are comparable with those for cognate programmes elsewhere; whether expected learning outcomes are properly covered by the schedule of assessments; whether quality assurance procedures, including the engagement of external examiners, are being followed through; and – perhaps – whether there is intrainstitutional consistency across subject areas as regards assessment. Some managerially oriented questions are given in Box 13.2.

The institution has to ensure that its systems function effectively and efficiently. Assessments must be both fit for purpose and properly handled. In this section, the focus is on the operation of the assessment system, i.e. efficiency. (In practice, there may be some cross-flow between fitness for purpose and operationalization, involving iteration between assessment design and the system for implementation because some design features may prove problematic to implement). Some things are operated at institutional level, others departmentally. There can be confusion as to ownership of responsibility, leading to duplication (not necessarily consistency) and/or 'gaps'. A example is cited by Yorke (1998b) in which the institutional examinations office and the department concerned each thought that the other was responsible for making the arrangements for laying out an examination room, which led to some frantic retrieval work and a delayed examination.

Box 13.2   Some questions for institutional managers

- In the assessment system, are the responsibilities of relevant postholders defined; how well do these responsibilities interlock; and are there any 'holes' which could cause trouble?
- Are the assessment regulations watertight (and have no internal holes or contradictions)?
- Are any external requirements[1] widely understood within the institution (and any partner institutions)?
- Are the duties of the examination boards clearly delineated, and do they interlock (without 'gaps', unnecessary duplication or complications)?
- Is the flow of information regarding assessment accurate, timely and appropriate to the task in hand? (This includes the provision of information to students and staff about assessments, and to examination boards. It also encompasses guidance regarding matters such as plagiarism and arrangements for students with disabilities.)
- In countries where there is a system of external examiners, does it function effectively?[2]
- Does the system for student complaints and appeals function properly?

1. In the UK, examples would be the Quality Assurance Agency's Code of Practice, the set of 'subject benchmarks' produced under the QAA's aegis, and the expectations of professional and statutory bodies.
2. In the UK it is expected that action will be taken in response to the comments of external examiners, and that externals will receive feedback on this.

Source: based on Yorke 2001c: 8–9

Another requirement is to have contingency plans. The oversleeping of a key-holder prevented access to an external examination venue on time, since an alternative keyholder could not be found quickly. The working assumption has to be 'if it can go wrong, it will' – hence the need to be prepared.

These examples – and readers will probably be able to add their own – are indicative of a need for a systems analysis that shows what is expected to happen against the flow of events that actually do happen. Coupled with a risk analysis regarding the functionality of the system, this would highlight the points at which the system might break down in future. One such pressure-point, particularly relevant to modular schemes, is the end-of-year assessments and the need for the information to be made available for the examinations board. Not only does the marking of assessments have to be done to tight deadlines (what happens if a marker is incapacitated?), but the data have to be entered correctly and presented in an appropriate format (is there time for proper checking, since perfection in data entry cannot be guaranteed?), with, ideally, some statistical analyses to guide the board in its deliberations.

However, as has been repeatedly said, assessment systems are not only about certifying attainments: they also have implications for learning – which is a matter that pushes the discussion back towards considerations of effectiveness. A frequent charge against modular schemes is that feedback reaches the student too late for it to be useful. The student may have already have had to make decisions regarding the next set of modules to be taken, or the feedback on an assignment (and, when it is made available, on an examination performance) is of limited practical value – the student has moved on to the next set of modules and has not got the time for a reprise of what has gone. As Knight (2002a) amongst others – points out, an important function of feedback is to indicate how the student can develop in respect of future work. The implication is that feedback needs to have a generic formative component as well as to provide a commentary on the performance being assessed. The institutional analysis of the assessment system needs to incorporate student learning as well as the more immediately obvious procedural matters.

The use of external examiners in the UK has been criticized from various perspectives (e.g. Warren Piper 1994; Silver *et al.* 1995). Suffice it to note here that the large growth in student numbers and the introduction of modular schemes are two factors which have made it more difficult for external examiners to pronounce on the standards attained by students. The expectations of external examiners have been codified by the QAA (2000a), thereby providing a framework against which institutions' use of them can be appraised.

Doing the right things

However, making sure that systems are working properly may be insufficient. As we have stressed, employability in particular makes fresh demands – of students and staff. Many personal qualities and achievements are not amenable to traditional modes of assessment (Chapter 2), and hence new institutional conceptions are needed of what assessment can (and cannot) be expected to do. Some institutions have in-house expertise in assessment available to them, in a department of education or an educational development unit, in which case it is incumbent on senior managers to make use of it. Where there is no in-house expertise, it may well be fruitful to bring expertise in from outside.

One issue is that of the relative amounts of coursework and examinations (dichotomizing what is, in reality, a less clear-cut variety of assessment practices). Elton (1998) suggested that the upward trend in honours degree classifications in the UK (HEQC, 1996; Yorke, 2002a: see Chapter 11) could be attributed (at least in part) to changes in institutions' approaches to assessment, moving towards counting a greater proportion of coursework in the determination of the level of the award. This suggestion receives some empirical support from a study by Bridges *et al.* (2002), whose research findings were consistent with the 'folk-wisdom' that coursework tends to attract higher grades than examination performances. The point as regards institutional action is not whether coursework is 'better' or 'worse' than examinations (such propositions are simplistic, and are contested for a range of reasons). It is about a set of interlinked issues: what educational purposes the use of coursework and examinations is intended to satisfy, whether the connection between purposes and assessment methodology stands up to scrutiny, and – if it does not – what the institution should do about the situation.

Dealing with cheating

Institutions are obliged to take cheating seriously if their awards are not to be compromised. Policies have been constructed and practices implemented. The better way of dealing with the problem is to approach it from a different direction, by constructing assessment tasks that require a unique response from the student[9] – one that is some way distant from the straightforward collection and presentation of material (which is amenable to plagiarism of the 'cut and paste' variety). As Stefani and Carroll (2001) suggest regarding plagiarism, the institutional response to the threat should include reviewing curricula to identify where the threat is at its greatest, and devising strategies to mitigate it.

Awards and standards

The grading of awards

It is standard practice, in summing up a learner's clutch of programme performances, to resort to averaging or 'profiling' which, in the case of the majority of students, is simply processed mechanically by the computer software.[10] However, we have suggested in previous chapters that some aspects of employability are not readily amenable to grading. If employability is to be taken seriously, then assessments will have to include non-graded elements. This has implications for awards in which graded components are combined to produce an overall graded performance, such as a grade-point average or an honours degree classification.

In the UK, the long-established classification of the honours degree is indefensible because of the idiosyncrasy of students' spectra of achievements, and there is a compelling argument to move towards an unclassified honours degree[11] coupled with some form of transcript documenting what a student has achieved. The inclusion of some (non-gradable) aspects of employability in a student's profile of achievements ought to assist in the demise of classification. Practical realism suggests that such a development could take place only if there were agreement across the UK higher education system that the classified honours degree had reached the end of its useful life, and that an alternative approach to the formalization of students' achievements commanded a substantial measure of support.

We noted in Chapter 8 that the degree award algorithms used in UK higher education lacked robustness. In addition, the degree classification is in any case a poor filter for employers, for whom the employability of a graduate involves not only the academic intelligence which the assessment system tends to index (albeit not unproblematically), but also the personal qualities and 'practical intelligence' (Wagner 1993) that contribute to a person's being effective in dealing with the kinds of challenge that employment tends to throw up.

Absolutism vs relativism in standards

There is a major tension underlying the concept of standards. Until perhaps the 1990s there was a general view in the UK that standards were absolute: an upper second class honours degree represented roughly the same level of achievement irrespective of the institution from which it was gained. The view was supported by the work of the Council for National Academic Awards (CNAA) in whose earlier days, particularly, the work of its subject panels led to standards in the polytechnics and colleges being consistent with those of the then universities. As CNAA's programme validation evolved into institutional accreditation, the responsibility for linking with a normative perspective on standards passed to the individual polytechnic or college. These institutions generally maintained the practices that they had adopted under CNAA, involving external advisers in programme validation events and maintaining the external examiner system. In some subject areas it was possible to find a commonality of perspective a number of years after the demise of CNAA,[12] which indicated, if not absolute standards, a considerable normative appreciation of what standards should be. However, the challenges to absolute standards strengthened during the 1990s. The idea of standards took a relativistic turn: an upper second class honours degree was no longer held to be the same irrespective of the institution – a view which employers had in any event adopted for some considerable time, as they overlaid their own valuations of institutions and programmes on the supposed gold standard. The teaching quality assessment process[13] and its successor, subject review, tacitly adopted a relativist position when the process was based on the institution's own aims and objectives for the programmes being appraised. Nevertheless, this will have been coloured by normative expectations, and by the later introduction of 'subject benchmarks'.[14]

The muddiness of this water is increased when the issue of 'value added' (CNAA/PCFC 1990) is brought into consideration. We noted in Chapter 12 that measures of value added were bedevilled by technical problems. However, from the point of view of employability, a putative employer might need to be aware of the basis of an individual graduate's success. This points towards the need for the graduate to be able to make (and sustain) a claim to have taken maximum advantage from their experience in higher education, i.e. to be able to explain their personal value added in qualitative terms, which may be of particular significance for someone who entered higher education from a disadvantaged background.

Learning institutions?

A critical issue for any institution is how it develops itself – in the context of this book, in respect of assessment. There are three components:

- How the institution learns from the experiences of its diverse departments and develops its practices.
- How it keeps itself informed about national and international developments.
- The development of its staff.

Box 13.3   Strategic questions for institutional managers

- Does the institutional policy or mission imply that its general approach to assessment should be changed? If so, in what way(s)?
- Are there any general institutional weaknesses in assessment (such as might have emerged from subject reviews or from internal reflection on practices and procedures) which need to be tackled?
- Since assessment is, by general consent, the least well understood and implemented aspect of curricula, what developmental activity needs to be instigated?
- In dealing with the preceding questions, is best use being made of existing expertise, both in-house and from outside. If not, why not?
- What, if anything, needs to be done to make the institutional system that surrounds assessment function effectively and be compliant with external expectations?
- How does the *institution* keep abreast of developments in assessment both nationally and internationally?
- How does the institution learn from its diverse experiences regarding assessment, and develop? (And how can this learning assist in the development of systems at the level of the higher education sector?)

Source: based on Yorke 2001c: 8

Some relevant strategic questions are set out in Box 13.3. Again, there is a need to bring appropriate expertise to bear on the issues, lest policy and practice are constructed on inadequate foundations.

Institutional research

In the USA, institutions typically have a group of staff whose task is to undertake institutional research because of the need to underpin institutional planning and decision-making with evidence. There is a tradition of data collection in the USA at all levels from the institutional to the national (where the National Center for Educational Statistics produces an impressive array of reports that enable institutions to benchmark their performances against their peers). The brief of the institutional research unit is much wider than assessment, of course.

In contrast, institutional research activity in the UK tends not to be the province of a designated unit. Such institutional research as is done is often commissioned on an ad hoc basis, perhaps in response to a crisis of some sort, with the consequence that institutional learning itself tends to be ad hoc. From the point of view of institutional strategy, this must be a weakness.

The Student Assessment and Classification Working Group (SACWG) has drawn upon national and institutional statistics to investigate patterns of gradings and degree classifications across the sector.[15] Similarly, the Northern Universities

Consortium for Credit Accumulation and Transfer has surveyed institutional practice in cumulating module performances into awards (Armstrong *et al.* 1998). These examples indicate that useful work on assessment can be done through collaborative endeavour, although to date this has not been focused on the relationship between assessment and employability.

Being informed about developments

Assessment is a complex topic that ranges both vertically (i.e. from the assessment of individual learning outcomes to awards) and horizontally across disciplines. A significant problem for an institution is keeping track of developments across both dimensions. Few academics have a wide specialist knowledge of assessment, and they may not be involved by institutions when policy and its implementation are being discussed. The Learning and Teaching Support Network (LTSN) in the UK offers a model which could be transferred to the institutional level. The LTSN's Generic Centre has the task of drawing information from, and feeding it out to, the 24 subject centres, each of which relates to a subject discipline or group of broadly cognate disciplines. Within an institution, an educational development unit (or similar) could function in a brokerage role analogous to that of the LTSN's Generic Centre. A necessary condition for success in that role would be the engagement of one or more persons with specialist knowledge of assessment. The virtue of the unit as broker would be that it would be in a prime position to take a lead in staff development activity.

Staff development

Precept 13 of the Code of Practice regarding assessment (QAA 2000a) is a blunt statement:

> Institutions should ensure that all staff involved in the assessment of students are competent to undertake their roles and responsibilities.

At one level, this can hardly be contentious. An organization should expect to operate competently across its range of functions. However, the challenges that assessment throws up, as demonstrated throughout this book, make the notion of competence more problematic than casual thought might suggest. We have aimed, in this book, to point out that the assessment practices that are adopted, often without searching inquiry, may not be fit for the purposes they are supposed to achieve. A significant component of the problem is that, by and large, academics are relatively untrained for tasks that demand a considerable level of sophistication and technical expertise. They may have learned about assessment through a process of acculturation in which the norms of assessment in the discipline are absorbed without necessarily being discussed, let alone being questioned. In pilot work, Yorke *et al.* (2000) found that some academics had gained their understanding of assessment methodology from the experience of having been assessed and/or from discussions with colleagues on matters such as how to go about the task of grading work. In their discussions of departmental leadership in higher education, Knight and Trowler (2001) argued that learning through collaborative working on assessment, learning, teaching and curriculum problems, with consultancy advice, could be the most powerful and extensive method of professional learning. They preferred this approach to the normal provision of workshops for those staff who volunteer for them. Subject associations and networks are potential sources of consultancy-type support.

Staff development for assessment is vital. At the crudest, an institution needs to take care that its assessment processes stand up to scrutiny which, in an increasingly litigious era, could involve significant cost. In one institution, an appeal against an examination board decision rumbled through a number of phases before reaching the courts. The fact that the appeal was eventually rejected was of little consolation to the institution which had spent some £30,000 in legal fees alone, not counting the opportunity costs of handling the series of appeal meetings. To put it in perspective, the visible cost represents roughly that of a lecturer for a year. Whilst the case sketched was extreme in terms of the time and cost involved, it takes relatively few smaller appeal events to 'use up' the equivalent of the annual salary of a member of staff. If things are 'not done right', the waste of resources may be more than trivial.

Staff development is, of course, far more than a defensive operation. The institution needs to ensure that new staff are inducted into the norms and expectations of their discipline: skill in assessment should not be left to chance and the unprepared mind. In the first instance, this should be a matter that is delegated to the relevant department, whose procedures should include a mechanism for assuring the senior member of staff in the institution who holds the 'assessment brief' that this has been done. Accommodating a new member of staff to the disciplinary norms is the first requirement, so that basic expectations can be met with confidence. However, the department needs, in turn, to put its assessment methodologies 'under suspicion', questioning whether they really are the most appropriate for the circumstances – a matter in the first instance for the more experienced staff. The need is for expertise in assessment methodology which perhaps only a minority of departments can find amongst their own ranks. For those departments not so blessed, relevant expertise may be found elsewhere in the institution, or beyond its borders.

Staff development activity related to assessment might include the actions listed in Box 13.4.

Changes to assessment regimes need to be thought through carefully before being implemented, particularly because of their impact on students' futures.

The impact on staff, too, of changing an assessment regime should not be overlooked. With hindsight (and, in truth, it ought to have been with foresight), the roughly doubled loading of summative assessment on staff because of the introduction of modularized or semesterized programmes in the UK was flawed. Not only did this take place when student numbers were growing, but also it had very adverse effects on student learning via formative assessment. The lessons from experiences such as this are clear: educational changes made in haste tend to be followed by later repentance.

Box 13.4   Some possible staff development actions

- Developing the general level of understanding in the institution (and any partner institutions).
- Developing technical expertise in assessment (and an understanding of what the limitations of assessment are).
- Identifying and sharing good practice within the institution (and its partners).
- Researching existing practices.
- Exploring the implications of changes in the expectations laid upon higher education (in the UK, examples include the government's policies on widening participation and employability).
- Scrutinizing the institutional assessment system in order to identify whether any changes are needed (this spans the academic and administrative components of the system).

Source: based on Yorke 2001c: 19

Working in partnership

The senior academic with the 'assessment brief' for the institution will need to work in partnership with colleagues in different parts of the institution if the assessment system is to work optimally. Whilst they may need to produce a new, or revise an existing, strategy, they will need to discuss developments with key people in academic and administrative departments. This has the potential to bring together the academic and administrative needs as regards assessment in an optimal way. However, catching academics' attention and gaining their commitment is problematic where the idea of academic freedom can be used as a bulwark against the changes that are being sought.

As is readily apparent from earlier in this book, assessment is an aspect – perhaps the main aspect – of the educational process that is in need of developmental work. Here the educational development unit (or similar) has a major part to play, though it may well have to draw on expertise from elsewhere within the institution (an education department) or from outside. The most profitable approach is likely to be when the educational development unit, with or without the support of expertise from elsewhere, as appropriate, works in partnership with a department or programme. Blanket coverage, as those who have worked in educational development units well know, is often dismissed with words like, 'Well, it's different in our particular department'. This provides an easy escape route from tackling problems.

Framing institutional assessment policy

The institutional response to the challenges of assessment has to be strategic, providing a policy framework within which the assessment methodologies of the various subject disciplines can be operated. At the level of the subject discipline (and quite properly), account will need to be taken of norms and of the expectations of external bodies that have a legitimate stake in the assessment process. The institution as a whole has to be concerned with matters such as those listed in Box 13.5.

Box 13.5 Some institutional policy considerations regarding assessment

- Ensuring that programmes undertaken by students provide a range of assessment tasks that will help students to develop and demonstrate their achievement across a variety of aspects of employability . . .
- . . . whilst at the same time not overassessing students (and, by extension, overburdening staff).
- Discouraging the belief that every aspect of employability can be assessed validly and reliably within the resources available . . .
- . . . and hence working towards the introduction of alternative approaches to summative assessment where traditional approaches fall short.
- Encouraging assessment methods that are, by their nature, inimical to cheating (and plagiarism in particular).
- Ensuring widespread understanding of the expectations of external bodies regarding assessment.
- Optimizing the methodology through which a student's performances are taken into account when determining their entitlement to an award.
- Setting in train appropriate staff development activity.

This list, which could quite easily be extended, indicates that there is a considerable agenda for the senior manager in an institution who has been given the assessment brief. Many of the issues facing that person interlock, and are not susceptible of an easy resolution: the ideal response to any individual issue may not be a realistic possibility. Whereas perfection in assessment is a chimera for a host of technical and practical reasons, it is practicable to make a sustained (and the complexity of assessment underscores 'sustained') commitment to enhancement.

So what can the senior manager holding the assessment brief actually do? We offer some answers below, acknowledging that they have relevance, *mutatis mutandis*, to others in managerial positions.

- *Place assessment well up the institutional agenda.*
- *Stimulate an institutional climate* in which a commitment to assessment development is valued, if it is not already present.

    - This includes a preparedness to reflect on the outcomes of assessment, where analysis of data can trigger developmental activity.

- *Look for what is feasible.*

    - Accept that there are some things that are simply not amenable to summative assessment given the available resources, and stimulate the hunt for other ways in which the assessment objective(s) might be reasonably well-satisfied.

- Advocate the optimizing of the effort devoted to assessment, e.g. avoiding duplication, looking for opportunities through which the assessment of something can be subsumed under the assessment of something else (word-processing skills within the assignment submission, and so on).
- Remember that a lot can be gained by incremental change – the 'low pain, high gain' approach. Do not assume that changes necessarily have to be showy, or 'big-bang', in character.

- *Support developmental work.*

  - Budget for it. Developmental work will include analyses of the current position as regards assessment, staff development needs, and so on. Expertise from outside the institution may be needed for some developmental activities.
  - Convene, or cause to be convened, groups (perhaps based on departments or programmes) tasked with looking at the present state of assessment in the institution in relation to the challenges posed by this book: to what extent are these challenges being met? Even more importantly, but consequentially, ensure that the question 'What now needs to be done?', is asked.
  - Identify colleagues in the institution who can act as leaders in developing assessment methodology, and make use of their expertise.
  - Remember that there is a need for examples to be provided of the kinds of performance that are associated with assessment criteria. Criteria are relatively easy to construct, but 'the devil is in the detail' of interpreting them in operational terms.

- *Do not take colleagues' work for granted.* The managerially underused words 'Thank you', sincerely and not over-effusively used, can go a long way towards creating or reinforcing the climate of commitment that is needed for the development of assessment (and, of course, of institutional provision more generally).

Notes

1. See Scott (1998) for a diverse collection of commentaries on globalization.
2. We noted earlier the growing power of the computing industry to determine assessment practice – to the extent that industrial certification, with a rigorous programme of updating to maintain currency, has taken over some of the terrain that was previously inhabited by higher education institutions (Adelman 2001).
3. These and other generic centre assessment resources can be read by following the link to Resources at http://www.ltsn.ac.uk/genericcentre/index.asp?id=17149 and searching under 'Assessment'.
4. See also www.cshe.unimelb.edu.au/assessinglearning
5. See McInnis (2001).
6. As an example, a mature student accepted £30,000 in an out of court settlement of his claim regarding inadequate provision on his programme of study (Baty 2002).

7. The provisions of SENDA extend to all aspects of institutional functioning and are expected to be fully operational by September 2005.
8. This approach is further developed in Yorke (2003b).
9. Note, though, that this is likely to require a greater level of attention on the part of assessors.
10. For those who merit special consideration due to personal circumstances, or because the performances *in toto* fall just below a borderline, the mechanism is overridden by a deliberative process in the examination board.
11. See the argument in Winter (1993a) and Yorke (2002b).
12. Business Studies is a good example: see Yorke *et al.* (1998).
13. Run at first by the funding councils in the UK, and later by the Quality Assurance Agency.
14. See the QAA website www.qaa.ac.uk for the current set of documents.
15. Examples of SACWG's work can be found in Woolf and Turner (1997); Bridges *et al.* (1999, 2002); Yorke *et al.* (1996, 2000, 2002a,b).

14

Conclusions

Key questions, and short answers

In this book we have been concerned with three overarching questions, to which we give short answers by way of summing up points that have been made throughout this book.

Question 1: How can assessment be used most effectively in the support of learning?

Answer 1: Almost tautologically, emphasize formative assessment. Ensure that the climate of the programme is one that encourages learning goals rather than performance goals. This may well necessitate some redesign of the curriculum.

Question 2: What are the limits of assessment as regards the warranting of learners' achievements?

Answer 2: Some achievements are simply not warrantable with the resources likely to be available. Be prepared to acknowledge this. Consider practical alternative ways in which students' achievements may be conveyed to others, such as the adoption of a claims-making approach.

Question 3: How can the effectiveness of summative assessments be maximized?

Answer 3: Ensure that the summative assessments really do assess what they are intended to assess. Invest in the *programme* arrangements needed to ensure high reliability. Reconfigure, or even drop, assessments that fail in this respect.

The following sections summarize the main lines of reasoning that have led to those answers.

Complexity

The greater prominence of employability in modern curricula, together with a resurgence of interest in curricular coherence (to some extent induced by national quality assurance systems), have brought sharply into view some problems regarding assessment that have been present in higher education for a very long time, but which have not been at the forefront of attention. We have demonstrated in this book that assessment methods may not deliver what they are commonly thought to deliver. In terms of the UK Advertising Standards Authority's code for advertising, current summative assessments have difficulty in completely satisfying the requirement to be 'legal, decent, honest and truthful'. Some may be dismayed to realize the extent of the problems with assessment.

The literature on assessment often looks more like the output of a cottage industry than the product of coordinated scholarship. There are many reports of experiences of using *this* technique in *that* module, or of the levels of reliability that can be attained by being scrupulous in the use of a certain method for certain purposes, or of experiences which made teacher and students feel that good learning had taken place. This is important but it is not sufficient unless we are prepared to see the undergraduate years as a farrago of unrelated modules taught without reference to systematic appreciations of the research literature on human learning in general and undergraduate learning in particular. Assessment, we have argued, is more complex than casual thinking might suggest. Without theories of what can be judged and how, of the relationship between assessment and learning, and of the ways in which judgements and claims can be represented, attempts to enhance assessment practices are built on sand.

Employability

The rise to prominence of employability in higher education has driven thinking in the UK down two rather different lines. The first involves the accountability of higher education to the originator of a substantial part of its funding: the government. Here we find particular reference to employment rates in the form of 'first destination statistics', in which graduates' employment status six months after graduating is indexed, though improvements are in train (Rushforth 2003). Whilst employment rates are probably the 'hardest' short-term indication available to a government regarding graduate outcomes, they are vulnerable to vicissitudes of the labour market and other factors. This line of thinking offers little guidance for the development of curricula.

The 'softer' concept of employability is probably more useful – especially to graduates – since it encompasses developments that ought to stand them in good stead for a lifetime. In our various writings on the topic, we have been at pains to point to the close relationship that exists between employability and good learning – not a new suggestion, since similar thinking can be found in Silver and Brennan (1988). The problem for the auditor is that it is difficult to produce a simple 'measure' of employability, as we have described it, not least because the true value of employability can only be ascertained over a considerable length of time.

Reflection on the implications of employability for the curriculum quickly raises the question of whether the curriculum is maximizing the opportunity for students to develop. We have argued that attention needs to be paid not only to understanding and skills-in-context, but also to the more personal aspects of development, such as self-efficacy and metacognition. These influence the characteristics that employers tend to say they want but which are not easily assessed in traditional ways.

Judgement, rather than measurement

There is a need to accept that many expected learning outcomes are intrinsically 'fuzzy', even though they may be expressed in apparently precise terms. The apparent precision usually evaporates as teachers and students come to interpret the outcomes for their different purposes. The 'obvious' solution – to seek ever tighter specification of the expected outcomes – merely leads into the entangling and disorienting jungle of detail as was experienced by those faced with the system of NVQs developed under the aegis of the National Council for Vocational Qualifications in the UK (and before that time, with the zealous application of behavioural objectives to curriculum design).

We have argued that much learning is complex, involving the integration of understanding and skilled practices from multiple sources. Complex learning requires a corresponding complexity in assessment. Some learning may be assessed in passing, on an 'adequacy assumed unless' basis.

Complex learning is likely to underpin 'authentic' achievements such as work placements or creative activity, where it is often inappropriate to state expected learning outcomes in any detail. As is particularly true with creativity, complex learning may also be 'divergent' in that it can lead a student into unexpected, but worthwhile, intellectual territory. The assessment system needs to be able to accommodate the student who can branch off the expected, perhaps well-mapped, path whilst remaining true to the general intentions of the programme on which they have enrolled.

In general, then, it is sensible to avoid straining after precision in specifying expected learning outcomes. Most assessments are *judgements* reached with reference to the assessment criteria – in effect, the result of a process of 'connoisseurship' (Eisner 1985) – and not measurements. Some judgements are highly definite at the pass/fail boundary, especially where the decision is of high importance (such as those on fitness to practice – for example, a student teacher's irresponsible and unauthorised demonstration in the school laboratory of the explosive nitrogen triiodide, the failure to insist on safety precautions in the use of equipment, and the exhibition of racial prejudice). Other judgements do not require clear-cut boundaries, since the assessment system allows compensation for weaknesses in one part of the assessed task if there are strengths elsewhere. This is often seen in the grading of essays, where the research literature suggests that the reliability of assessments continues to be a problem. In some circumstances, as when a report on a work placement is taken as the best available proxy for the learning that has taken place, judgements have to be so highly inferential that their validity must come quite seriously under question.

If many assessment judgements cannot be robust, doubt must fall on the gradings given in respect of curricular components, and, wherever these are computed, on overall gradings for the programme, such as the honours degree classification used in the UK. We suggest that assessment practices often fall into the trap of grading to a fineness that cannot be justified by the methods in use – the error of misplaced precision.[1] The difficulties with precision are compounded where institutions vary in the way in which they cumulate gradings for award purposes (Armstrong *et al.* 1998; Yorke *et al.* 2002a), and where operations on numerical data (especially percentages) are undertaken on the basis of unwarranted assumptions regarding their mathematical properties (Dalziel 1998). The conclusion is inescapable: overall assessments can be of only limited usefulness, since they represent different ways of trying to mix achievements that are epistemologically different and incommensurable to greater or lesser degrees. Since, for a variety of reasons, these are often 'high-stakes' judgements for graduates and employers, we believe it necessary to consider alternative ways of summing up and presenting achievements.

Reducing the tension between formative and summative assessment

There is an ever-present tension between the formative and summative components of a programme, as we have shown in earlier chapters. This is most sharply seen in the higher education teacher's dual role: as formative assessor, the teacher is concerned to engage with the learner to facilitate development, whereas the role of summative assessor obliges them to stand back and provide disinterested judgements. The production of gradings in some national systems (for example, those in the UK and the USA), accentuates the distancing of the teacher from the learner.

The tension cannot be *eliminated* unless summative assessment is detached from the teacher's role, which is an unrealistic proposition in higher education for a variety of reasons which include the difficulties of constructing summative assessments from 'outside' the curriculum;[2] in recruiting assessors; and with the basic benefit/cost ratio of adopting this course of action, let alone the implications for a 'state curriculum' that would hover over the process. However, the tension could be reduced if:

- overall gradings (where used) were abolished;
- the learning process explicitly sought to assist students to develop their capacity to claim achievements and to support their claims with evidence;
- the claims-making approach, supported by an institutional certification of the study units in which the learner had engaged, were to become accepted by employers and others outside the academy.

Whilst teachers would be required to make summative judgements about performances on individual curricular components, these judgements could be cited by the learner as evidence of achievement. The teacher's broader purpose, that of supporting learning, would be given a dominance that it typically lacks.

Implied in these suggestions are the following:

- *A curricular culture that accentuates the facilitation of learning.* The key word here is 'facilitation', since all curricula are presumed to increase students' learning, whether they are expected to achieve this in, say, the Humboldtian manner of students learning from the lectures of experts or from a problem-based approach. There is substantial evidence to show that formative assessment is effective, and hence curricula should emphasize it.
- *A valuing in curricula of the complex, 'soft' achievements* valued by employers and which generally help a person to deal with issues in broader life.
- *A curriculum that acknowledges the varied starting points of those who enrol.* Two groups that differ from the norm of students entering higher education more or less directly from school at around 18 years of age – those entering from 'access' programmes (who are typically 'mature') and young people who enter higher education from disadvantaged backgrounds – will probably have learning needs that are, in some respects, different from the normative group. They will, as a consequence, benefit from an approach to formative assessment that is differentiated according to need. This is particularly relevant to the first year of full-time experience in higher education, which is a 'make or break' period for some students.
- *A lessened concern with the 'exactness' of summative gradings* at study-unit level, although for progression purposes student performances will have to reach an acceptable standard. Lessening the emphasis on grading would help to reduce the likelihood of students adopting performance goals, since there would be no point in aiming for a predetermined overall grade by obtaining an appropriate grade profile. The importance of learning goals should emerge more strongly and, if anything, ought to lead to an enhancement of students' performances.
- *Broad acceptance of ungraded awards.* The world beyond the academy would need to accept that students' achievements can properly be indexed through an ungraded award that the graduate can elaborate in terms of claims supported by evidence (some from 'traditional' summative assessments, and some from experiences such as work placements).

Programme-level thinking and subsidiarity

Throughout this book we have been at pains to stress the importance of assessment at the programme level, for two main reasons. First, whereas students can achieve the outcomes expected of them at study-unit level, these achievements do not necessarily add up to the achievements they make across the programme as a whole: the whole can be rather more than the sum of the parts, since it can more easily accommodate the learning that takes a considerable time to come to fruition. Secondly, whereas the achievements in study units may be of interest to an employer, it is likely to be the totality of the graduate's gain from higher education that is of greater interest – not only the achievements in the subject discipline, but also those extradisciplinary achievements that are less easy to assess. The employer, understandably, would like the outcomes of assessment – the certification of achievement – to be generalizable to the graduate's potential performance in the job. If assessments are to have this predictive validity, then they need to be reliable, which implies repeated estimates are made of target achievements, and they need to be fair representations of student learning that has addressed outcomes that employers value. Just as advertisements for financial services now warn that past performance is no guarantee of future success, experience suggests to us that assessments undertaken in higher education do not always have full transfer value. This is one reason why we have been prompted to consider alternatives to summative assessment.

We do, however, caution against simplistic changes to assessment approaches, mindful of the possibility of unintended consequences when one part of the complexity is changed without thinking through the systemic implications. An action that appears good from one angle may turn out to have collateral effects that undercut the hoped-for gain. For example, making assessment of the first semester of a full-time programme formative, rather than summative, could have damagingly negative effects if students' perceptions of the situation do not accord with that of the staff – they could fail the whole year at one go and have more difficulty in retrieving their positions than if the failure had become apparent to them much earlier. (The response in this case should be that formative assessment earlier in the programme should have picked up the potential for failure and initiated attempts to forestall it.)

We insist that taking a systemic approach to assessment need not be tantamount to 'hard managerialism', with its emphasis on 'command and control' strategies. 'Soft managerialism', with an emphasis on agreeing goals and then helping others to meet them in the ways they judge most fit for purpose and context, lies closer to the notion of subsidiarity. Relatively few academic leaders (or teachers in general) can claim to be experts in assessment, yet all in leadership positions at module, programme, department and institution levels bear responsibilities in respect of it. Much that happens under the label of 'assessment' has a traditional ring about it. We have demonstrated that assessment is more problematical than perhaps many appreciate. It is to be hoped that a new emphasis in England on improving the management of universities and colleges will reach down to programme leaders and heads of department.

Some directions for curriculum redevelopment

Our analysis of assessment, if followed through, has significant implications for the further development of curricula.

Tightly unitized curricula need to be relaxed to accommodate the 'slow learning' that might be missed when the focus of assessment is on relatively small curricular chunks. Projects and dissertations may go some way in this respect, but are likely to pick up slow *academic* learning and to miss the development of 'soft' skills (which, if provided with a proper theoretical footing, can fulfil requirements for academic rigour).

A strengthened emphasis on formative assessment implies the commitment of more teacher time, which will have to be repaid from elsewhere in the curricular 'budget'. This constitutes a redistribution of the teaching effort (formative assessment is, after all, a vehicle for teaching) which would raise questions about how best to use the other available teaching time. The restriction of summative assessment to those components where it can satisfy technical requirements reasonably well ought to create some time for more formative work.

As we noted in Chapter 11, the development students' capacity for claims-making requires the use of some curricular time. It also requires students' commitment. Whilst we support the general intentions of the personal development planning (PDP) that is scheduled to be part of UK higher education in 2005–06, we have doubts about the extent to which both students and institutions will commit themselves to it, given the other pressures on them. The experience with Records of Achievement in schools suggests that they have been seen as low-status activities with relatively little pay-off in the employment environment. However, if PDP can be established as a vehicle through which students can build up their CVs, and also construct their claims to 'graduateness', then its future could be rather brighter.

Whilst pilot work may have pointed to the value of PDP, it is quite a different matter to scale up any educational innovation by a couple of orders of magnitude. Enthusiasm for its adoption is likely to run less vigorously across a whole sector than in self-selected pilot institutions. The development of a curricular model along the general lines of the 'capability envelope' – even if the 'envelope' were redesigned in the process – is one way which support for the development of CVs and claims-making might be gained.

Quality assurance and quality enhancement

Our analysis has subverted the assumption that assessment is an instrument of quality assurance because it has challenged the credibility of the (summative) data that quality assurance processes consume. There is no reason why summative assessment data should not *inform* quality assurance but it is exceptional for the data to be robust enough to allow fine distinctions to be drawn or small differences between cohorts, departments and modules to be taken very seriously.

On the other hand, we have strongly implied that good assessment practices are bound up with quality enhancement. We take quality enhancement to be about continuing attempts to improve learning, teaching, assessment and the curriculum more generally. In many ways, assessment is the key to quality enhancement,[3] with changes to assessment practices probably having more potential impact on student learning than any other sorts of intervention. Clearly, apparently poor summative assessment scores can signal that something may be amiss and lead to deliberation about whether teaching quality is inadequate or whether there are other plausible explanations, such as a change in module or programme recruitment patterns.

However, assessment has a more fundamental role than this in quality enhancement. Where assessment tasks extend to the full range of outcomes associated with a module or, on a larger scale, with a programme, then the 'assessment backwash' encourages students to engage with those outcomes, always assuming that the assessment load is reasonable and that overassessment does not prompt students towards using coping strategies. Conversely, changes to teaching or learning that are not matched by assessment changes may have some impact when led by charismatics, but are likely to have marginal impact in other cases. Yet, whilst suggesting that changes to assessment practices may be the most promising way of enhancing the quality of student learning, we need to recall that assessment changes are not easily made. Figures 2.1 and 2.2 in Chapter 2 showed assessment practices as networks of rules, tools, people and relationships. For change to have a good chance of 'sticking', attention needs to be paid to as many elements of the assessment system as possible. To use the language of Table 4.3 (Chapter 4), learners and teachers have to be enrolled in new assessment cultures. The Alverno College experience shows both that this is possible and that it takes a coherent and coordinated approach to succeed (Mentkowski and Associates 2000).

Innovation is not easy, especially when it involves orchestrating the work of teachers who are often accustomed to running their own modules. Intuitive approaches to innovation on this scale will have some successes but we would prefer good leaders to operate on the basis of theories of innovation that are informed by systematic research evidence.

Innovation and leadership

Research findings do not tell leaders what to do, although they do provide some generalizations about what tends to be most effective. For example, reviewing the literature on educational change, Trowler *et al.* (2003) drew ten conclusions:

1. Thinking about 'changing' is more productive than concentrating on 'change' because dynamism is always involved – 'innovations' will change as they are developed.
2. Responses to change on the ground will be strongly influenced by the different pre-existing situations there, including different histories. We can therefore expect the same intentions to work out quite differently in different contexts.
3. Innovations come loaded with meaning and emotional baggage. They may be welcomed warmly or viewed with suspicion or as a threat. Sometimes, predicting responses is rather difficult, but it is worth the effort to try to make educated guesses about the probabilities of different sorts of outcome emerging.
4. Changes threaten to disrupt the distribution of power in higher education, including the relations between teachers and students (depending on the nature of the innovation). Expect opposition from 'losers'.
5. Innovations have a greater chance of success if they are seen as profitable (in a broad sense) by staff in the areas that matter to them – or that are made to matter to them.
6. Sometimes, the time for a change has come – the time is right. Changes which are successfully embedded at one time and place may not be so in another time and place.

7. Existing cultures are extremely tenacious: cultural sensitivity is extremely important in devising change strategies. This makes the transfer of innovation hard.
8. Mandated changes may produce compliance, but professionals have considerable scope for compliance-without-change, resistance and subversion.
9. Small, incremental changes are more likely to be successful in the longer term than big bangs.
10. Expect those involved in planning change to lose sight of the detail of constraints and issues on the ground, even if they are practitioners themselves. The planning process itself imposes blinkers on the vision of the planners because of the generalizing bias of planning itself. Thinking separately and creatively about the issues can help smooth the implementation process.

A message here is that quality enhancement, innovation and assessment reform are best seen as slow projects, not so much to be delivered through managerial *chutzpah*, as the outcome of leadership that encourages small, incremental changes that move things in appropriate directions. Some things, such as programme frameworks, learning intentions and the principle of subsidiarity, often need forceful advocacy and tenacious guardianship but, once such principles are in place, leadership for innovation seems to be a matter of supporting, encouraging and enabling rather than the exercise of managerial power. And if Bascia and Hargreaves are to be believed, it also seems to involve humility:

> . . . educational policymakers have not learned anything from these decades of research, whose recurring theme has been the complexity (if not outright failure) of educational change and the inadequacy of so many reform ideas . . . we have so little evidence that anyone has learned anything new about the processes of teaching and schooling beyond the confines of their own personal locations.
>
> (Bascia and Hargreaves 2000: 20)

So, we draw this book to a close not by focusing directly on assessment, learning and employability, but by pointing to the importance of leadership. Leaders are supposed to make a difference. To make a constructive difference, they need to be well-informed. Our overall aim in writing this book has been to point out some of the problems with assessment, and to put forward some ideas regarding how they might be ameliorated. It will have been abundantly apparent where our particular preferences lie. Others will have different preferences. Our book will be successful to the extent that those in leadership roles reflect on what we have said, and use what we have offered here in the development of assessment practices at the level for which they hold responsibility. We wish them every success.

Notes

1. Sometimes the error of misplaced provision is seen in attempts to make judgements any finer than 'provisionally adequate' and 'not adequate'.

2. 'Content-free' assessments, as in the general tests of reasoning, intelligence or 'graduate-ness', may be reliable descriptions of something but, by definition, not of what students have learned through a particular programme. There are suggestions that they tend to describe students' pre-existing levels of cultural capital and, as such, embody distinct cultural biases.

3. Angelo and Cross (1993) describe a series of classroom assessment techniques that are intended to provide teachers with swift indications of the impact of their teaching so that shortfalls can be quickly made good.

References

Abramson, M. and Jones, P. (2001) Getting students off to a flying start: improving the retention of advanced GNVQ students entering higher education. *Widening Participation and Lifelong Learning* 3(2): 34–7.

Adams, C. and King, K. (1995) Towards a framework for student self-assessment. *Innovations in Education and Training International* 32(4): 336–43.

Adelman, C. (ed.) (1990) *A College Course Map: Taxonomy and Transcript Data*. Washington, DC: US Government Printing Office.

Adelman, C. (2001) The medieval guild in cyberclothes: international dimensions of industry certification in information technology. *Tertiary Education and Management* 7(3): 277–92.

Adey, P. and Shayer, M. (1994) *Really Raising Standards*. London: Routledge.

Airasian, P. (1988) Symbolic validation: the case of state-mandated high stakes testing. *Educational Evaluation and Policy Analysis* 10(4): 301–13.

Anderson, L.W. and Krathwohl, D.R. (2001) *A Taxonomy for Learning, Teaching and Assessment*. New York: Addison Wesley Longman.

Anderson, L.W. and Sosniak, A. (eds) (1994) *Bloom's Taxonomy: A Forty-year Retrospective. Ninety-third Yearbook of the National Society for the Study of Education*. Chicago: University of Chicago Press.

Angelo, T.A. and Cross, K.P. (1993) *Classroom Assessment Techniques: A Handbook for College Teachers*. San Francisco: Jossey-Bass.

Argyris, C. and Schön, D. (1974) *Theory in Practice: Increasing Professional Effectiveness*. San Francisco: Jossey-Bass.

Armstrong, M., Clarkson, P. and Noble, M. (1998) *Modularity and Credit Frameworks: The NUCCAT Survey and 1998 Conference Report*. Newcastle upon Tyne: Northern Universities Consortium for Credit Accumulation and Transfer.

Ashworth, P., Bannister, P. and Thorne, P., with others (1997) Guilty in whose eyes? University students' perceptions of cheating and plagiarism in academic work and assessment. *Studies in Higher Education* 22(2): 187–203.

Astin, A.W. (1991) *Assessment for Excellence: The Philosophy and Practice of Assessment and Evaluation in Higher Education*. New York: Macmillan.

Astin, A.W. (1997) *Four Years that Matter: The College Experience Twenty Years On*. San Francisco: Jossey-Bass

Atkins, M. (1999) Oven-ready and self-basting: taking stock of employability skills. *Teaching in Higher Education* 4(2): 267–80.

Atkins, M.J., Beatty, J. and Dockrell, W.B. (1993) *Assessment Issues in Higher Education*. Sheffield: Employment Department.

Atlay, M. and Harris, R. (2000) An institutional approach to developing students' 'transferable' skills. *Innovations in Education and Training International* 37(1): 76–81.

Ausubel, D.P. (1968) *Educational Psychology: A Cognitive View*. London: Holt, Rinehart & Winston.

Averill, J.R. (2000) Intelligence, emotion, and creativity, in R. Bar-On and J. Parker (eds) *The Handbook of Emotional Intelligence*. San Francisco: Jossey-Bass, pp. 277–98.

Bandura, A. (1997) *Self-efficacy: The Exercise of Control*. New York: Freeman.

Barach, J.A and Eckhardt, D.R. (1996) *Leadership and the Job of the Executive*. Westport, CT: Quorum Books.

Barnett, R. (1997) *Higher Education: A Critical Business*. Buckingham: SRHE/Open University Press.

Barr, R.B. and Tagg, J. (1995) From teaching to learning – a new paradigm for undergraduate education. *Change* Nov/Dec, pp. 13–25.

Bascia, N. and Hargreaves, A. (2000) Teaching and leading on the sharp edge of change, in N. Bascia and A. Hargreaves (eds) *The Sharp Edge of Educational Change: Teaching, Leading and the Realities of Reform*. London: Routledge/Falmer, pp. 3–26.

Baty, P. (2002) 'I blame government,' says £30,000 winner. *The Times Higher Education Supplement* No. 1549 (2 August), p. 6.

Baume, D. and Yorke, M. (2002) The reliability of assessment by portfolio on a course to develop and accredit teachers in higher education. *Studies in Higher Education* 27(1): 7–25.

Baume, D. and Yorke, M. , with Coffey, M. (forthcoming) What is happening when we assess, and how can we use our understanding of this to improve assessment? *Assessment and Evaluation in Higher Education*.

Bennett, N., Dunne, E. and Carré, C. (2000) *Skills Development in Higher Education and Employment*. Buckingham: SRHE/Open University Press.

Bercuson, D., Bothwell, R. and Granatstein, J.L. (1997) *Petrified Campus: The Crisis in Canada's Universities*. Toronto: Random House.

Biggs, J. (1999) *Teaching for Quality Learning at University*. Buckingham: SRHE/Open University Press.

Birnbaum, R. (1992) *How Academic Leadership Works*. San Francisco: Jossey-Bass.

Black, P. (1998) Formative assessment: raising standards. *School Science Review* 80(291): 39–46.

Black, P. and Wiliam, D. (1998) Assessment and classroom learning. *Assessment in Education* 5(1): 7–74.

Black, P. and Wiliam, D. (2002) *Standards in Public Examinations*. London: King's College London.

Blackwell, A., Bowes, L. Harvey, L. Hesketh, A. and Knight P.T. (2001) Transforming work experience in higher education. *British Educational Research Journal* 26(3): 269–86.

Blasko, Z. with Brennan, J., Little, B. and Shah, T. (2002) *Access to What? Analysis of Factors Determining Graduate Employability*, A report to HEFCE. London: Centre for Higher Education Research and Information, Open University.

Bligh, D. (1998) *What's the Use of Lectures?* 5th edition. Exeter: Intellect.

Bloom, B.S. (1956) *Taxonomy of Educational Objectives. Handbook 1: Cognitive Domain*. London: Longman.

Bloom, B.S., Hastings, J.T. and Madaus, G.F. (1971) *Handbook on Formative and Summative Evaluation of Student Learning*. New York: McGraw-Hill.

Booth, A. (2001) Developing history students' skills in the transition to university. *Teaching in Higher Education* 6(4): 487–503.

Boud, D. (1995) Assessment and learning: contradictory or complementary?, in P. Knight (ed.) *Assessment for Learning in Higher Education*. London: Kogan Page, pp. 35–48.

Boud, D. (2000) Sustainable assessment: rethinking assessment for the learning society. *Studies in Continuing Education* 22(2): 151–67.

Boud, D. and Falchikov, N. (1989) Quantitative studies of self-assessment in higher education: a critical analysis of findings. *Higher Education* 18(5): 529–49.

Boud, D. and Feletti, G.E. (eds) (1997) *The Challenge of Problem-based Learning*, 2nd edition. London: Kogan Page.

Bourdieu, P. and Passeron, J.C. (1977) *Reproduction in Education, Society and Culture*. London: Sage.

Bourner, T., O'Hare, S. and Barlow, J. (2000) Only connect; facilitating reflective learning with statements of relevance. *Innovations in Education and Training International* 37(1): 68–75.

Bowker, G.C. and Star, S.L. (1999) *Sorting Things Out*. Cambridge, MA: MIT Press.

Breland, H.M. (1999) From 2 to 3Rs: the expanding use of writing in admissions, in S.J. Messick (ed.) *Assessment in Higher Education: Issues of Access, Quality, Student Development and Public Policy*. Mahwah, NJ: Lawrence Erlbaum Associates, pp. 91–111.

Brennan, J. and Little, B. (1996) *A Review of Work-based Learning in Higher Education*. Sheffield: DfEE, and London: Quality Support Centre/Open University.

Brennan, J., Johnstone, B., Little, B., Shah, T. and Woodley, A. (2001) *The Employment of UK Graduates: Comparisons with Europe and Japan*. London: Higher Education Funding Council for England.

Bridges, D. (1993) Transferable skills: a philosophical perspective. *Studies in Higher Education* 18(1): 43–51.

Bridges, P., Bourdillon, B., Collymore, D., *et al.* (1999) Discipline-related marking behaviour using percentages: a potential cause of inequity in assessment. *Assessment and Evaluation in Higher Education* 24(3): 285–300.

Bridges, P., Cooper, A., Evanson, P., *et al.* (2002) Coursework marks high, examination marks low: discuss. *Assessment and Evaluation in Higher Education* 27(1): 35–48.

Briggs, J. and Peat, F.D. (1999) *Seven Life Lessons of Chaos*. New York: Harper Collins.

Broadfoot, P. (2000) Assessment and intuition, in T. Atkinson and G. Claxton (eds) *The Intuitive Practitioner: On the Value of Not Always Knowing What One is Doing*. Buckingham: Open University Press, pp. 199–219.

Broadfoot, P. (2002) Assessment for lifelong learning: challenges and choices. *Assessment in Education* 9(1): 5–7.

Brockbank, A. and McGill, I. (1998) *Facilitating Reflective Learning in Higher Education*. Buckingham: Open University Press.

Brown, G., Bull, J. and Pendlebury, M. (1997) *Assessing Student Learning in Higher Education*. London: Routledge.

Brown, J.S. and Duguid, P. (2000) *The Social Life of Information*. Cambridge, MA: Harvard University Press.

Brown, P. and Scase, R. (1994) *Higher Education and Corporate Realities: Class, Culture and the Decline of Graduate Careers*. London: UCL Press.

Brown, P., Hesketh, A. and Williams, S. (2002) Employability in a knowledge-driven economy, in P. Knight (ed.) *Innovation in Education for Employability: Notes from the 13th June 2002 Skills plus Conference*, Manchester Metropolitan University, pp. 5–25. Available at http://www.open.ac.uk/vqportal/Skills-Plus/home.htm (accessed 24 August 2002).

Brown, S. (1999) Institutional strategies for assessment, in S. Brown and A. Glasner (eds) *Assessment Matters in Higher Education: Choosing and Using Diverse Approaches*. Buckingham: SRHE/Open University Press, pp. 3–13.

Brown, S. and Knight, P. (1994) *Assessing Learners in Higher Education.* London: Kogan Page.

Bruner, J. (1985) Vygotsky: a historical and conceptual perspective, in J.V. Wertsch (ed.) *Culture, Communication and Cognition: Vygotskian Perspectives.* Cambridge: Cambridge University Press, pp. 21–34.

Bruner, J.S. (1970) Some theories on instruction, in E. Stones (ed.) *Readings in Educational Psychology.* London: Methuen, pp. 112–24.

Bruner, J.S. (1974) *Beyond the Information Given: Studies in the Psychology of Knowing* (ed. J.M. Anglin). London: Allen & Unwin.

Brunson, B.I. and Matthews, K.A. (1981) The Type-A coronary-prone behavior pattern and reaction to uncontrollable stress: an analysis of performance strategies, affect, and attributions during failure. *Journal of Personality and Social Psychology* 40(5): 906–18.

Bryman, A. (2001) *Social Research Methods.* Oxford: Oxford University Press.

Cambridge, B.L. (2001) Electronic portfolios as knowledge builders, in B.L. Cambridge (ed.) *Electronic Portfolios: Emerging Practices in Student, Faculty and Instructional Learning.* Washington DC: American Association for Higher Education, pp. 1–11.

Campbell, D. and Russo, M.J. (2001) *Social Measurement.* Thousand Oaks, CA: Sage.

Campbell, D.T. and Stanley, J.C. (1963) *Experimental and Quasi-experimental Designs for Research.* Boston, MA: Houghton Mifflin.

Carroll, J. (2002) Using assessment to deter plagiarism, *Link* (journal of the LTSN hospitality, leisure, sport and tourism subject centre), No. 5: 12–14.

Carroll, M. (1995) Formative assessment workshops: feedback sessions for large classes. *Biochemical Education* 23(2): 65–7.

Chambers, E. (1992) Work load and the quality of student learning. *Studies in Higher Education* 17(2): 141–53.

Chambers, D. and Glassman, P. (1997) A primer on competency-based education. *Dental Education* 61(8): 651–66.

Chanock, K. (2000) Comments on essays: do students understand what tutors write? *Teaching in Higher Education* 5(1): 95–105.

Chappell, C., Farrell, L., Scheeres, H. and Solomon, N. (2000) The organization of identity: four cases, in C. Symes and J. McIntyre (eds) *Working Knowledge: The New Vocationalism and Higher Education.* Buckingham: SRHE/Open University Press, pp. 135–52.

Checkland, P. (1981) *Systems Thinking, Systems Practice.* Chichester: John Wiley.

Checkland, P. and Scholes, J. (1990) *Soft Systems Methodology in Action.* Chichester: John Wiley.

Cherniss, C. (2000) Social and emotional competence in the workplace, in R. Bar-On, and J. Parker (eds) *The Handbook of Emotional Intelligence.* San Francisco: Jossey-Bass, pp. 433–58.

Clark, C.M. and Peterson, P.L. (1986) Teachers' thinking processes, in M. Wittrock (ed.) *Handbook of Research on Teaching,* 3rd edition. New York: Macmillan, pp. 255–96.

Claxton, G. (1998) *Hare Brain, Tortoise Mind.* London: Fourth Estate.

CNAA/PCFC (1990) *The Measurement of Value Added in Higher Education.* London: Council for National Academic Awards and the Polytechnics and Colleges Funding Council.

Coffield, F. (2002) Skills for the future: I've got a little list. *Assessment in Education* 9(1): 39–43.

Coleman, S. and Keep, E. (2001) *Background Literature Review for PIU Project on Workforce Development.* London: Cabinet Office Performance and Innovation Unit.

Cooke, R. (2003) *Final Report of the TQEC on the Future Needs and Support for Quality Enhancement of Learning and Teaching in Higher Education.* London: Higher Education Funding Council for England, Universities UK and the Standing Conference of Principals.

Cooper, R.K. and Sawaf, A. (1997). *Executive EQ.* London: Orion Business Books.

Cowan, J. (1998) *On Becoming an Innovative University Teacher: Reflection in Action.* Buckingham: SRHE/Open University Press.

Cowie, B. and Bell, B. (1999) A model of formative assessment in science education. *Assessment in Education* 6(1): 101–16.

Cronbach, L.J. and Meehl, P.E. (1955) Construct validity in psychological tests. *Psychological Bulletin* 52: 281–302.

Cuming, J. and Maxwell, G. (1999) Contextualising authentic assessment. *Assessment in Higher Education* 6(2): 177–94.

Dalziel, J. (1998) Using marks to assess student performance. *Assessment and Evaluation in Higher Education* 23(4): 351–66.

Davies, H. and Nutley, S. (2002) *Evidence-based Policy and Practice: Moving from Rhetoric to Reality*. St Andrews: Research Unit for Research Utilisation.

Davies, M. and Fleiss, J.L. (1982) Measuring agreement for multinominal data. *Biometrics* 38: 1047–51.

Davies, P. (2002) Levels of attainment in geography. *Assessment in Education* 9(2): 185–204.

Denzin, N.K. and Lincoln, Y.S. (eds) (1994) *Handbook of Qualitative Research*. London: Sage.

Desforges, C. (1989) *Testing and Assessment*. London: Cassell.

DfES (Department for Education and Skills) (2003) *The Future of Higher Education* (Cm. 5753). Norwich: The Stationery Office.

Dochy, F., Segers, M. and Sluijsmans, D. (1999) The use of self-, peer and co-assessment in higher education: a review. *Studies in Higher Education* 24(3): 331–50.

Doyle, W. (1983) Academic work. *Review of Educational Research* 53(2): 159–99.

Dweck, C.S. (1999) *Self-theories: Their Role in Motivation, Personality and Development*. Philadelphia: Psychology Press.

Dweck, C.S. and Leggett, E.L. (1988) A social-cognitive approach to motivation and personality. *Psychological Review* 95(2): 256–73.

Easterby-Smith, M. (1997) Disciplines of organizational learning: contributions and critiques. *Human Relations* 50(9): 1085–113.

EC (2002) *'Best procedure' project on education and training for entrepreneurship*, Final Report of the Expert Group. Brussels: European Commission. Available at http://europa.eu.int/comm/enterprise/entrepreneurship/support_measures/training_education/education_final.pdf (accessed 20 January 2003).

Ecclestone, K. (2001) I know a 2:1 when I see it: understanding criteria for degree classifications in franchised university programmes. *Journal of Further and Higher Education* 5(3): 301–13.

Ecclestone, K. (2002) *Learning Autonomy in Post-16 Education: The Politics and Practice of Formative Assessment*. London: Routledge/Falmer.

Ecclestone, K. and Swann, J. (1999) Litigation and learning: tensions in improving university lecturers' assessment practice. *Assessment in Education* 6(3): 377–89.

Eisner, E.W. (1985) *The Art of Educational Evaluation: A Personal View*. London: Falmer.

Elliott, E. and Dweck, C. (1988) Goals: an approach to motivation and achievement. *Journal of Personal and Social Psychology* 54(1): 5–12.

Elton, L. (1998) Are UK degree standards going up, down or sideways? *Studies in Higher Education* 23(1): 35–42.

Engeström, Y. (2001) Expansive learning at work: towards an activity theoretical reconceptualization, *Journal of Education and Work* 14(1): 133–56.

Engineering Professors' Council (2002) *The EPC Engineering Graduate Output Standard*, Final Report of the EPC Output Standards Project. Coventry: Engineering Professors' Council.

Entwistle, A.C. and Entwistle, N.J. (1992) Experiences of understanding in revising for degree examinations. *Learning and Instruction* 2(1): 1–22.

Entwistle, N.J. and Marton, F. (1994) Knowledge objects: understandings constituted through intensive academic study. *British Journal of Educational Psychology* 64(1): 161–78.

Eraut, M. (1994) *Developing Professional Knowledge and Competence*. London: Falmer Press.

Evans, J. and Benefield, P. (2001) Systematic reviews of educational research: does the medical model fit? *British Educational Research Journal* 27(5): 527–41.

Farrell, J.P. (2000) Why is educational reform so difficult? *Curriculum Inquiry* 30(1): 83–103.

Feinstein, L. (2000) *The Relative Economic Importance of Academic, Psychological and Behavioural Attributes Developed in Childhood*. London: Centre for Economic Performance, London School of Economics.

Fischer, K., Kenny, S. and Pipp, S. (1990) How cognitive processes and environmental conditions organise discontinuities in the development of abstractions, in C. Alexander and E. Langer (eds) *Higher Stages of Human Development*. Oxford: Oxford University Press, pp. 71–96.

Fiske, J. (1990) *Introduction to Communication Studies*, 2nd edition. London: Routledge.

Franklyn-Stokes, A. and Newstead, S.E. (1995) Undergraduate cheating: who does what and why? *Studies in Higher Education* 20(2): 159–72.

Fransella, F. and Adams, B. (1966) An illustration of the use of repertory grid technique in a clinical setting. *British Journal of Social and Clinical Psychology* 5(1): 51–62.

Fullan, M. (1991). *The New Meaning of Educational Change*. London: Cassell.

Gaff, J.G. and Ratcliff, J.L. (eds.) (1996) *Handbook of the Undergraduate Curriculum*. San Francisco: Jossey-Bass.

Ganesan, R., Edmonds, G. and Spector, M. (2002) The changing nature of instructional design for networked learning, in C. Steeples and C. Jones (eds) *Networked Learning: Perspectives and Issues*. London: Springer-Verlag, pp. 93–110.

Gardner, H. (1983) *Frames of Mind*. New York: Basic Books.

GCCA (2002) *The Course Experience Questionnaire 2001*. Melbourne: Graduate Careers Council of Australia.

Gee, J.P. and Lankshear, C. (1997) Language, literacy and the new work order, in C. Lankshear (ed.) *Changing Literacies*. Buckingham: Open University Press, pp. 83–101.

Gibbons, M., Limoges, C., Nowotny, H., Schwartzman, S., Scott, P. and Trow, M. (1994) *The New Production of Knowledge: The Dynamics of Science and Research in Contemporary Societies*. London: Sage.

Gibbs, G. (1999) Using assessment strategically to change the way students learn, in S. Brown and A. Glasner (eds) *Assessment Matters in Higher Education: Choosing and Using Diverse Approaches*. Buckingham: SRHE/Open University Press, pp. 41–53.

Gibbs, G. and Simpson, C. (2002) Does your Assessment Support Student Learning? Unpublished paper, Centre for Higher Education Practice, The Open University, Milton Keynes.

Gibson, G.W. (1992) *Good Start: A Guidebook for New Faculty in Liberal Arts Colleges*. Boston, MA: Anker.

Gipps, C.V. (1994) *Beyond Testing: Towards a Theory of Educational Assessment*. London: Falmer Press.

Goldstein, H. and Woodhouse, G. (2000) School effectiveness and educational policy, *Oxford Review of Education* 26(3/4): 253–363.

Goleman, D. (1996). *Emotional Intelligence*. London: Bloomsbury.

Goleman, D. (1998). *Working with Emotional Intelligence*. New York: Bantam Books.

Goodyear, P. (2002) Psychological foundations for networked learning, in C. Steeples and C. Jones (eds) *Networked Learning: Perspectives and Issues*. London: Springer-Verlag, pp. 49–76.

Gosling, D. and Moon, J. (2001) *How to Use Learning Outcomes and Assessment Criteria*. London: Southern England Consortium for Credit Accumulation and Transfer.

Gray, J., Hopkins, D., Reynolds, D., Wilcox, B., Farrell, S. and Jesson, D. (1999) *Improving Schools: Performance and Potential*. Buckingham: Open University Press

Greatorex, J. (1999) Generic descriptors: a health check. *Quality in Higher Education*, 5(2): 155–66.

Guile, D. and Young, M. (1998) Apprenticeship as a conceptual basis for a social theory of learning. *Journal of Vocational Education and Training* 50(2): 173–92.

Haney, C. and Zimbardo P.G. (1997) The socialization into criminality: on becoming a prisoner and a guard, in J.L. Tapp and F.L. Levine (eds) *Law, Justice and the Individual in Society: Psychological and Legal Issues*. New York: Holt, Rinehart & Winston, 198–223.

Hargreaves, D. (2001) A capital theory of school effectiveness and improvement. *British Educational Research Journal* 27(4): 487–503.

Harlen, W. and James, M. (1997) Assessment and learning: differences and relationships between formative and summative assessment. *Assessment in Education* 4(3): 365–79.

Harvey, L. (2002) The end of quality? *Quality in Higher Education* 8(1): 5–22.

Harvey, L., Moon, S. and Geall, V., with Bower, R. (1997) *Graduates' Work: Organisation Change and Students' Attributes*. Birmingham: Centre for Research into Quality/Association of Graduate Recruiters.

Haug, G. and Tauch, C. (2001) *Trends in Learning Structures in Higher Education II*, Follow-up report prepared for the Salamanca and Prague Conferences of March/May 2001. Available at http://www.oph.fi/publications/trends2/trends2.html. (accessed 25 July 2002).

Hawkins, P. and Winter, J. (1995) *Skills for Graduates in the 21st Century*. Cambridge: Association of Graduate Recruiters.

Hedlund, J. and Sternberg, R. (2000) Too many intelligences?, in R. Bar-On and J. Parker (eds) *The Handbook of Emotional Intelligence*. San Francisco: Jossey-Bass, pp. 136–67.

HEFCE (2002) *Performance Indicators in Higher Education in the UK, 1999–2000, 2000–1*, Report 2002/52. Bristol: Higher Education Funding Council for England.

Heller, J.I., Sheingold, K. and Myford, C.M. (1998) Reasoning about evidence in portfolios: cognitive foundations for valid and reliable assessment. *Educational Assessment* 5(1): 5–40.

HEQC (1996) *Inter-institutional Variability of Degree Results: An Analysis in Selected Subjects*. London: Higher Education Quality Council.

HEQC (1997) *Graduate Standards Programme: Final Report* (2 vols). London: Higher Education Quality Council.

Herman, J.L., Gearhart, M. and Baker, E.L. (1993) Assessing writing portfolios: issues in the validity and meaning of scores. *Educational Assessment* 1(3): 201–24.

Hesketh, A.J. (2000) Recruiting an elite? Employers' perceptions of graduate education and training. *Journal of Education and Work* 13(3): 245–71.

Heywood, J. (2000) *Assessment in Higher Education: Student Learning, Teaching, Programmes and Institutions*. London: Jessica Kingsley.

Hillage, J. and Pollard, E. (1998) *Employability: Developing a Framework for Policy Analysis*. London: Department for Education and Employment.

Hinchliffe, G. (2002) Situating skills. *Journal of Philosophy of Education* 36(2): 187–205.

Hirsch, E.D. (1967) *Validity in Interpretation*. New Haven, CT: Yale University Press.

Hirsch, F. (1977) *Social Limits to Growth*. London: Routledge & Kegan Paul.

Hochschild, A.R. (1993) *The Managed Heart: The Commercialization of Human Feeling*. Berkeley, CA: University of California Press.

Hockett, C. and Asher, R. (1964) The human revolution. *Current Anthropology* 5(3): 135–47.

Holmes, L. (1996) Reframing the ability-based curriculum in higher education. Unpublished paper, University of North London.

Holmes, L. (2001) Reconsidering graduate employability: the graduate identity approach. *Quality in Higher Education* 7(2): 111–19.

Hounsell, D., McCulloch, M. and Scott, M. (eds) (1996) *The ASSHE Inventory*. Edinburgh: University of Edinburgh and Napier University.

Hoyles, C. (1990) Neglected voices: pupils' mathematics and the national curriculum, in P. Dowling and R. Noss (eds) *Mathematics* versus *the National Curriculum*. Basingstoke: Falmer Press, pp. 191–213.

Hult, C. (2001) Using on-line portfolios to assess English majors at Utah State University, in B.L. Cambridge (ed.) *Electronic Portfolios: Emerging Practices in Student, Faculty and Instructional Learning*. Washington DC: The American Association for Higher Education, pp. 60–70

Izard, J. (2002) Achieving comparability between assessments of different regions or nations: practical strategies. Paper presented to the Association of Commonwealth Examinations and Accreditation Bodies, Mauritius, 4–8 September. Available at http://www.nzqa.govt.nz/aceab/docs/Jones.pdf (accessed 19 July 2002).

Jackson, N. and Lund, H. (2000) *Benchmarking for Higher Education*. Buckingham: SRHE/Open University Press.

Jackson, S., Lunt, T. and Margham, P. (1998) Accrediting sandwich training: the City and Guilds Licentiateship, in J. Stephenson and M. Yorke (eds) *Capability and Quality in Higher Education*. London: Kogan Page, pp. 77–84.

James, R., McInnis, C. and Devlin, M. (2002) *Assessing Learning in Australian Universities: Ideas, Strategies and Resources for Quality in Student Assessment*. Melbourne: CSHE, University of Melbourne, and Canberra: Australian Universities Teaching Committee.

Jenkins, P. (2001) Development of electronic portfolios for nursing students, in B.L. Cambridge (ed.) *Electronic Portfolios: Emerging Practices in Student, Faculty and Instructional Learning*. Washington DC: The American Association for Higher Education, pp. 71–5

Jessup, G. (1991) *Outcomes: NVQs and the Emerging Model of Education and Training*. London: Falmer Press.

Jones, B. (2002) Comparability between examinations: a review of some of the issues. Paper presented to the Association of Commonwealth Examinations and Accreditation Bodies, Mauritius, 4–8 September. Available at http://www.nzqa.govt.nz/aceab/docs/Jones.pdf (accessed 19 July 2002).

Kahn, P.E. and Hoyles, C. (1997) The changing undergraduate experience: a case study of single honours mathematics in England and Wales. *Studies in Higher Education* 22(3): 349–62.

King, P.M. and Kitchener, K.S. (1994) *Developing Reflective Judgment: Understanding and Promoting Intellectual Growth and Critical Thinking in Adolescents and Young Adults*. San Francisco: Jossey-Bass.

Klein, N. (2001) *No Logo*. London: Flamingo.

Klenowski, V. (2002) *Developing Portfolios for Learning and Assessment: Processes and Principles*. London: Routledge Falmer.

Knight, P. (2000) The value of a programme-wide approach to assessment. *Assessment and Evaluation in Higher Education* 25(3): 237–51.

Knight, P.T. (2001a) Complexity and curriculum: a process approach to curriculum-making, *Teaching in Higher Education* 6(2): 371–83.

Knight, P.T. (2001b) *Key Concepts: Formative and Summative, Norm and Criterion-referenced Assessment*. York: Learning and Teaching Support Network.

Knight, P.T. (2002a) *Being a Teacher in Higher Education*. Buckingham: SRHE/Open University Press.

Knight, P.T. (2002b) *Assessment for Learning: Practices and Programmes*, A reader for programme H850. Milton Keynes: The Open University.

Knight, P.T. (2002c) Summative assessment in higher education: practices in disarray, *Studies in Higher Education* 27(3): 275–86.

Knight, P.T. (2002d) *Small-scale Research*. London: Sage.

Knight, P.T. and Trowler, P.R. (2000) Academic work and quality. *Quality in Higher Education* 6(2): 109–14.

Knight, P.T. and Trowler, P.R. (2001) *Departmental Leadership in Higher Education*. Buckingham: SRHE/Open University Press.

Knight, P.T. and Yorke, M. (2002) Employability through the curriculum. *Tertiary Education and Management* 8(4): 261–76.

Knight, P.T. and Yorke, M. (2003) *Learning, Curriculum and Employability in Higher Education*. London: Routledge Falmer.

Kohlberg, L. (1964) *The Philosophy of Moral Development: Moral Stages and the Idea of Justice*. San Francisco: Harper & Row.

Koretz, D. (1998) Large-scale portfolio assessments in the US: evidence pertaining to the quality of measurement. *Assessment in Education* 5(3): 309–34.

Koretz, D., Stecher, B., Klein, S. and McCaffrey, D. (1993) *Interim Report: The Reliability of Vermont Portfolio Scores in the 1992–93 School Year*. Santa Monica, CA: RAND Institute on Education and Training.

Latour, B. (1999) On recalling ANT, in J. Law and J. Hassard (eds) *Actor Network Theory and After*. Oxford: Blackwell, pp. 14–25.

Laurillard, D. (1993) *Rethinking University Teaching: A Framework for the Effective Use of Educational Technology*. London: Routledge.

Leadbeater, C. (2000) *Living on Thin Air*. London: Penguin.

Leithwood, K., Jantzi, D. and Steinbach, R. (1999) *Changing Leadership for Changing Times*. Buckingham: Open University Press.

LeMahieu, P., Gitomer, D.H. and Eresh, J.T. (1995) Portfolios in large-scale assessment: difficult but not impossible. *Educational Measurement: Issues and Practices* 14(1): 11–16, 25–8.

Leon, P. (2002) Graduates say degrees leave them short of skills. *The Times Higher Education Supplement* No. 1565 (22 November), p. 6.

Lester, S. (1999) Assessing the self-managing learner: a contradiction in terms?, in D. O'Reilly, L. Cunningham and S. Lester (eds) *Developing the Capable Practitioner: Professional Capability through Higher Education*. London: Kogan Page, pp. 99–108.

Linn, R. (2000) Assessments and acountability. *Educational Researcher* 29(2): 4–16.

Luhmann, N. (1995) *Social Systems* (trans. J. Bednarz and D. Baecker). Stanford, CA: Stanford University Press.

Marzano, R.J. (1998) *A Theory-based Meta-analysis of Research on Instruction*. Aurora, CO: Mid-continent Regional Educational Laboratory.

Mayer, J.D., Caruso, D.R. and Salovey, P. (2000a) Selecting a measure for emotional intelligence: the case for ability scales, in R. Bar-On and J. Parker (eds) *The Handbook of Emotional Intelligence*. San Francisco: Jossey-Bass, pp. 320–42.

Mayer, J.D., Salovey, P. and Caruso, D.R. (2000b) Emotional intelligence as zeitgeist, as personality and as a mental ability, in R. Bar-On, and J. Parker (eds) *The Handbook of Emotional Intelligence*. San Francisco: Jossey-Bass, pp. 92–117.

McCarthy, D. and Hurst, A. (2001) *A Briefing on Assessing Disabled Students*, Assessment Series No. 8. York: Learning and Teaching Support Network.

McInnis, C. (2001) *Signs of Disengagement? The Changing Undergraduate Experience in Australian Universities*. Melbourne: Centre for the Study of Higher Education, University of

Melbourne. Available at http://www.cshe.unimelb.edu.au/downloads/InaugLec 23_8_01.pdf (accessed 25 July 2002).

McLeman, P. and Smith, P. (1998) The career management initiative at Buckinghamshire Chilterns University College, in J. Stephenson and M. Yorke (eds) *Capability and Quality in Higher Education*. London: Kogan Page, pp. 102–111.

McPherson, A. (1997) Measuring added value in schools, in A. Harris, N. Bennett and M. Preedy (eds) *Organizational Effectiveness and Improvement in Education*. Buckingham: Open University Press, pp. 184–90.

Mentkowski, M. and Associates (2000) *Learning that Lasts: Integrating Learning Development and Performance in College and Beyond*. San Fancisco: Jossey-Bass.

Miller, C.M.L. and Parlett, M. (1974) *Up to the Mark: A Study of the Examination Game*, Monograph 21. London: Society for Research into Higher Education.

Moon, J. (1999) *Reflection in Learning and Professional Development*. London: Kogan Page.

Moon, J. (2003) *Reflection and Employability*. York: Learning and Teaching Support Network.

Morgan, G. (1997) *Images of Organization*, 2nd edition. Thousand Oaks, CA: Sage.

Morley, L. (2001) Producing new workers: quality, equality and employability in higher education. *Quality in Higher Education* 7(2): 131–8.

Moshman, D. (1999) *Adolescent Psychological Development*. Mahwah, NJ: Lawrence Erlbaum Associates.

Naylor, R. and Smith, J. (2002) Schooling effects on subsequent university performance: evidence for the UK university population, Warwick Economic Research Papers No. 657. Coventry: Department of Economics, Warwick University.

NCIHE (1997) *Higher Education in the Learning Society, Report of the National Committee of Inquiry into Higher Education* (The Dearing Report). Norwich: HMSO.

NICATS (2002) *Designing Learning Programmes: A Credit-based Approach*. Belfast: Northern Ireland Credit Accumulation and Transfer System.

Nystrand, M., Cohen, A.S. and Dowling, N.M. (1993) Addressing reliability problems in the portfolio assessment of college writing. *Educational Assessment* 1(1): 53–70.

O'Donovan, B., Price, M. and Rust, C. (2000) The student experience of criterion-referenced assessment. *Innovations in Education and Teaching International* 38(1): 74–85.

Osborne, C., Davies, J. and Garnett, J. (1998) Guiding the student to the centre of the stakeholder curriculum: independent and work-based learning at Middlesex University, in J. Stephenson and M. Yorke (eds) *Capability and Quality in Higher Education*. London: Kogan Page, pp. 85–94.

Otter, S. (1992) *Learning Outcomes in Higher Education*. London: Unit for the Development of Adult Continuing Education.

Page, B. (1998) The new capability curriculum at the University of North London, in J. Stephenson and M. Yorke (eds) *Capability and Quality in Higher Education*. London: Kogan Page, pp. 35–41.

Palloff, R.M. and Pratt, K. (1999) *Building Learning Communities in Cyberspace*. San Francisco: Jossey-Bass.

Pascarella, E.T. and Terenzini, P.T. (1991) *How College Affects Students*. San Francisco: Jossey-Bass.

Pawson, R. (2001) *Evidence Based Policy. II: The Promise of 'Realist Synthesis'*. London: UK Centre for Evidence Based Policy and Practice, Queen Mary College, University of London.

Pellegrino, J., Chudowsky, N. and Glaser, R. (eds) (2001) *Knowing What Students Know: The Science and Design of Educational Assessment*. Washington DC: National Academy Press.

Perry, W.G. (1998/1970) *Forms of Ethical and Intellectual Development in the College Years* (Reprint of 1970 text, with a new introduction by L.L. Knefelkamp.) San Francisco: Jossey-Bass.

Peterson, C., Maier, S.F. and Seligman, M.E.P. (1993) *Learned Helplessness: A Theory for the Age of Personal Control.* New York: Oxford University Press.

Peterson, P.L. (1979) Direct instruction reconsidered, in P.L. Peterson and H.J. Wahlberg (eds) *Research on Teaching.* Berkeley, CA: McCutcheon, pp. 59–67.

Pietroni, R. and Millard, L. (1997) Portfolio-based learning, in D. Pendleton and J. Hasler (eds) *Professional Development in General Practice.* Oxford: Oxford University Press, pp. 81–93.

Pintrich, P.R. (2000) The role of goal orientation in self-regulated learning, in M. Boekaerts, P. Pintrich and M. Zeidner (eds) *Handbook of Self-regulation.* New York: Academic Press, pp. 451–502.

Pintrich, P.R. (2002) The role of metacognition in learning, teaching and assessing. *Theory into Practice* 41(4): 219–25.

Pitts, J., Coles, C. and Thomas, P. (1999) Educational portfolios in the assessment of general practice trainers: reliability of assessors. *Medical Education* 33(7): 515–20.

Polanyi, M. (1958) *Personal Knowledge: Towards a Postcritical Philosophy.* London: Routledge & Kegan Paul.

Price, M. and Rust, C. (1999) The experience of introducing a common criteria assessment grid across an academic department. *Quality in Higher Education* 5(2): 133–44.

Purcell, K. and Pitcher, J. (1996) *Great Expectations: The New Diversity of Graduate Skills and Aspirations.* Coventry: Institute for Employment Research, University of Warwick.

Purcell, K., Morley, M. and Rowley, G. (2002) *Recruiting from a Wider Spectrum of Graduates.* London: Council for Industry and Higher Education, and Bristol: ESRU, Bristol Business School.

QAA (1999) *Policy on Programme Specifications.* Gloucester: Quality Assurance Agency for Higher Education.

QAA (2000a) *Code of Practice for the Assurance of Academic Quality and Standards in Higher Education.* Gloucester: Quality Assurance Agency for Higher Education.

QAA (2000b) *The National Qualifications Framework for Higher Education Qualifications in England, Wales and Northern Ireland: A Position Paper.* Gloucester: Quality Assurance Agency for Higher Education.

QAA (2001a) *Subject Overview Report: Business and Management*, QO5/2001. Gloucester: Quality Assurance Agency for Higher Education.

QAA (2001b) *Subject Overview Report: Education*, QO10/2001. Gloucester, Quality Assurance Agency for Higher Education.

QAA (2001c) *The Framework for Higher Education Qualifications in England, Wales and Northern Ireland.* Gloucester: Quality Assurance Agency for Higher Education.

QAA (2001d) *Guidelines for HE Progress Files.* Gloucester: Quality Assurance Agency for Higher Education.

Reich, R.B. (1991) *The Work of Nations.* London: Simon & Schuster.

Reich, R.B. (2002) *The Future of Success.* London: Vintage.

Resnick, L.B. and Resnick, D.P. (1992) Assessing the thinking curriculum, in B.R. Gifford and M.C. O'Connor (eds) *Changing Assessments: Alternative Views of Aptitude, Achievement and Instruction.* Boston: Kluwer, pp. 37–75.

Richards, B. (1993) A degree of self-fulfilment. *The Times Higher Education Supplement* 20 August, p. 10.

Richardson, R. (1999) *Performance Related Pay in Schools. An Evaluation of the Governments' Evidence to the School Teachers' Pay Review Body.* London: National Union of Teachers.

Robbins, L. (Chairman) (1963) *Higher Education, Report of the Committee appointed by the Prime Minister under the chairmanship of Lord Robbins, 1961–63.* London: Her Majesty's Stationery Office.

Robertson, D. (1993) Flexibility and mobility in further and higher education: policy continuity and progress. *Journal of Further and Higher Education* 17(1): 68–79.

Robertson, D. (2002) *Intermediate-level Qualifications in Higher Education: An International Assessment.* Available at www.hefce.ac.uk/Pubs/RDreports/Downloads/report12.htm (accessed 12 January 2003).

Rolfe, I. and McPherson, J. (1995) Formative assessment: how am I doing? *Lancet* 345(8953): 837–9.

Rosenholtz, S. (1989) *Teachers' Workplace.* New York: Macmillan.

Rowntree, D. (1987) *Assessing Students: How Shall We Know Them?* London: Kogan Page.

Rudduck, J. and McIntyre, D. (eds) (1998) *Challenges for Educational Research.* London: Paul Chapman.

Rushforth, J. (2003) Letter. *The Times Higher Education Supplement* No. 1576 (14 February), p. 15.

Sadler, D.R. (1989) Formative assessment and the design of instructional systems. *Instructional Science* 18(2): 119–41.

Sadler, D.R. (1998) Formative assessment: revisiting the territory. *Assessment in Education* 5(1): 77–84.

Sadler, D.R. (2002) Learning dispositions: can we really assess them? *Assessment in Education* 9(1): 45–51.

Salmon, G. (2000) *E-moderation. The Key to Teaching and Learning Online.* London: Kogan Page.

Savin-Baden, M. (2000) *Problem-based Learning in Higher Education: Untold Stories.* Buckingham: SRHE/Open University Press.

Schratz, M. and Walker, R. (1995) *Research as Social Change.* London: Routledge.

Schwartz, P. and Webb, G. (eds) (2002) *Assessment: Case Studies, Experience and Practice from Higher Education.* London: Kogan Page.

Scott, P. (1995) *The Meanings of Mass Higher Education.* Buckingham: SRHE/Open University Press.

Scott, P. (ed.) (1998) *The Globalization of Higher Education.* Buckingham: SRHE/Open University Press.

Seldin, P. (1997) *The Teaching Portfolio.* Boston, MA: Anker.

Sennett, R. (1998) *The Corrosion of Character.* New York: Norton.

Shaw, M. (1996) . . . from rhetoric to reality. Paper prepared for the Higher Education for Capability Assessment Meeting, Institute of Education, University of London, 11 July (mimeo).

Sheffield Hallam University (1996) *A Partnership Approach to Integrating NVQs and Academic Awards in the Engineering Industry, Report on a Project Undertaken for the Department for Education and Employment.* Sheffield: Sheffield Hallam University.

Shepard, L.A. (2000) The role of assessment in a learning culture. *Educational Researcher* 29(7): 4–14.

Silver, H. and Brennan, J. (1988) *A Liberal Vocationalism.* London: Methuen.

Silver, H., Stennett, A. and Williams, R. (1995) *The External Examiner System: Possible Futures.* London: Quality Support Centre, Open University.

Simon, M. and Forgette-Giroux, R. (2000) Impact of a content selection framework on portfolio assessment at the classroom level. *Assessment in Education* 7: 83–101.

Squires, G. (1990) *First Degree: The Undergraduate Curriculum.* Buckingham: SRHE/Open University Press.

Stark, R., Gruber, H., Renkl, A. and Mandl, H. (1998) Instructional effects in complex learning. *Learning and Instruction* 8(2): 117–29.

Stecher, B. (1998) The local benefits and burdens of large-scale portfolio assessment. *Assessment in Education* 5(3): 335–51.

Steering Group for the NRA Review (1997) *Report of the Steering Group*, Report No. NRAR1. Department for Education and Employment.

Stefani, L. and Carroll, J. (2001) *A Briefing on Plagiarism*, Assessment Series No. 10. York: Learning and Teaching Support Network.

Stephenson, J. (1998) The concept of capability and its importance in higher education, in J. Stephenson and M. Yorke (eds) *Capability and Quality in Higher Education*. London: Kogan Page, pp. 1–13.

Stephenson, J. (2001) Ensuring a holistic approach to work-based learning: the capability envelope, in D. Boud and N. Solomon (eds) *Work-based Learning: A New Higher Education?* Buckingham: SRHE/Open University Press, pp. 86–102.

Stephenson, J. and Yorke, M. (1998) Creating the conditions for the development of capability, in J. Stephenson and M. Yorke (eds) *Capability and Quality in Higher Education*. London: Kogan Page, pp. 193–225.

Sternberg, R.J. (1997) *Successful Intelligence: How Practical and Creative Intelligence Determine Success in Life*. New York: Plume.

Sternberg, R.J. and Grigorenko, E.L. (2000) Practical intelligence and its development, in R. Bar-On and J. Parker (eds) *The Handbook of Emotional Intelligence*. San Francisco, CA: Jossey-Bass, pp. 215–243.

Stowell, M. (2001) Equity, justice and standards: assessment decision making in higher education. Paper presented at the Society for Research into Higher Education Annual Conference, University of Cambridge (mimeo).

Supovitz, J.A., MacGowan, A. and Slattery, J. (1997) Assessing agreement: an examination of the interrater reliability of portfolio assessment in Rochester, New York. *Educational Assessment* 4(3): 237–59.

Swann, J. and Ecclestone, K. (1999) Improving lecturers' assessment practice in higher education: a problem-based approach. *Educational Action Research* 7(1): 63–84.

Sylva, K. (1994) School influences on children's development. *Journal of Child Psychology and Psychiatry* 35(1): 135–70.

Taylor, I., Thomas, J. and Sage, H. (1999) Portfolios for learning and assessment: laying the foundations for continuing professional development. *Social Work Education* 18(2): 147–60.

Tinto, V. (1993) *Leaving College: Rethinking the Causes and Cures of Student Attrition*, 2nd edition. Chicago: University of Chicago Press.

Topping, K., Holmes, E.A. and Bremner, W. (2000) The effectiveness of school-based programs for the promotion of social competence, in R. Bar-On, and J. Parker (eds) *The Handbook of Emotional Intelligence*. San Francisco: Jossey-Bass, pp. 411–32.

Torrance, H. (ed) (1995) *Evaluating Authentic Assessment*. Buckingham: Open University Press.

Torrance, H. and Pryor, J. (1998) *Investigating Formative Assessment: Teaching, Learning and Assessment in the Classroom*. Buckingham: Open University Press.

Torrance, H. and Pryor, J. (2001) Developing formative assessment in the classroom: using action research to explore and modify theory. *British Educational Research Journal* 27(5): 615–31.

Trowler, P.R. (ed.) (2002) *Higher Education Policy and Institutional Change*. Buckingham: SRHE/Open University Press.

Trowler, P., Saunders, M. and Knight, P.T. (2003) *Change Thinking, Change Practices*. York: Learning and Teaching Support Network.

UUK (2002) *Reducing the Risk of Student Suicide: Issues and Responses for Higher Education Institutions*. London: Universities UK.

Valsiner, J. and van der Veer, R. (2000) *The Social Mind: Construction of the Idea*. Cambridge: Cambridge University Press.

van Geert, P. (1994) *Dynamic Systems of Development: Change between Complexity and Chaos.* Hemel Hempstead: Harvester Wheatsheaf.

Vaz, M., Avadhany, S.T. and Rao, B.S. (1996) Student perspectives on the role of formative assessment in physiology. *Medical Teacher* 18(4): 324–6.

Vygotsky, L.S. (1978) *Mind in Society: The Development of Higher Psychological Processes.* Cambridge, MA: Harvard University Press.

Wagner, R.K. (1993) In search of intraterrestrial intelligence. *Journal of Cooperative Education* 28(2): 18–21.

Wakeford, N. (1994) Becoming a mature student: the social risks of identification. *Journal of Access Studies* 9(2): 241–56.

Walvoord, B.E. and Anderson, V.J. (1998) *Effective Grading: A Tool for Learning and Assessment.* San Francisco: Jossey-Bass.

Warren Piper, D. (1994) *Are Professors Professional? The Organisation of University Examinations.* London: Jessica Kingsley.

Watton, P. and Collings, J. (2002) Developing a framework for independent work experience, in P. Watton, J. Collings and J. Moon (eds) *Independent Work Experience: an Evolving Picture,* SEDA Paper 114. Birmingham: Staff and Educational Development Association, pp. 25–34.

Watton, P., Collings, J. and Moon, J. (eds) (2002) *Independent Work Experience: An Evolving Picture,* SEDA Paper 114. Birmingham: Staff and Educational Development Association.

Weick, K. (1995) *Sensemaking in Organizations.* Thousand Oaks, CA: Sage.

Weick, K.E. (1976) Educational organizations as loosely-coupled systems. *Administrative Science Quarterly* 22(1): 1–19.

Wenger, E. (1998) *Communities of Practice: Learning, Meaning and Identity.* Cambridge: Cambridge University Press.

Wertsch, J.V. (1998) *Mind as Action.* Oxford: Oxford University Press.

West, M. (2000) Supporting school improvement. *School Leadership and Management* 20(1): 43–60.

Winter, R. (1993a) Education or grading? Arguments for a non-divided honours degree. *Studies in Higher Education* 18(3): 363–77.

Winter, R. (1993b) The problem of educational levels (Part 1). *Journal of Further and Higher Education* 17(3): 90–104.

Winter, R. (1994) The problem of educational levels (Part 2). *Journal of Further and Higher Education* 18(1): 92–106.

Winter, R. and Maisch, M. (1996) *Professional Competence and Higher Education: The ASSET Programme.* London: Falmer Press.

Wolf, A. (1995a) Authentic assessments in a competitive sector: institutional prerequisites and cautionary tales, in H. Torrance (ed.) *Evaluating Authentic Assessment.* Buckingham: Open University Press, pp. 88–104.

Wolf, A. (1995b) *Competence-based Assessment.* Buckingham: Open University Press.

Wolf, A. (1998) Portfolio assessment as national policy: the National Council for Vocational Qualifications and its quest for a pedagogical revolution. *Assessment in Education* 5(3): 413–45.

Wolf, A. (2002) *Does Education Matter? Myths about Education and Economic Growth.* London: Penguin.

Wolf, A., Harrison, A., Jones, P., Sylva, K. and Wakeford, R. (1997) *Assessment in Higher Education and the Role of 'Graduateness'.* London: Higher Education Quality Council.

Wolfe, E.W. (1996) *A Report on the Reliability of a Large-scale Portfolio Assessment for Language, Arts, Mathematics and Science,* ERIC ED 399 285.

Wood, D., Bruner, J.S. and Ross, G. (1976) The role of tutoring in problem-solving. *Journal of Child Psychology and Psychiatry* 17(2): 89–100.

Wood, R. (1987) *Measurement and assessment in Education and Psychology: Collected Papers 1967–87.* London: Falmer Press.

Wood, R. and Power, C. (1987) Aspects of the competence–performance distinction: educational, psychological and measurement issues. *Journal of Curriculum Studies* 19(5): 409–24.

Woolf, H. and Cooper, A., *et al.* (1999) Benchmarking academic standards in history: an empirical exercise. *Quality in Higher Education* 5(2): 145–54.

Woolf, H. and Turner, D. (1997) Honours classifications: the need for transparency. *The New Academic* (Autumn), pp. 10–12.

Wright, W.A. and O'Neil, C. (1995) *Teaching Improvement Practices: International Perspectives*, in W.A. Wright and Associates, *Teaching Improvement Practices*. Boston, MA: Anker, pp. 1–57.

Wright, W.A. and Knight, P.T. with Pomerleau, N. (2000) Portfolio people: teaching and learning dossiers and the future of higher education. *Innovative Higher Education* 24(2): 89–102.

Yorke, D.M. (1985) Administration, analysis and assumption: some aspects of validity, in N. Beail (ed.) *Repertory Grid Technique and Personal Constructs: Applications in Clinical and Educational Settings.* London: Croom Helm, pp. 383–99.

Yorke, M. (1998a) Assessing capability, in J. Stephenson and M. Yorke (eds) *Capability and Quality in Higher Education.* London: Kogan Page, pp. 174–91.

Yorke, M. (1998b) The management of assessment in higher education. *Assessment and Evaluation in Higher Education* 23(2): 101–16.

Yorke, M. (1998c) Performance indicators relating to student development: can they be trusted? *Quality in Higher Education* 4(1): 45–61.

Yorke, M. (1999a) Editorial. *Studies in Higher Education* 24(3): 277–8.

Yorke, M. (1999b) *Leaving Early: Undergraduate Non-completion in Higher Education.* London: Falmer Press.

Yorke, M. (1999c) The skills of graduates: a small enterprise perspective, in D. O'Reilly, L. Cunningham and S. Lester (eds) *Developing the Capable Practitioner.* London: Kogan Page, pp. 174–83.

Yorke, M. (1999d) *Getting It Right First Time.* Cheltenham: Universities and Colleges Admissions Service.

Yorke, M. (2000a) A cloistered virtue? Pedagogical research and policy in UK higher education. *Higher Education Quarterly* 54(2): 106–26.

Yorke, M. (2000b) Benchmarking the student experience, in N. Jackson and H. Lund (eds) *Benchmarking for Higher Education.* Buckingham: SRHE/Open University Press, pp. 67–84.

Yorke, M. (2001a) Formative assessment and its relevance to retention. *Higher Education Research and Development* 20(2): 115–26.

Yorke, M. (2001b) Telling it as it is? Massification, performance indicators and the press. *Tertiary Education and Management* 7(1): 57–68.

Yorke, M. (2001c) *Assessment: A Guide for Senior Managers.* York: Learning and Teaching Support Network.

Yorke, M. (2002a) Degree classifications in English, Welsh and Northern Irish Universities: trends, 1994/95 to 1998/99. *Higher Education Quarterly* 56(1): 92–108.

Yorke, M. (2002b) Remaking the grade. *The Times Higher Education Supplement* No. 1565 (22 November), p. 16.

Yorke, M. (2002c) Subject benchmarking and the assessment of student learning. *Quality Assurance in Education* 10(3): 155–71.

Yorke, M. (2003a) Formative assessment in higher education: moves towards theory and the enhancement of pedagogic practice. *Higher Education* 45(4): 477–501.

Yorke, M. (2003b) Going with the flow: first-cycle higher education in a lifelong learning context. *Tertiary Education and Management* 9(2): 117–30.

Yorke, M. and Knight, P. (2003) *Embedding Employability into the Curriculum*. York: Learning and Teaching Support Network. [Provisional title]

Yorke, M. and Knight, P. (2003) Self-theories: some implications for teaching and learning in higher education. *Studies in Higher Education* 29 (forthcoming).

Yorke, M., Cooper, A., Fox, W., *et al.* (1996) Module mark distributions in eight subject areas and some issues they raise, in N. Jackson (ed.) *Modular Higher Education in the UK in Focus*. London: Higher Education Quality Council, pp. 105–7.

Yorke, M., Bourdillon, B., Bridges, P., *et al.* (1998) Benchmarking academic standards: a pilot investigation, in N. Jackson (ed.) *Pilot Studies in Benchmarking Academic Practice*. Gloucester: Quality Assurance Agency for Higher Education, pp. 33–50.

Yorke, M., Bridges, P. and Woolf, H., *et al.* (2000) Mark distributions and marking practices in UK higher education: some challenging issues. *Active Learning in Higher Education* 1(1): 7–27.

Yorke, M., Barnett, G., Bridges, P., *et al.* (2002a) Does grading method influence Honours degree classification? *Assessment and Evaluation in Higher Education* 27(3): 269–79.

Yorke, M., Barnett, G., Ecclestone, K., *et al.* (2002b) How are honours degree classifications affected by the award algorithm? Paper presented at the annual conference of the British Educational Research Association, Exeter (mimeo).

Index

The Society for Research into Higher Education

The Society for Research into Higher Education (SRHE), an international body, exists to stimulate and coordinate research into all aspects of higher education. It aims to improve the quality of higher education through the encouragement of debate and publication on issues of policy, on the organization and management of higher education institutions, and on the curriculum, teaching and learning methods.

The Society is entirely independent and receives no subsidies, although individual events often receive sponsorship from business or industry. The Society is financed through corporate and individual subscriptions and has members from many parts of the world. It is an NGO of UNESCO.

Under the imprint *SRHE & Open University Press*, the Society is a specialist publisher of research, having over 80 titles in print. In addition to *SRHE News*, the Society's newsletter, the Society publishes three journals: *Studies in Higher Education* (three issues a year), *Higher Education Quarterly* and *Research into Higher Education Abstracts* (three issues a year).

The Society runs frequent conferences, consultations, seminars and other events. The annual conference in December is organized at and with a higher education institution. There are a growing number of networks which focus on particular areas of interest, including:

Access	Learning Environment
Assessment	Legal Education
Consultants	Managing Innovation
Curriculum Development	New Technology for Learning
Eastern European	Postgraduate Issues
Educational Development Research	Quantitative Studies
FE/HE	Student Development
Funding	Vocational Qualifications
Graduate Employment	

Benefits to members

Individual

- The opportunity to participate in the Society's networks
- Reduced rates for the annual conferences
- Free copies of *Research into Higher Education Abstracts*

- Reduced rates for *Studies in Higher Education*
- Reduced rates for *Higher Education Quarterly*
- Free copy of *Register of Members' Research Interests* – includes valuable reference material on research being pursued by the Society's members
- Free copy of occasional in-house publications, e.g. *The Thirtieth Anniversary Seminars Presented by the Vice-Presidents*
- Free copies of *SRHE News* which informs members of the Society's activities and provides a calendar of events, with additional material provided in regular mailings
- A 35 per cent discount on all SRHE/Open University Press books
- The opportunity for you to apply for the annual research grants
- Inclusion of your research in the *Register of Members' Research Interests*

Corporate

- Reduced rates for the annual conference
- The opportunity for members of the Institution to attend SRHE's network events at reduced rates
  - Free copies of *Research into Higher Education Abstracts*
- Free copies of *Studies in Higher Education*
- Free copies of *Register of Members' Research Interests* – includes valuable reference material on research being pursued by the Society's members
- Free copy of occasional in-house publications
- Free copies of *SRHE News*
- A 35 per cent discount on all SRHE/Open University Press books
- The opportunity for members of the Institution to submit applications for the Society's research grants
- The opportunity to work with the Society and co-host conferences
- The opportunity to include in the *Register of Members' Research Interests* your Institution's research into aspects of higher education

Membership details: SRHE, 76 Portland Place, London
W1B 1NT, UK Tel: 020 7637 2766. Fax: 020 7637 2781.
email: srhe@mailbox.ulcc.ac.uk
world wide web: http://www.srhe.ac.uk./srhe/
Catalogue: SRHE & Open University Press, McGraw-Hill Education,
McGraw-Hill House, Shoppenhangers Road, Maidenhead,
Berkshire SL6 2QL. Tel: 01628 502500. Fax: 01628 770224.
email: enquiries@openup.co.uk – web: www.openup.co.uk

BEING A TEACHER IN HIGHER EDUCATION

Peter T. Knight

Being a Teacher in Higher Education draws extensively on research literatures to give detailed advice about the core business of teaching: instruction, learning activities, assessment, planning and getting good evaluations. It offers hundreds of practical suggestions in a collegial rather than didactic style.

This is not, however, another book of tips or heroic success stories. For one thing Peter Knight appreciates the different circumstances that new, part-time and established teachers are in. For another, he insists that teaching well (and enjoying it) is as much about how teachers feel about themselves as it is about how many slick teaching techniques they can string together. He argues that it is important to develop a sense of oneself as a good teacher (particularly in increasingly difficult working conditions); and it is for this reason that the final part of this work is about career management and handling change.

This is a book about doing teaching and being a teacher: about reducing the likelihood of burn-out and improving the chances of getting the psychic rewards that make teaching fulfilling. It is an optimistic book for teachers in universities, many of whom feel that opportunities for professional fulfilment are becoming frozen.

Contents
Part 1 People, times and places – Being at work in higher education – Learning teachers, learning students – Being a new teacher – Feeling motivated – Maintaining teaching vitality – Part-time teaching – Part 2 Teaching practices – Instruction – Learning tasks – Creating feedback – Designing for learning – Getting good evaluations – Part 3 Times of change – Change, experiencing change and making change happen – Managing your career – Being a teacher in higher education – References – Index – The Society for Research into Higher Education.

256pp   0 335 20930 0 (Paperback)   0 335 20931 9 (Hardback)

SKILLS DEVELOPMENT IN HIGHER EDUCATION AND EMPLOYMENT

Neville Bennett, Elisabeth Dunne and Clive Carre

The last decade has seen radical changes in higher education. Long held assumptions about university and academic autonomy have been shattered as public and political interest in quality, standards and accountability have intensified efforts for reform. The increased influence of the state and employers in the curriculum of higher education is exemplified by the increasing emphasis on so-called core or transferable skills; an emphasis supported by the Dearing Report which identified what it called 'key' skills as necessary outcomes of all higher education programmes. However, there is little research evidence to support such assertions, or to underpin the identification of good practice in skill development in higher education or employment settings. Further, prescription has outrun the conceptualization of such skills; little attention has been paid to their theoretical underpinnings and definitions, or to assumptions concerning their transfer.

Thus the study reported in this book sets out to gain enhanced understandings of skill acquisition in higher education and employment settings with the aim of informing and improving provision. The findings and analyses provide a clear conceptualization of core and generic skills, and models of good practice in their delivery, derived from initiatives by employers and staff in higher education. Student and graduate employee perspectives on skill delivery and acquisition are presented, together with a clearer understanding of the influence of contexts in skill definition and use in workplace settings. Finally, important questions are raised about institutional influences and constraints on effective innovation, and the role that generic or key skills play in traditional academic study, and in workplace effectiveness.

Contents
Generic skills in the learning society – A conceptualization of skills and course provision – Beliefs and conceptions of teachers in higher education – The practices of university teachers – Student perceptions of skill development – Employer initiatives in higher education – Employer's perspectives on skills and their development – The graduate experience of work – The challenges of implementing generic skills – Appendices – References – Indexes.

208pp   0 335 20335 3 (Paperback)   0 335 20336 1 (Hardback)

ASSESSMENT MATTERS IN HIGHER EDUCATION
CHOOSING AND USING DIVERSE APPROACHES

Sally Brown and Angela Glasner (eds)

Assessment really does matter in higher education. Internationally, academics – and those who support them – are seeking better ways to assess students, recognizing that diverse methods are available which may solve many of the problems associated with the evaluation of learning.

Assessment Matters in Higher Education provides both theoretical perspectives and pragmatic advice on how to conduct effective assessment. It draws clearly on both relevant research and on its contributors' practical first hand experience. It asks, for example:

- How can assessment methods best become an integral part of learning?
- What strategies can be used to make assessment fairer, more consistent and more efficient?
- How effective are innovative approaches to assessment, and in what contexts do they prosper?
- To what extent can students become involved in their own assessment?
- How can we best assess learning in professional practice contexts?

This is an important resource for all academics and academic managers involved in assessing their students.

Contents
Preface – Contributors – Part one: Systems approaches to assessment – Institutional strategies for assessment – Innovations in student assessment: a system-wide perspective – Assessment and evaluation: a systems approach for their utilization – Using assessment strategically to change the way students learn – Part two: Exploring the effectiveness of innovative assessment – Why assess innovatively? – The experience of innovative assessment: student perspectives – Biases in marking students' written work: quality? – Part three: Assessing practice – Assessing practice – Assessment of key skills – Using portfolios for assessment in teacher preparation and health sciences – Group-based assessment: an evaluation of the use of assessed tasks as a method of fostering higher quality learning – Dimensions of oral assessment and student approaches to learning – Part four: Towards autonomous assessment – Towards autonomous assessment: using self and peer assessment – Self and peer assessment – Peer assessment of undergraduate seminar presentations: motivations, reflection and future directions – Using peer and self assessment for the first time – Conclusion – Index.

224pp   0 335 20242 X (Paperback)